THE BOND

THE THREE DOCTORS

SAMPSON DAVIS, M.D.,

GEORGE JENKINS, D.M.D., *and*

RAMECK HUNT, M.D., *with Margaret Bernstein*

THE BOND

THREE YOUNG MEN LEARN TO

FORGIVE AND RECONNECT

WITH THEIR FATHERS

RIVERHEAD BOOKS
a member of Penguin Group (USA) Inc.
New York
2007

RIVERHEAD BOOKS
Published by the Penguin Group
Penguin Group (USA) Inc., 375 Hudson Street, New York, New York 10014, USA • Penguin
Group (Canada), 90 Eglinton Avenue East, Suite 700, Toronto, Ontario M4P 2Y3, Canada
(a division of Pearson Penguin Canada Inc.) • Penguin Books Ltd, 80 Strand, London WC2R 0RL,
England • Penguin Ireland, 25 St Stephen's Green, Dublin 2, Ireland (a division of Penguin Books
Ltd) • Penguin Group (Australia), 250 Camberwell Road, Camberwell, Victoria 3124, Australia (a
division of Pearson Australia Group Pty Ltd) • Penguin Books India Pvt Ltd, 11 Community
Centre, Panchsheel Park, New Delhi–110 017, India • Penguin Group (NZ), 67 Apollo Drive,
Rosedale, North Shore 0632, New Zealand (a division of Pearson New Zealand Ltd) • Penguin
Books (South Africa) (Pty) Ltd, 24 Sturdee Avenue, Rosebank, Johannesburg 2196, South Africa

Penguin Books Ltd, Registered Offices:
80 Strand, London WC2R 0RL, England

Library of Congress Cataloging-in-Publication Data

Davis, Sampson.
The bond : three young men learn to forgive and reconnect with their fathers / Sampson Davis,
George Jenkins, and Rameck Hunt ; with Margaret Bernstein.
p.   cm.
ISBN 978-1-59448-957-0
1. Davis, Sampson—Family.   2. Jenkins, George—Family.   3. Hunt, Rameck—Family.
4. Fathers and sons—United States—Case studies.   5. African American physicians—Biography.
6. Physicians—United States—Family relationships—Case studies.   I. Jenkins, George.
II. Hunt, Rameck.   III. Title.
HQ755.86.D37   2007   2007022947
306.874'2092396073—dc22
[B]

Printed in the United States of America
3   5   7   9   10   8   6   4   2

BOOK DESIGN BY NICOLE LAROCHE

While the authors have made every effort to provide accurate telephone numbers and Internet addresses
at the time of publication, neither the publisher nor the authors assume any responsibility for errors,
or for changes that occur after publication. Further, the publisher does not have any control over and
does not assume any responsibility for author or third-party websites or their content.

Dedicated to the memory of Kenneth Davis, Sampson's father,
in hopes more of us will discover our father's stories. Miss you, Dad!

—SAMPSON

For Alim Bilal . . . To a man whose dreams were snuffed out way too early, but
who had the courage and strength to reignite them. Your courage and strength
has inspired us all. I love you, Dad.

—RAMECK

In honor of my grandfather who passed away, Robert Williams.

—GEORGE

Contents

Introduction

THE THREE OF US grew up in a world where it seemed normal for men to abandon their children. Fathers weren't important in our lives at all.

For us and for a lot of the kids in our Newark neighborhood, Father's Day was never a big deal. We hardly knew when it fell, and rarely celebrated it when it occurred. To us, Father's Day was "kind of like Rosh Hashanah," as Rameck puts it. "It seemed like a celebration for other people, a day that belonged to another culture." To this day, George remembers the humiliation of having to ask a classmate how to tie a necktie because his father wasn't around to help him learn. And Sampson knows firsthand the destructive lure of the streets and how valuable a father's steadying influence would have been when times got tough and he found himself out there.

Our dads weren't our heroes. In many ways, they were the guys we hoped we'd never be like. So fatherhood and the crucial role it plays in the lives of children and families weren't important to us as kids, because we didn't know any better.

We do now.

Not having fathers left gaping holes in our lives. George rarely saw his father after his parents split up when he was a toddler. Rameck's father was hooked on drugs when Rameck was born, so he spent his time either locked up or out on the streets searching for a fix. And Sampson's father moved out when he was still a child, leaving Sampson's mom with the job of rearing a houseful of kids on her own. It was inevitable that we tripped in these holes every day of our lives. Rameck forced himself to sign up for Pop Warner football because it was something he thought boys were supposed to do and was so embarrassed that he didn't know how to put on his shoulder pads he quit football instead of asking for help. Sampson ventured out into the streets in search of male role models because he couldn't get his emotionally distant dad to pay attention to him. He allowed friends to hustle him down the path of crime and easy money, until he found himself locked up in the juvenile detention center for a summer. And George had to gulp down his pride many times to ask friends to help him learn even the simplest tasks such as how to shave.

In our world, it was our mothers and grandmothers who had to do the heavy lifting of parenting. They fed us, clothed us, hugged us, and fretted over us. As we grew, they tried their best to drill positive values into us, lecturing us to go to school and stay off the streets. Though they tried, they couldn't teach us everything we needed to know. It was an exhausting job to raise us, and it was scary watching them get worn down by poverty and stress.

In many ways, we ended up replacing our absentee dads on our haphazard journey to manhood with one another. In high school and college, we pooled our limited knowledge and shared our strengths. Together we figured out many of life's mysteries, from how to treat women to how to pick out a graduation suit.

But while this is a book about the profound emptiness of life without a father, it's also a book about hope. While we explore how vitally important fathers are to a child's development, we also celebrate that it's never too late to connect with your father. In these pages, we speak frankly about the sense of loss that the three of us felt as fatherless kids, and we explore a lot of questions most fatherless children ask: Why did you leave me? Did you ever wonder if I was missing you? Did you miss me? Was I on your mind? Why didn't you call more? Why didn't you send for me? We also explain how as adults we made a conscious effort to create relationships with our fathers that we didn't have as children, and how that connection has changed us and our fathers.

This book is written from a male perspective. Although we know that fatherless daughters struggle with their own issues of loss and compensation, this is our story, so we focused on our own feelings and experiences to illuminate the points we want to make.

You'll find that this book is divided into three distinct sections, so that each of us can explain our own relationship with our father. In Chapter 1 of each section, we share our experiences growing up without fathers. In Chapter 2, you'll hear from our dads themselves as they explain what went wrong in the father-son relationship. One thing we realized through the process of researching and writing this book is that although these men contributed half our DNA, we knew precious little about them and their history. We were stunned to find that all three of our fathers share common traits that account for a great deal about their inability to be devoted dads.

We resume our own stories in Chapter 3, letting you know where we stand emotionally with the information we've gleaned about our fathers. In Chapter 4 you'll meet real people who have impressed us by taking a bold stand to stop the cycle of fatherlessness in their own lives. They're people who didn't have fathers in their lives as kids, but they were smart enough to decide not to pass on the pain to another generation. We admire these people and want to banner their success so more people can learn from it. Little by little, one victory at a time, is the best way to put an end to this harmful trend.

In the final chapter of each section, we offer ideas that you can put to work immediately to help reduce the harm being done by absentee dads and to welcome these missing fathers back into their children's lives.

Remember, this is a book of hope. We refuse to give up hope that things can change. Thousands of young people who read our first book, *The Pact,* told us that positive friendships have the power to push a young person to success.

Once again, we're putting our faith in friendship. We believe there's no stronger force for change. We're confident that our nation's men are strong enough to put other influences aside and live lives in which children come first. That's where they have always belonged.

We believe a new era is possible, and that adults can successfully band together to form a bond and to wash away the crippling legacy of absentee fatherhood. *It can happen,* if we wake up and voice the hard truth to one another that it's a heartless thing to deprive a child of a father who should rightfully be a protector and a cheerleader.

We compare it to a quest. And there are tasks that must be completed to be a healthy, complete man. First you must teach yourself to succeed. Then you must teach yourself to become a father, even without a role model. And last, if you can find it in your heart, forgive your father. In the coming chapters, we will provide our best advice to you on how to achieve all of these goals.

Every time we see one of our friends break through the baggage of his past and become a loving and loyal guardian of his kids, it energizes and excites us. These are the good guys who prove that change is possible. Watching them, we know the truth: There is unrivaled joy in being a father who provides the stability and attention that encourage all children to soar.

SECTION ONE

GEORGE

Chapter 1

GEORGE JENKINS
The Beginning

T HERE ARE a thousand things I'd rather do than venture out of the tiny comfort zone that my father and I have created. I haven't seen my dad, George Jenkins, Sr., since my graduation from dental school in 1999. He and I have always been friendly but distant: he lives in another state, and we've never really connected as father and son. My lifelong strategy has been to not think too deeply about our relationship, to keep from actively resenting him.

It was my mom's firm desire to rear Garland, my older brother, and me in a stable environment that led her away from her short-lived marriage to my father. My mother disapproved of my dad's heavy drinking during the time we lived together as a family in my dad's hometown in rural South Carolina. One day when I was a toddler, Mom abruptly packed our bags, grabbed my hand and my brother's, and led us to the bus station. She delivered Garland and me to her parents in North Carolina to take care of us, then headed to Newark, where we eventually joined her after she landed a job.

I don't think I've seen my father a dozen times since we got on that bus.

As a child, I convinced myself that I was cool with my dad's absence. After all, hardly any of my friends had a father, either. As a grown man, I know better. Yet when we decided to write this book, I stalled, switched gears, and finally stopped writing altogether. It was hard to grasp how deeply I had buried things and how unwilling I was to disclose them. Not having a full-time father, I realized, made me vulnerable in ways that I would rather not announce to the world.

My mom, Ella Jenkins Mack, was a twenty-three-year-old single mother living in Rahway, New Jersey, when she met my father. At the time, she was on her own, caring for baby Garland. My parents were introduced by my father's sister, Rosa Lee, who lived down the street from my mom. My parents hit it off from the start: my mother was intrigued by handsome George Jenkins and his engaging conversations. He had been to college and seemed knowledgeable about so many things. As they spent time together, going to movies and parties, Mom thought they would make a good couple. Within a year, they married, in 1972. My dad returned to his native South Carolina to run his father's country store, and Mom and Garland soon followed him. I was born in 1973, not long after they moved.

The marriage didn't last long, which is why I have almost no memory of living with my dad. He had a drinking problem, and my mom got fed up quickly. They had little money, the electricity often got cut off because he hadn't paid the bill, and my father refused to let her work although she longed to bring in extra income. After I was born, her patience with him wore even thinner. She didn't want to raise children in an unhealthy environment.

When my mother asked my father if he would consider going to Alcoholics Anonymous, he irritatedly replied that he would drink as long as he wanted to. He would quit, he informed her, when he got good and ready.

There wasn't anything left to discuss after that for my determined mom, born into a large, close-knit family who worked hard to build a good life for their children. She couldn't see how we were ever going to find the good life if we stayed with him. That was the moment she realized it was time to "giddyup," as she puts it.

She packed a trunk and a suitcase with our stuff. It wasn't much to carry, she says with a laugh, because we had so few belongings at the time. And that day while my father was working at the store, she took us to the bus station. I wasn't quite two years old. Garland was three.

Our mom never looked back. She says she felt wonderfully free at that moment, even though our future was uncertain.

We headed for her parents' home in Warrenton, North Carolina, a small country town about fifty miles outside of Raleigh, where Mom's family welcomed us. It was a comfortable refuge, filled with loving relatives, but I didn't know what to make of all the changes. "Where's Daddy?" I asked Mom over and over again.

After a few months, Mom headed north to Newark, where she knew she could find a job. She also knew that her parents could watch us full-time until she carved out a stable life in New Jersey. Mom was gone for an entire year, but she visited us often. She always had a hard time tearing herself away when she had to return to work. It broke her heart the day she realized I had started calling her sister "Mommy."

My dad never came after us. When I was young, I felt he never sought us out to make sure we were safe. We could have been hungry or homeless. It seemed like he didn't care.

In 1977, when I was three and Garland was four, Mom showed up triumphantly, ready to move us north. She had been in such a tremendous hurry to pick up her babies that she got a speeding ticket along the way, in Virginia.

She moved us into an apartment in the Stella Wright projects on Muhammad Ali Boulevard in Newark. Mom was working in a factory back then, and a friend at work happened to mention that he knew someone who was looking for kids to babysit. That's how Mom met Willa Mae, our loyal and longtime babysitter who lived just a few blocks from us. "She was an angel. God sent her to me," my mom has often said, declaring it one of the luckiest moments of her life when she met Willa Mae.

Although Willa Mae lived in a notorious housing project nicknamed

"Little Bricks," I have only the warmest memories of my time there. I loved going over to her apartment, where her daughters helped care for us. I remember sitting on the couch next to Willa Mae, keeping her company while she watched her soap operas. She always kept boxes of chocolate and strawberry Nestlé Quik in the cupboard, and I used to drink so much of that flavored milk that I'm sure I'll have strong bones for life. (Now that I'm a dentist, I don't recommend such sugary drinks, though.) Willa Mae was like a member of the family. Mom could lean on her. She would take us to the doctor or dentist if we had to go, and once she even kept us for an entire week when Mom was sick.

The Stella Wright projects were noisy all night long with music blaring and basketball games being played at all hours. The hallways smelled of urine. Mom had no intention of living there for long. After a while, she took an office job at Chubb Federal Insurance and went to work every day determined to save enough money to move. Within three years, she had enough stashed away to buy into a co-op apartment, which was just across the street but seemed like a different world. The windows of our new two-bedroom place in High Park Gardens overlooked a peaceful, attractive yard landscaped with grass and flowers. Hardworking people lived in our building on Quitman Street, and they didn't party all night. But I had a constant reminder that I hadn't moved very far. Every time I looked out my window, I could see the Stella Wright high-rise. The projects blocked out the rest of the view and served as my daily backdrop.

As I grew up, I watched Mom bust her behind to take care of us. She had a rigorous schedule: wake up, dress us, and take us to Willa Mae's house, go to work all day, pick us up, come home to fix dinner, shop for groceries in the middle of the night when we were asleep, and do laundry on Saturdays. I suffered with asthma as a kid, so sometimes I disrupted Mom's routine with my wheezing episodes. On many nights, she had to drop everything to drive me to the emergency room, with Garland in tow. It took a few hours for the medicine to take effect, but I'd feel better by morning and then sleep for hours at the babysitter's house. Mom didn't get to rest. If the next day was a weekday, she would have to hurriedly comb her hair, throw on her work clothes, and go in for her eight-hour shift.

I never felt then that my dad visited much, and he rarely sent money. Mom knew that my father didn't earn a lot running his store, so she didn't push him to send more child support. "Why aggravate myself to get whatever little he has?" she would say.

She had a village helping her out to raise the two of us. Her eight siblings, who had all moved north, chipped in to help. Mom's family had a big influence on me, instilling a huge respect for hard work and higher learning. Four of my mother's sisters went to college, and I have two aunts, Catherine and Mary, who have master's degrees. It baffled me that my mother never went to college, so I started nagging her about it. "Go to school, Ma," I told her repeatedly. I couldn't understand why she didn't get a degree. It would have sent me an even stronger message about the importance of staying in school and getting an education. I also had an ulterior motive—secretly, I wanted her to get a college degree so she could earn more and buy me more Christmas presents.

When I was about eleven, my mother reunited with Garland's father. The two of them got married, and he moved into our apartment. I had my fantasies about what a father would be like—I had observed my friends' fathers and also had watched plenty of TV dads over the years—but the new addition to our house didn't exactly fit my expectations. Heyward Mack was a quiet man who just didn't communicate much. One day, five years after he arrived, he moved out without much warning to any of us.

As I've gotten older, I've begun to appreciate what he actually did for us. He pitched in to chauffeur me to my dental appointments after I got braces in my early teens. He always bought me Italian hot dogs after my orthodontist visits although I couldn't eat because the tightened braces made my teeth tender. Heyward generously shared his family with me. I loved going over to his parents' house, especially at holidays when his mother would cook a big pot of the best greens I ever tasted. I think Heyward is like many men of his generation. He was a provider but a businesslike one. I won't forget how he picked me up from college every semester when it was time to move out of the dorm and helped me lug all my stuff back and forth. He showed his love through action, not by flowery talk. While I was in college, he and Mom reconciled, and he remains a big presence in my life.

Yet I never called him Dad. That wasn't the way our relationship worked. I usually called him Heyward, and, on rare occasions, I felt comfortable enough to call him Pop. Mom knew she had to step in and be both a father and a mother to Garland and me. Bluntly, she told us about the facts of life. She would remind us often, and quite matter-of-factly, to wear condoms. "Look here, let me tell you," she would say. "You're growing up—so make sure to wrap that thing up. When you lay down with somebody, what you do could lead to a baby, and that means you're tied to that person for the rest of your life. So if you're eyeing a girl and it's not someone you want to be with next year and the year after that, then I suggest you keep walking."

In case any doubt remained, she'd tack on a final warning: "Don't bring no babies here." She said it so often that to this day I'm still haunted by those warnings.

Mom made it clear what *not* to do, but I still needed some instruction on what *to* do. I needed somebody to explain things. At age fifteen, I found one in Reggie, a dude I worked with at Murray Steaks, a frozen food company. I respected Reggie because it seemed like he knew how to handle his business. Only eighteen and already a father, Reggie was holding down a job, taking college classes, and caring for his young family. A good-looking guy, he'd had plenty of women chasing him in his earlier days so he had lots of expertise to share when we weren't unloading meat trucks or stocking shelves. He gave me my first condom, which I kept in my wallet. Eventually, it got so wrinkled that I couldn't use it, but it had done its duty by then, serving as an educational tool. Before Reggie, I'd had some experimental encounters, always rushed due to the fear that somebody's parents would bust in on us. Thanks to his coaching, I got a better sense of what to do when the opportunity presented itself and how to prevent an unwanted pregnancy.

Mom never shied away from the tough parts of parenting, but a woman can't show you how to be a man. The older I got, the more I found myself scavenging in the streets to pick up the basics of male behavior. Everyday situations mystified me. For one thing, I never felt confident when dealing with the constant confrontations that arise when you live in a neighborhood like mine. Somebody's always losing his temper; somebody's always getting shoved around. The root of these beefs is usually something so trivial or petty that I just couldn't get worked up about it.

I taught myself to sidestep confrontation, either by talking my way out of it or by just walking away, allowing my opponent to feel big and bad. But misgivings always nagged at me when I took the nonviolent approach. Should I have popped him in the eye? Did I look soft when I walked away? I never knew for sure. I could have used a father's advice to teach me where to draw the line and guide me through the minefields on Newark streets, where fistfights could ignite in a flash.

Newark was a tough town, the kind of place where it felt as if danger was all around you. In the Brick City, as it's been called, you always stood a good chance of being in the wrong place at the wrong time, even if you avoided obvious trouble and minded your own business. The city Rameck, Sampson, and I grew up in became synonymous with poverty and violence during our formative years, as Newark's white middle class fled to the suburbs. During the 1970s, the black population grew, and the city erected tall brick housing projects that teemed with poor people. In 1975, *Harper's Magazine* dubbed Newark the worst city in America. The city was still recovering from the deadly riots of 1967, and over the coming decades continued to be torn apart by drugs, poverty, unemployment, and hopelessness.

It was normal to see teenagers take stolen cars and spin them out, which we called "locking it up." We could be standing at the bus stop, and all of a sudden we might see a Honda Accord zoom down the street doing sixty or seventy. When the driver slammed on the brakes and turned the wheel sharply, the car would do a complete 180-degree turn. Even though we all knew the cars were stolen, we would watch admiringly. We even had a dance called the "lock it up." We also had fun watching cop chases. TV shows and movies are full of high-speed pursuits today, but we could see real action from our street corner. One big difference between Hollywood and our Newark reality was that the thieves usually got away. Everybody knew that the police couldn't go over a certain speed in residential areas because it would put the public at risk.

The crime-ridden brick housing projects towered over our neighborhoods, limiting our ambitions. I didn't understand a world beyond the Newark projects until I was in third grade at Louise A. Spencer School. There, I encountered an unforgettable teacher, Mrs. Viola Johnson. She took us on field trips to New York City and sent us postcards when she traveled. I became particularly fascinated with England because Mrs. Johnson had formed a Shakespeare club and had us inner-city kids holding weekly meetings to discuss Shakespeare's plays and sonnets. I was the club's president. I remember dreaming of exploring England's grand theaters and palaces.

Suddenly, with Mrs. Johnson's help, I knew that the world had more to offer and that it was up to me to go after it.

By the time I got out of elementary school, I had made up my mind to go to college. "George, you're bright enough to earn a scholarship," Mrs. Johnson often told me. Her words influenced me for a lifetime.

In sixth grade, my school recommended that I take the entrance exam for University High, a prestigious magnet school in Newark. It was a lucky break for me. I had no desire to go to our local high school; it didn't seem as though it adequately prepared students for college or even tried to challenge them.

I passed the test and entered University High in seventh grade. I remember being overwhelmed at seeing the high school seniors walking around. They were so much bigger and seemed so cool. University High in so many ways was a haven for a kid like me. I was surrounded by students who wanted to achieve. It was here that I met Sam and Rameck, who would change and challenge me.

Despite those positive influences, Newark's violence still intruded on my daily life. There was no escaping it. The incident I remember most vividly happened when I was in tenth grade. I had left school with my girlfriend and a longtime friend who lived near me. We were at the bus stop with a bunch of kids from my school, all waiting for the number 13 bus. One of the guys at the bus stop was a "pretty boy" type with a refined look, not very tough at all.

Then some kids showed up from Hawthorne Avenue, a few blocks away. Loud and rowdy, they had a reputation for harassing students from our magnet school. They looked ready to fight. I recognized one of the guys rolling with them because he was in the special education program at my school. We made eye contact, but he didn't mess with me. Relief flooded through me. Special-ed kids had their own classes on the third floor and they took a lot of teasing for not being able to keep up with the rest of us academically. I never joined in the taunts—bullying other kids never appealed to me—plus, I had played basketball in the gym against this guy and held my own. Those are the only two reasons I can think of that gained me enough of his respect to make him nod to me and keep it moving past me and my friends.

He and about eight of his friends went right for the pretty boy and started picking on him. I have no idea why. Maybe the pretty boy made fun of the special-ed kid in the past, or maybe he just looked weak. Whatever the reason, they lifted him up by his collar and pushed him against a fence. But they didn't hit him or rob him, I noticed with surprise. As after-school altercations go, this one seemed extraordinarily mild. As I watched, I told myself, "I don't know that guy. As long as my friends aren't in it, I don't need to get involved." But I wished the bus would hurry up and come.

But then the friend with us did the unthinkable. He walked up to the guy who had the pretty boy pinned up by the collar and put his hand on the guy's back, as if to ask him to please leave the kid alone. I couldn't believe it. It was essentially a suicide mission. The whole situation had seemed so benign, on the verge of blowing over. But by jumping in, my friend instantly took it to another level. I recognized the rhythm of street fights: now the bully would feel like his manhood was in question if he let the kid go.

I was right. The crowd turned on my friend and started beating the crap out of him. To make matters worse, other people from the vicinity joined in, so now it looked as if fifteen people were wailing away on him.

I wish I could rewrite this story and tell you that I jumped in heroically and took on half the crowd for him. But I wasn't that great of a fighter, and I knew my assistance wouldn't have helped matters. So I did what I thought I had to do, and that was escort my girl right on the bus, which arrived just as the fight was ending. Later, she told me I did the right thing. "He had no business crossing the line like that," she insisted. Although the friend who suffered the beating never criticized me, I never forgave myself for being a bystander.

To be honest, I didn't like fighting. I still don't. Although I knew I had to be ready to defend myself, I didn't believe fighting really resolved anything. I guess my outlook had something to do with growing up inside High Park Gardens, where my neighbors shared a strong work ethic and knew how to be civil to one another. To this day, I marvel at how I managed to make it through my teen years without getting loaded down with all the hostility and violent behavior that statistics show are tied tightly to fatherlessness.

Somehow, I felt immune to the peer pressure. When our neighborhood basketball games ended and everybody got bored, I'd head home to read a book while the other guys walked down the street to steal a car. Nobody bothered me, and I didn't bother them. Possibly it was the street credibility I earned for being an aggressive athlete, scratching my knees up for life on the concrete parking lots where we played football and basketball. Or maybe it was my streetwise cousins who lived nearby and made it clear that nobody should mess with George. For some reason, I didn't have to fight for my honor every time I went outside. I didn't bully anybody, or gossip, or laugh at the special-ed kids. I just tried to be straight up with everybody. Eventually I got labeled as a cool dude who studied hard and was sure to make it out of the ghetto one day. On my block, everybody knew that school was my hustle, instead of the streets, and they grew to respect me for it.

What I know of self-defense, I learned from my best friend from the neighborhood, Cash. He was the best fighter I knew, thanks to his father, Shahid Jackson, Sr., a Newark police officer who made sure that Cash worked out at the Police Athletic League every day. I watched Cash win all kinds of boxing trophies and tournaments. I learned the hard way about Cash's skills when we were playing a boxing game called "hard to the body." The object is to throw closed-fist blows to punch your opponent in the stomach, chest, and arms—no face shots. Thinking I would be able to hold my own, I tried to throw a punch. But before I could get my shot off, he hit me fast with three stomach and chest blows. Gasping for air, I didn't know what to do with myself. I couldn't even continue the game.

Over the coming months, Cash showed me some of the fundamentals of boxing and I became good at slap boxing: I had good instincts and my long arms were assets. I tried to soak up all the knowledge I could when Cash gave me lessons, but I couldn't help thinking he had an asset I lacked, a father to instill the self-assurance that helped Cash navigate the confrontations of daily life, while I second-guessed everything.

Luckily for me, Cash's dad didn't mind letting me borrow him.

Once we moved into High Park Gardens, I hung out nearly every day at Cash's house. Since I was always around, his father kind of adopted me. He was a former boxer who ran the Newark police's youth athletic league. He was well known in the entertainment world, as well, having served as bodyguard to stars like Kool & the Gang and Smokey Robinson.

He was well respected in our neighborhood. One day Cash and I came running into Shahid's house to tell him that the kids in the projects had jumped us on our way home from baseball practice, stealing our bats and gloves. Shahid was dressed only in his pajamas at the time but he swung into action. He walked right up to the projects and loudly announced that his boys better get their stuff back right away—or else. He stood outside the apartment building and waited. Within minutes, a window on a nearby apartment opened and the missing bats and gloves were returned, including some we didn't even own.

Shahid did the things for me that I thought a father should do. He put me on the sports teams he coached, and he took me to boxing matches and to Continental Airlines Arena to see the Nets play. Whenever he bought tickets to take his sons to an event, he always bought one for me.

Many's the time that he and his wife took me out to dinner. He loves a good meal, and he introduced me to the joys of a fine steak. When I was seventeen, I had to hide my astonishment the first time Shahid tossed me the keys to his gold LeBaron. "You guys can go to the mall, just don't wreck the car," he said, nonchalantly giving us permission to go out without him. Here I was getting a chance to drive the family car before Cash, who was ten months younger, got to slide behind the wheel. The trust Shahid showed in me meant a lot.

He listened when I had something to say. I didn't have to put up a macho front when I talked to Shahid. I could ask questions freely, share my insecurities, and get good advice.

It was Shahid whom I excitedly talked to on the fateful day when I met a caring dentist who took the time to show me his office and instruments. It was the first day I ever dreamed of becoming a dentist. Shahid still remembers the enthusiasm in my voice. To this day, it's Shahid I go to for fatherly advice. I'll always see him as larger than life, a broad-shouldered hero of a man with refined taste but a down-to-earth attitude.

Caring fathers like Shahid were rare in my neighborhood. But during my younger years, I brushed up against a few good men whom I studied closely as if they were rare biology specimens, always looking to pluck insights on how men should behave. My friends Anthony and Al lived with both their parents, and I admired how they got along with their father. Whenever I came over for their dad's poker parties, I paid close attention, watching how he treated his male friends, how he trained his sons and me to play the game, and mimicking the fine art of talking trash while playing cards.

Al and Ant were considered the rich kids on my block. Their father had a well-paying job with benefits, and his mother made additional money caring for foster children. They had five-hundred-dollar Mongoose and Diamondback bikes outfitted with lugs on the wheels that they used to do wheelies and other hot tricks. Man, how I wished I was in their shoes when they zipped up and down the street on those bikes, the two-wheeled equivalents of Ferraris.

Their shoes were ultra-fly, too. Al and Ant actually created fashion trends in our neighborhood because they wore the hottest styles before anybody else could afford them. I remember clearly they showed up with ninety-dollar Fila sneakers before we'd ever heard of them. You could count on Al and Ant to sport brand-new leather and sheepskin jackets as soon as the weather turned cold. I remember one winter day somebody pulled a shotgun on Al and coat-jacked him. Having everything they ever wanted brought these guys a lot of unwanted attention.

As soon as they got their driver's licenses, they found cars waiting for them in the driveway. Ant jumped right out of the box with an Infiniti, and Alan got a 300Z. It was incredible seeing my peers pushing rides like these as soon as they got their licenses. They had cars as nice as the hustlers and drug dealers in our neighborhood.

But I could never hate on them. Al and Ant's mother was sweet and invited me on family trips. Once, they took me with them to Atlanta, where I got to see Dr. Martin Luther King, Jr.'s memorial and the church he pastored. Also, their family had a vacation home in the Poconos and they took me there with them. They loved traveling and didn't mind sharing their world with me.

To me, Anthony and Al's lifestyle was like a fairy tale. It didn't resemble the economics of my single-mom-headed household at all. Hanging out with them taught me one clear-cut perk of having a full-time dad: added income for the family. Having a father in residence could be a definite asset in a lot of ways.

THE FUNNY THING IS, if my dad and I had lived in the same city, I think we would have been tight. When we talk on the phone occasionally, it's always friendly and warm. But 675 miles separated us—a distance my father didn't bridge very often.

In my early years, Dad used to come to his sister's house in nearby Rahway, New Jersey, and we would spend some time together. During one visit when I was twelve or thirteen, he let me drive his used Cadillac around the block. It was my first time stepping on the accelerator of a car. I won't forget it—that huge steering wheel looked like the wheel on a boat. "Wow, my dad's pretty cool to let me do something like this," I thought to myself.

But as I got older, his visits became less frequent. He came north only for my graduations from high school, college, and dental school. Years would slip by, years when I struggled to maintain my focus in school while my mother worked two jobs to help pay my tuition and fees. Earning a dentistry degree so I could write those precious three letters, DMD—doctor of dental medicine—after my name was not easy.

Although I didn't have much of a relationship with Dad, I'm thankful I had the good fortune to become friends with two guys who bring out the best in me. Sampson Davis and Rameck Hunt became my sidekicks at University High. They were just like me—fun-loving, but they knew when to buckle down and get their schoolwork done. One fateful day during our senior year, we happened to get shooed into a room where a recruiter from Seton Hall University in nearby South Orange, New Jersey, was talking about the school's new pre-medical/pre-dental program for minorities.

The funny thing about it is we hadn't really planned to be in that room that day. We actually tried to skip out of the presentation to play basketball. But a teacher caught us, shoved us into the library, and told us to take a seat. I'm convinced that God wanted us to hear that recruiter's message.

As we lounged in our seats at a back table, the female recruiter said something that grabbed my attention: Seton Hall's Pre-Medical/Pre-Dental Plus Program would provide assistance with all aspects of the college experience, from admissions to tuition. As the recruiter spoke, I could see my future becoming more certain than I'd ever dared to envision it. "This is it!" I thought to myself. As a young boy, I had declared that I wanted to grow up and be a dentist. Now, the perfect opportunity had presented itself, like a genie granting a wish.

"Man, we could go to college for free," I told Sam and Rameck. "Let's do this together."

That was the day we made our pact. The three of us promised to apply to the program and stick together until we came out on the other end as doctors.

When Sam, Rameck, and I were accepted in 1991 to the Seton Hall program, we knew that we had signed on for eight years of intense studying. Yet there was one thing we didn't think we had to worry about: money. The program had been created to encourage minorities from disadvantaged backgrounds to go into the medical field, and it came with a promise of free tuition. But that promise wasn't kept. While we were undergraduates at Seton Hall, the scholarship fund for our program was found to have been mismanaged. The university threw together a mix of grants, loans, and scholarships that paid in part for our undergraduate expenses, but we had to foot the rest of the bill.

Just getting through college ended up costing us thousands, and our unpaid tuition and fee bills piled higher and higher every year. But my mom didn't let that derail my dream. Her attitude was "Go for it, George. Just do your best. We'll make a way." And she did. She took a second job to help pay for my education. Her days became exhausting. She woke up before dawn to go to work at the insurance company. When she got off there at four P.M., she'd head over to her second job at Bell Atlantic to be ready to start at five. She usually got home after nine P.M.

At both jobs, she served as a customer service representative, talking to people on the phone. Sometimes the callers were irate and it was Mom's job to defuse them. She burned herself out solving other people's problems for seventy hours a week. Her blood pressure shot up, she tired easily, and she had no life except for getting to work and back. After a few years, her exhaustion began to show. She would fall asleep whenever she slowed down, like during church or a hair appointment. One day she went out with her sisters and found herself too winded to keep up with their leisurely pace. Eventually she got so sick that she had to quit her night job. By then I was almost done with dental school, and we knew that we had made it to the top of the mountain.

But more than once, Mom dipped into her retirement savings to help me out. Once when I called her for help, she quietly closed out her membership in an investment club, liquidating the stock she had proudly bought. I felt bad going to Mom when I needed money, but she never hesitated. "If I have it, you got it" was her philosophy.

I remember one day during those lean times, I opened my mail and out fell a postcard from my father from Jamaica. I couldn't believe it. Here Mom and I were scraping and stressing, and he was having a great time on a cruise. Years later, I decided that I had overreacted—after all, everybody's entitled to a vacation—but for some reason that day, seeing that glossy postcard made me wonder: How could he afford a cruise and not help me out with school expenses? Even if he had spent years saving for the trip, why hadn't he been disciplined enough to do the same thing and put some money aside for me?

As a teenager, I wasn't bitter about him not being around. I just figured that if he could be by my side, he would be. He must have a good reason for not showing up, I told myself.

But as I grew older, those long-repressed feelings of resentment came pouring out. I couldn't choke them back. On my own, I had managed to defy most of the statistics facing me: Growing up without a father tends to intensify a boy's aggression, and it doubles the chance that a child will drop out of school.

But not having my father in my life, I realized, had created one persistent problem that I couldn't figure out how to conquer. Not having a father to encourage me, to give me unconditional support, seemed to have sapped me of the confidence I needed to take risks and approach new situations fearlessly. As a result, every step I took on the Seton Hall University campus was shaky.

I felt bombarded from the first day that my mom and her mother dropped me off, just gazing at my new world of manicured lawns, tall buildings, and white kids everywhere. Though the school was just a few miles west of Quitman Street in Newark, it was totally different from the all-black, low-income community I had left behind. I felt out of place at Seton Hall, and although I had Rameck and Sam with me, even their support didn't help me overcome the feelings of inadequacy.

How do I maneuver here? How do I integrate into this world? Everything caused anxiety for me, from registering for classes to figuring out the social scene and the campus racial dynamics. I couldn't get over the fact that it seemed like the white students looked through me as if I didn't exist. I would say, "Hi, how are you?" yet white kids would walk past without replying. That really confused me. Although I made many white friends who didn't treat me that way, including my freshman roommate, I still felt I didn't belong. I didn't have the confidence to walk on campus acting as if I owned the place.

Just opening the door of my dorm room every day meant I had to steel my nerves. I hated that feeling, yet I couldn't figure out how to feel more comfortable. I felt adrift, trying to figure out a million mysteries. Why didn't anybody warn me what to expect before I got here? Although I needed to focus on my classes, a hodgepodge of distractions came flying at me. In the past, I'd taken my cues from my friends and family, but all that seemed worthless now.

I relied heavily on Sam and Rameck, who shared a room across the hall. We talked every night, studied together, and helped one another adjust to all the challenges being flung at us. When I needed to buy a car, for instance, Rameck went to the dealership and helped me through the hassles of bargaining and financing. I chose a used Volkswagen Jetta, and picked one with a manual transmission since it was cheaper than an automatic. The next day, Rameck stayed loyally at my side as I sputtered and stalled, trying to pick up the rhythm of driving a stick shift. With his help, I finally felt the thrill of driving my own car.

I had my mind on money constantly. At times, I worried if I'd be able to afford to finish school. I let these kinds of pressures distract me, and things only seemed to worsen when I graduated from Seton Hall and headed off to the New Jersey Dental School. For one thing, I didn't have Rameck and Sam by my side anymore. They had already branched off to start medical school early. The pressures of dental school seemed overwhelming. For one thing, the bills were higher. I already owed $50,000 in school loans, and dental school was shaping up to cost double that amount. There were a couple of times when I buried my head in my hands, just worn down by the whole ordeal. The classes were painfully difficult, I was racking up thousands of dollars in debt, and I was essentially compromising my mother's health by forcing her to work two jobs to pay for dental school. At times like this, when I was ready to give up, I never even thought of calling my father. He and I just didn't have that kind of relationship.

Dental school also forced me to change my look. During our dental clinics, when we met with the public, students were expected to look like professionals. For starters, I didn't know how to shave. I found a barber to tighten me up every couple of weeks, but between visits, I fumbled around trying to come up with a do-it-yourself approach. Without reliable advice on how to apply aftershave and avoid razor bumps, I wasted a lot of money trying out different drugstore products. Isn't this what a father is supposed to show you? My mirror became my silent partner, keeping secret my attempts to imitate the techniques that I'd insisted my barber demonstrate to me. But I never got my face as smooth as I wanted.

Also, dental students were required to wear ties, and I didn't know how to tie one. Once again, I had to force myself past the nervousness of asking someone to show me the things my father should have taught me. "Whatever it takes, I'll do," I'd tell myself. "I'm not going to let this hold me back." This time I dropped my pride, showed up to a class early, and asked a white classmate to show me how it was done. He graciously gave me a tie-tying lesson in the bathroom, and we never spoke of it again.

I needed even more help than that to transform my look from laid-back college student to professional. Then a teacher all three of us knew from our high school days named Mr. Charles strutted on the scene like a fashion savior. I had admired Mr. Charles for his suaveness since the first day I glimpsed him stepping out of his Mercedes-Benz in Gucci shoes and a perfectly tailored Armani suit. A native of Haiti, he taught French at University High. He was without a doubt the best-dressed person I'd seen up to that point. His look reeked of quality and professionalism. From the little I knew of designer clothes, I didn't think I'd ever be able to afford a fraction of Mr. Charles's style.

When I got to Seton Hall, I found out that Mr. Charles had a business up the street. He owned a men's clothing boutique within walking distance of my dorm. He made custom suits, even going to Milan twice a year to shop for fancy fabrics. The first thing I bought at his store was a versatile knit shirt. I could wear it as a casual shirt or a jacket with a mock turtleneck underneath. He must have chopped half the retail price off for me because he knew I loved it.

Needing his expertise while in dental school, I'd stop by whenever I was in the vicinity, help myself to a beer in his private refrigerator, and sit down for a chat. He always welcomed me warmly and schooled me on fashion details I had never heard before: the proper fit of a suit, exactly where a belt should lie on your torso, how much shirt sleeve should show at the end of your jacket.

If I had a big event coming up, I would tell him and he would help me pull together a great look. For an annual dental school dance that we called "The Tooth Ball," he custom-fitted me with tan slacks and a navy blue blazer with subtle checks in the fabric. I got Sam and Rameck hooked on his boutique, and they started shopping there, too. He loved seeing us walk in the door, and he always gave us healthy discounts since we usually had more lint than money in our pockets.

He knew we had to scrape to afford our education. After the Newark *Star-Ledger* ran a front-page story about our pact on the day we graduated from medical and dental school, we ran into Mr. Charles. "Saw you in the paper," he said with pride. "I want you to come by the store later on." When we arrived, he told us he wanted to give each of us a pair of custom-made slacks. "It's my gift," he said.

I couldn't help but think he had shown me more support than my own father had.

My late lessons in shaving, grooming, dressing—the things my father should have taught me—turned out to be things that most embarrassed me. To be twenty-three and not know how to tie a tie? That screamed to the world that my father wasn't in my life. But I knew I had to get over it. I had to ask for help, despite the pain, because I wanted desperately to move my life forward.

It didn't help my state of mind to see so many of my dental school peers from the middle class who had the steadying influence of both parents and were lucky enough to take it for granted. I saw classmates with trust funds and kids with fathers who were well-connected businessmen. Watching them live their more privileged lives bothered me, because these kids had their futures all lined up. I felt I couldn't compete; I barely knew anything about the professional world that awaited me. I knew only to keep putting one foot in front of the other and hope to God that my career would fall into place if I could just manage to graduate.

It wasn't that I needed my dad to be rich. I just needed him to be there. He might not have been able to pay my tuition or hire me in the family dental practice, but what burned me up was that he didn't know or care about my pressures. He left the whole ordeal on my mom's shoulders when he should have been helping her out. I wish he could have provided an additional source of advice, resources, anything, so I could have given my mother a break. Instead, he just put his hands in his pockets. And that's why, like the professional athletes who send shout-outs to their moms on camera, it's become important to me to let Mom know how much I appreciate her for all her sacrificing. That's why I now make it my business to send her on an annual vacation. She's earned it. I know that even now, she's got my back.

On the positive side, I do believe that not having a father present in my life made me more of a go-getter. Since I was a kid, I've always been on the lookout for opportunities to put myself on the road to success. Having never had a dad to go to for advice or assistance, I knew I would have to chip away at the obstacles in my path by myself. That's what made me tune in to the message of the Seton Hall recruiter that day, when Rameck and Sam were cutting up and not really listening. Sometimes I wonder if I would have turned out this way if I had had a strong father in my life. It's impossible to know. As a longtime observer of father-son relationships, I can say that I've seen fathers push their children in ways that aren't always positive. I've witnessed some friends make life-altering decisions to please their fathers that they otherwise would not have made. Several of my classmates became dentists just to make Daddy happy. That was one thing I didn't envy. I was always my own man, chasing my dream because I wanted it. I could take a more relaxed approach, setting my own goals because I answered only to myself.

That go-getter side of me pulled me through the tough times, but it also ended up taking me from a kind of benign neutrality toward my father to outright resentment. Where was *his* hustle? Where was his second job? My mom's attitude was "You just focus on school, George, I'll worry about the bills." Where was his paternal instinct? He was just as responsible for my existence as my mother was. If he had done half of what my mom did, or even a quarter, I might have respected him. Heck, show me some effort, if it's only that you tried to bring in some extra cash but it didn't work out.

After dental school graduation, there were still mountains to climb. My classmates hit the ground running after dental school. But I hit the ground with a serious thud. It cost $1,000 to take the licensing exam: Mom had to dig into her retirement savings again to help me with the fee. Again, no help from Dad. During my dental residency, my self-doubt got worse. I felt deflated. Now that I was finally in the workplace, I felt completely out of place. Did I reach too far out of my league? To get into this profession, you need contacts and some money. I didn't have either. And nobody was holding out a hand to show me the ropes.

To this day, I feel there are repercussions from not having a father that handicap me. I've been taken advantage of by people claiming they want to be my mentor. I crave guidance and direction so much that it has left me vulnerable. It's a stressful way to operate. I feel unprotected and sometimes just plain lost. I later found that research shows conclusively that children without fathers are less confident and more anxious when placed in unfamiliar settings. I didn't need a university study to tell me this. It was my reality and it still is. To this day, I'm constantly looking for approval, feeling unsteady in the workplace. And, unfortunately, that kind of support tends to be in short supply.

Not being confident also made me a late bloomer when it came to approaching women. In high school, I had a steady girlfriend, and she served as a security blanket. I didn't have to put myself out there on the dating scene and face rejection. But when I got to college, I decided it was time to solve this problem, the same way I had willed myself past all my other obstacles. I paid close attention to Sam, watching how he easily started conversations with the most beautiful women in the room. "Stop limiting yourself," I told myself. "Take a risk, get out there and introduce yourself." Change came slowly.

It shocked the life out of me when Cash called me during freshman year to ask me to come to his wedding. "What are you talking about?" I gasped. I convinced myself that he had to be joking. I hadn't even mastered the art of asking a woman out, and here he was getting married? I didn't go to the wedding. I regret that to this day, but honestly, I couldn't fathom the idea that Cash, my peer, my oldest friend, had popped the question to his girlfriend at age nineteen.

He's still happily married, and he and his wife just had their fourth child, little Malcolm. Cash's success at being a husband is a prime example of something I've long noticed: My only friends who are happily married right now are the few I know who were raised in a two-parent household.

It's the most valuable perk, I believe, of growing up in an intact family. For Cash and Al and Anthony (who are married, too), the necessary skills to be part of a satisfying partnership come easily. They can take for granted a gift that all of us don't possess. I'm still confounded by the mystery of how to make a long-term relationship work. As I steeled myself to break into dentistry, I've had to create a don't-mess-with-me zone. That mind-set helped me crash through career barriers and kept me moving through adversity, but it doesn't help in my relationships with women.

I never got a chance to see how to treat a lady every day, how to compromise, how to make a relationship work while raising a family. I never saw a man and woman work out even the smallest problems such as when he wants eggs, bacon, and waffles and she wants cereal.

So many people like me, reared without fathers, have been deprived of knowing how to behave in a relationship. It's like an intangible, invisible heirloom that fatherless children will never inherit.

To this day, it affects me. Ever since college, I've had so many demands on my time and attention that it makes my head swim. I'm even busier now, with a full-time job in dentistry plus the travel and community responsibilities of our work as The Three Doctors. I've never figured out how to give a girlfriend the attention she wants while handling the rest of my business effectively.

Once I had a girlfriend I liked a lot. She caught my attention at a book signing. A former track athlete, she looked like a walking sculpture of perfection to me. Her father was a dentist and she was considering going to dental school so it seemed we had a lot in common. Not long after we met, she took an interest in decorating my apartment. It could use a little sprucing up, I admitted, so I gave her my credit card. First, she bought curtains for my bedroom, something I'd been too busy to do. She even installed them. I loved it. Then she started walking in the door with new salt and pepper shakers, oven mitts, candles and towels and shower curtains. Just bags and bags full of new stuff. Okay, I dug the candles, but suddenly things seemed to be happening without my permission. I'm really not a color-coordinated, salt-and-pepper-shaker kind of guy. Things had gotten out of control. I started getting itchy.

She lived about an hour away, so we tried to see each other on weekends. At first she seemed to understand my career demands and took it in stride if I couldn't make it. And I pushed myself to go see her, even when I was dog-tired. But after a while, I couldn't keep up the pace. There were weekends when I felt so worn out I just wanted to chill. She let me know that I wasn't putting as much energy into the relationship as she expected. A few more missed weekends and she got mad and blew up. It's a cycle I know very well. Typically, my relationships start, hit full bloom, and then flame out, all within about four months.

Women, I've learned, want to be my number one priority. It bothers me that I haven't figured out how to deliver the attention they want and still keep myself afloat. At first, when a girlfriend objects to my busy schedule, I manage to put out the fire by ignoring my other duties and focusing on her. But I can't keep all the balls in the air at the same time, and her complaints get louder and louder. So I shut it down.

Can a relationship feel more natural and less like hard work? I have no idea. I've taught myself to master a lot of things over the years, but I've never gotten on top of this dilemma.

But I'm trying to teach myself to grow. Right now I'm in a situation that seems different from all the others.

My new lady has been a friend of mine for eight years and only now are we cautiously moving to the romantic stage. And it strikes me that it's our bond of friendship that's giving our new relationship its durability. She's already irreplaceable to me because she's stood by me for years and been such a good friend. The way I feel about her reminds me of the way I feel about Sam and Rameck: I'm going to take good care of this relationship because we have a history of being loyal to each other. There's nothing she can do that will push me away.

Being with her makes me think that friendship is what's missing from a lot of modern-day hookups. When you head straight to the bedroom, then that's a fragile bond that's too weak to withstand the inevitable disagreements. But when you become my friend, you're more precious to me than anything.

I'm still a juggler, frantically trying to manage my many priorities, but I'm holding this budding relationship in my hands much more delicately. I'm trying very hard to make it work. If this one doesn't work out, I don't want it to be my fault.

Is this love? Honestly, I don't know. I've never had a relationship last long enough for me to even consider buying an engagement ring and popping the question. I have told a girl "I love you" before. Yet I'm not sure I meant it. This is the kind of thing I dream of asking a father about. "How did it feel when you fell in love? How did you know she was the one?"

The thought of voicing these questions out loud makes me feel even more foolish than the day I asked for help tying a tie. These are the kinds of things that a son learns from a father. And when the father is missing, the lesson goes unlearned.

One of my college friends, Dax, got a letter from his dad in 2003 that shook him up. At the time, Dax had been dillydallying around in a long-term relationship with his girl, Candice, getting all the benefits of a live-in girlfriend without progressing to a true commitment. His father's letter told him, with all due respect, that good women like that don't come along every day. "I see how much effort you put into your career. You have to value your relationship the same way and put the same amount of effort into it," his father wrote. The gentle but frank letter made Dax stop and think. What's the right thing to do? He pondered it, then went and bought a ring. Today he's been married two years. It takes a real man, he realized, to make the responsible choice, instead of giving in to all the outside influences that emphasize sex without commitment.

Only a few months after Dax asked Candice to marry him, his father was diagnosed with brain cancer. He held on until the wedding, when he flew to St. Thomas to serve as Dax's best man. By that point, the tumor had stolen much of his ability to speak. He passed away shortly after that. Dax treasures those wordless moments he and his father shared as Dax crossed an important threshold in his life. By then, his father had done his job admirably. He didn't have to speak a word.

Since I became an adult, I've visited my father only once. In 1997, I volunteered to ride down south with a dental school friend from South Carolina, because he had to drive to Charleston to handle some paperwork related to his dental license. My dad picked me up and drove me to his home, where I spent half a day with him. He took me to meet some relatives and showed me where his store had been. Fragments of memories started stirring for me. I knew that I had been there before, although I couldn't remember much about it. As always, it was a pleasant visit but nothing lasting came of it.

Once I saw my paternal grandmother's picture. It shocked me to see that I look just like her. But to this day, I know almost nothing about her. Family history is important—people get strength from the things that happened in their past. When I was in dental school, I could have used some strong stimuli like that to keep me going. But I know so little about my father and his family. I don't even know my father's birthday.

My dad and I enjoy occasional talks on the phone. I never have a problem opening up when we chat. Anyone listening to our conversation would think that we have a real relationship. We tell each other we're going to keep in better contact, and then we hang up. But he doesn't follow through, and neither do I.

I have my own opinions about what a real father is supposed to be, and this isn't it. A father is supposed to sacrifice himself for his child. His willingness to do that should be so powerful that it latches the two of you together inseparably. That's what I've missed out on, that sense of sacrifice that lets me know I belong to my dad and there's nothing he wouldn't do for me. Not having it is what robbed me of my confidence and what continues to hamper me. It's tough to even think of advancing our father-son relationship without that foundation of security for it to rest on.

Over the years, it seemed as if the space I had reserved for him got filled by the people who were substitutes for him—like my mother and Shahid, then Sam and Rameck. By the day I finally donned a cap and gown and proudly placed the initials DMD after my name, I had no place left in my heart to put my father.

Now that I've forced myself over all the hurdles in my way, I just don't want anyone to make the mistake of thinking that my father had something to do with the success I've experienced. So I admit that I have put up a wall between us. To my easygoing father, everything probably seems fine. But for me, it's an oddly superficial feeling to have the outer shell of the relationship but not the bones. For me, the building blocks of our relationship are missing. And there can be no true bond without it.

Chapter 2

GEORGE JENKINS, SR.

The Beginning

IF YOU WOULD have told me when I was a young man that my son and I would have grown up to be this distant, I wouldn't have believed you. I always pictured myself having a close relationship with my child—much closer than I was ever able to have with my own parents.

When I search my soul honestly, I have to say there were several reasons why things turned out this way. But more than anything else, it was sheer geography that robbed me of my closeness with my son. I've spent most of my adult life in a rural South Carolina town called Woodrow. It's a humble little place with just one main street, Highway 441, running through it. The population is about ninety percent black, and families have lived here for generations. I was born here on February 3, 1942, and today I'm still living in the home that my family built. Once my wife departed, taking George and Garland with her and leaving me with an empty home, I wasn't in a position to travel up north often to visit them. If only George and I had lived closer, I feel certain that things would have turned out differently. I know that we would have spent time together and created the kind of memories that he ended up missing out on.

George is my only child and I am proud of him. I also admire the national reputation he is earning. I think *The Pact* tells a wonderfully original story: He and his two classmates had such a tight friendship that they kept one another from falling by the wayside.

Yet it was painful for me to read his book, and to see my role in my son's life reduced to just a handful of paragraphs. And unflattering paragraphs at that.

I can't deny that I haven't been the most attentive and affectionate of fathers. It's not something I'm proud of. However, I didn't have much of a road map to follow.

My parents weren't married. In truth, the facts behind my birth probably set a lot of tongues to wagging in my small town: My mother, a widowed schoolteacher, was having a baby. And the father of her child was the well-to-do married proprietor of the town's general store. This sort of news was totally out of the ordinary back then, and especially among the town's black professional class. I notice that today, this type of thing has become much more accepted.

My mom, Rosa Lee Blanding Jenkins, chose to give me the respectable last name of her deceased husband, Henry Jenkins, who had been a businessman and farmer. But I'm sure that my arrival had to be an inconvenience. What was she to do? She was already a mother of six who worked two jobs, as a teacher and also keeping afloat the little store that her deceased husband had owned. She didn't have time to care for an infant. So when I was just a few weeks old, she shipped me off to another town, deep in the South Carolina woods, to be cared for by a friendly couple. I lived in the home of Annie and David Dennis until I was old enough to attend school, and I almost never saw my blood family during those early years. I thought the Dennises were my family, because when I opened my eyes every morning, that's who I saw.

I cried buckets when Mr. Dennis died, when I was about six years old. My sister, who was married to the embalmer who handled Pop's body, spoke to me sharply that day. "What are you crying for?" she asked. "That's not your father. Elijah Prince is your father." Yes, I knew that Mr. Dennis wasn't related to me. But that didn't stop the feelings I had for the old man, the first that I knew as a father. A few years later, my mother would pass away before I had a real chance to bond with her. The Dennises would forever be the parents I felt the most love for when I was a child.

When I was old enough to attend school, I came back to Woodrow. I lived with my mom and finally got to know my six brothers and sisters. They were all much older than me, and most of them had married and gone out on their own. My sister Dorothy, a recent college graduate, was the only one still living at home. Eventually she married and left, too, and then it was just my mother and me. It was the only opportunity I would ever get to live with a biological parent.

I remember my mom as a busy and very businesslike lady. During the precious few years we had together, she taught me to read and write very well. And at night, when she closed the little country store that she had inherited from her husband, she would turn it into a math lesson for me. Together we would count the coins. I'd do the pennies and nickels, she would count the larger coins. But she didn't lavish a lot of attention on me. She was just too busy, with her jobs and the backbreaking work of keeping a household running. Back then, that's how parenting was done. Your parents would tell you what to do and they'd be quick to chastise you if you didn't do it correctly, but they wouldn't go overboard showing affection. Love was like an unspoken thing. I didn't understand it then, but I understood it later. And eventually I would see that it would influence my own parenting style.

Back then, of course, schools were segregated, so I went to the local school for colored children, a four-room building where several grades were taught in the same room. In those days, blacks had to support their own schools financially, and when there was no money, the school shut down. And that's exactly what happened. By the time I completed fifth grade, my school ran out of funds and had to close its doors. It's the story of my life: I had to leave my mother again. This time Mom took me to Sumter to live with my uncle, Charles Blanding, and attend school there.

I came home for Christmas break when I was eleven, in 1953, and I found that my mother was terribly sick, so much so that my sister had taken over the store. Mom was bedridden, weakened by diabetes and heart disease.

One night during that holiday break, I was minding the store with my sister when my mother's brother, my uncle Charles, walked in the door and delivered the news: He had gone in to check on my sleeping mother and found her dead. I was devastated. In that fatal, fateful instant, my childhood was gone. Earlier, as I bounced from one house to another, my rearing had always been left up to chance. But I always could maintain a slim hope that one day I would know how it feels to be enfolded in a mother's embrace and know that softness. I longed for softness, to combat all these hard knocks.

But from that point on, what happened in my life was up to the Good Master and me.

My sister Lanie stepped in to become my guardian after Mom died. She wanted me to continue with my schooling, so she enlisted the help of my biological father to send me away to a school she had heard about, in Camden, South Carolina. Mather Academy, a boarding school for Negro children established by the Methodist Church, had a great reputation. My father agreed that it would be the right thing to do, and he paid my tuition.

Elijah Prince and I weren't strangers to each other.

As I grew older, we would see each other occasionally. We both knew that we were father and son. But we never really talked about it when I was a child. My father was one of the most powerful men in Lee County, with a lot of important business holdings. In addition to his store, he owned a big farm on which he grew corn, peanuts, soybeans, and tobacco. A major employer in our community, he oversaw a team of men who farmed his land. Some summers, he would hire me to work in his fields. It gave me a chance to see him every day, although he always treated me impersonally, the way a boss handles an underling. I understood that. My father needed to command respect from his workers, and he couldn't afford to give me special treatment.

His wife wasn't happy that her husband had stepped out on her, fathering a child with another woman. She didn't seem to approve of me, nor the occasional overtures that my father made toward me. My father, who subscribed to the newspaper, knew that I enjoyed reading the comics, so he let me know that he was saving the funny papers for me. I would drop by his house every once in a while to pick them up. But his wife did her best to humiliate me when I stopped by. When I would ring the front doorbell, she would tell me, in a pointed voice, to come around to the back door—as if she were a white woman and I was the hired help. This was her way of putting me in my place. It hurt to be treated like this. From that point, I vowed that if I ever got married and had children, I would make sure they had the emotional security of knowing they belonged to a family.

I felt orphaned and lonely as well at Mather Academy. There were so many adjustments to make. Having grown up under rigid segregation, it was my first time ever seeing white teachers. I was immersed in a college preparatory environment, and expectations for the students were high. It was a tough course load, and although I didn't excel in all my classes, I discovered how much I enjoyed foreign languages. Latin and French were my favorite classes. Inside the halls of Mather Academy, my country accent eventually faded away. I learned to speak more crisply, to say "going" instead of "gwine." I tried to fit in. In my senior year I applied to colleges, as I saw my peers doing. I got accepted to Benedict College in Columbia, South Carolina, and I proudly enrolled there in 1959.

But quickly, the luster of the college experience wore off. I felt as if I were in a foreign land and that I didn't belong. I looked the part of a country hayseed, with holes in my shoes, and I was struggling to afford necessities. After I finished my sophomore year, I found myself impatient to have a wad of dollars in my pocket. I had been working since childhood, picking cotton, peanuts, or tobacco, and I knew that I could easily find a job. I was a grown man and I was hungry to start living like one, with a car and some nice clothes. I was tired of being broke and of living in the South, where black men were relegated to menial jobs that paid little. Also, I was acutely aware that there was nothing tying me to South Carolina anymore—my sister Lanie had moved away. I was ready to make my exit, too.

So I dropped out of college in 1961, telling myself that I was just taking off a semester, and headed for Kansas City, where Lanie had moved. She had met a guy in the service there, and they had married; they invited me to stay with them. I arrived in November and promptly had my Southern sensibilities attacked by a brutal Midwest winter. I found a job at a grocery store, and every morning at four-thirty I had to go through the teeth-chattering ritual of catching a bus across town in subzero weather.

Before long, I was ready for a job change. My brother-in-law worked at a railway terminal in Kansas City and he let me know there were openings there. Just getting the job was a test of my endurance: I waited in line from eleven A.M. to five P.M. to get hired. When I finally made it to the front of the line, all they asked me was if my back was straight and strong. The job was to move mailbags with heavy stuff inside like Sears, Roebuck catalogues. I was hired on the spot, and I ended up working there for four years.

At that time, the Vietnam War was going on. I opened my mailbox one day and there was a draft notice waiting for me. I was seeing a doctor then for a stomach ulcer, so I asked for a note confirming that fact. Still, I didn't think a lousy ulcer was enough to keep me out of the war. So before I was scheduled to report for induction, I took a week of vacation from my job to hang out and party. On my final night of freedom, a friend came over and we had a great time listening to music on my stereo till the wee hours.

The next day, I got up and couldn't find my doctor's note anywhere. Resigned to the fact that soon I'd be carrying a rifle and stepping through rice paddies, I reported to the army induction center and got in line. I stepped up halfheartedly when they asked if anyone had a medical reason why they could not serve their country—but I wasn't very confident because I couldn't find that blasted doctor's note. The induction officer was nice enough to call the doctor's office to confirm my stomach ulcer story, but the doctor was out that day. The sergeant told me sternly, "Jenkins, I'll give you one hour to find that note. If you're not back here by ten A.M., you're automatically a soldier."

I sped home and looked everywhere. The minutes were clicking by. Just before my time was up, it occurred to me to think, "What was I doing when I last had the note in my hand?" I searched near the stereo, and there it was, buried under some albums. I'll always consider that a moment of divine intervention. I put the note in my pocket and rode back down to the center. I carried it to the sergeant and handed it to him. It wasn't long before he announced, "Mr. Jenkins, you can go home." I didn't stay to ask any questions. Black men were getting killed left and right in that war. We could see it in the newspaper and on the nightly news. For some reason, God had blessed me with a reprieve.

Now, after surviving that close brush with fate, I had absolutely no desire to go back to work on Monday. So I took another week of vacation just to celebrate!

I admit I was running pretty wild back then, in my twenties. When I would get off work, I always looked forward to letting off some steam by partying with friends, listening to music, and having a few drinks. The thing that settled me down was when my sister Lanie and her husband started having problems. In 1967, she made up her mind to leave him, and she asked me to move away with her. Lanie was my only blood relative in Kansas City. When I thought about her trying to get reestablished in a new city, I thought I better go along to give her moral support. She had two daughters to raise.

She and I headed east, to check out the cities where our siblings were living. First we visited our brother Bobby in Washington, D.C. Lanie didn't like it, and decided to move back home to South Carolina. But I loved the excitement of the big city, and I wasn't ready to give it all up and go back to farm life with its dull days of backbreaking work. I decided to head for Rahway, New Jersey, where my sister Rosa Lee lived.

I lived in New Jersey from 1968 to 1972. I found a good-paying job at Esso Oil and started to become more settled and stable. It was a sobering period in U.S. history, a time when blacks bonded together to demand change, and when assassination bullets flew. I think the social climate affected me a lot. The nation was making a sharp turn, and I took note of the fact that serious change was needed in my life, too. I was in my early thirties, and no longer full of youthful immortality. I took an interest in an attractive neighbor of Rosa Lee's named Ella, and started thinking about giving up the bachelor life.

She was a smart young lady with plenty of common sense. A lot of young ladies I had met seemed frivolous by comparison. She was in her early twenties, but mature beyond her years. We could talk easily and for long hours. I enjoyed being in her company.

She had a baby boy, whom I accepted without question and treated like my own. I paid for his diaper service and bought the formula he needed. I wanted to be in her life. I asked Ella to marry me in 1972, when I was about thirty years old.

Around the same time, I got word that my father was gravely ill with leukemia, and that he wanted me to open his store back up for him and to keep it running. I quit my job without hesitation and moved back to Woodrow in the winter of 1972. A few months later, I married Ella and moved her and Garland down south to be with me.

My father lived until 1976, in the house behind his country store. I've told a lot of people that I wouldn't trade those four years I got to spend with him for anything. Finally, we had a chance to talk and interact, and I could see what type of man he was. As he trained me in the way he wanted his business to run, I realized he was a deeply principled man. During that time, it was common for shop owners to take advantage of poor black customers, but he refused to cheat people. A tireless entrepreneur, he believed in working long hours, but he also had a good sense of humor that made the time fly.

At the same time that I was carving out a first-time relationship with my father, my own son arrived. George, as it turned out, was born during one of the worst snowstorms in South Carolina history. He was born on a Wednesday at a hospital in Sumter, about sixteen miles away. The hospital discharged his mother that Friday, but the doctors wanted to keep George for observation. As I drove Ella home from the hospital, snowflakes started falling from the sky. And it snowed and snowed, for two days straight. This being South Carolina, there was no equipment or salt available to clear it from the roads. The snow kept falling, creating a huge impassable barrier between us and our new baby. People couldn't even get out of their driveways. So we had to wait what seemed like forever to welcome home little George. I believe that the doctors were ready to discharge him on Saturday, but we weren't able to get there until Tuesday.

After George was born, I made it a ritual to close the store at a certain time in the afternoon every day, to come home and spend an hour or two playing with him. I loved throwing him up in the air and catching him, and he loved our game, too.

Once we had a real emergency with him that could have been tragic. George was a toddler at the time, just starting to walk. My two young nieces were supposed to be taking care of him, but somehow he got hold of a costume-jewelry ring, a good-sized one. He put it in his mouth, of course, and it got lodged in his throat.

Someone from the house ran to get me at the store and told me that I better come quick. In a matter of minutes, we were in the car, making the long drive to the hospital in Sumter. My sister Lanie drove, and I jumped in the backseat with George, who was crying. It must have hurt bad, having a ring like that stuck in his windpipe. I was afraid that the thick ring would block his air passageway, so I stuck my finger down his throat and searched for it as gently as I could. It wasn't easy; George was sputtering and crying, and the ring was wedged pretty far down. We were halfway to Sumter before I finally touched the ring and eased it out of his throat. I was so relieved that he didn't choke on it. It seemed like a miracle.

I used to drink some when I lived in New Jersey, mostly on weekends. When I returned to South Carolina, my drinking picked up quite a bit. My brother-in-law operated a juke joint in Woodrow, and I would hang out there after work instead of going home. I started staying out late and drinking, the way I did when I was single. I guess I convinced myself that I wasn't doing anything wrong because I wasn't chasing women.

But when I would get home, I would be accused of all kinds of wrongdoing. I couldn't understand back then why my wife was so disapproving. I realize now that my thinking was pretty clouded by alcohol.

But even in my hazy state, I knew something was amiss one night in 1976 when I got home and the house was totally quiet. It's a funny thing; I could feel deep inside me that something was wrong the minute I pulled up in front of the house. I walked in and saw right away that a few things were missing. I walked into the kitchen and found that Ella had fixed me a full dinner and left it on the stove.

My family was gone, without a word. I had no forewarning, no nothing.

I went to both of my sisters, who spent a lot of time with Ella, and neither seemed to know what was going on. So I decided to take a week's vacation in Washington, D.C., in order to swing through her hometown in North Carolina and talk to Ella face-to-face. But as I drove through North Carolina, it occurred to me that maybe it wouldn't be a good idea to go to Ella's family's house. As I mulled the situation over, I convinced myself that I was the victim. After all, she hadn't told me she was leaving or where she was going; I wasn't even sure she and the boys were in Warrenton. Also, her parents were sure to be angry with me. As I drove, I considered the possibility that my presence might create a stormy situation. In the end, I opted to drive past Warrenton without stopping, and I headed for Washington, D.C., for the week.

That was a very, very hurtful period for me. At first I felt anger, and then I felt pain. I wished that Ella had told me what her plan was. I felt that I deserved a chance to talk about what was going on in her mind, and maybe we could have saved the marriage. But the way it went down, I was defenseless as well as helpless. I didn't know where my family was, until a child support notice arrived from the State of New Jersey more than a year later.

Those first years after she left, I drank even more heavily. I didn't contest the divorce when the papers arrived. I felt like a failure, to an extent. There had to be something I wasn't doing right.

And that really colored my thinking over the next years, when it came to having input into young George's life. Since Ella left when he was just a little boy, George seemed far out of my reach in New Jersey during the critical child-rearing years that followed. Although Ella's disappearance had hurt me, I certainly thought she was a fine mother, and I admired the good job she was doing with George and Garland. I didn't want to confuse George by intervening and possibly contradicting the principles she was raising him by. And I'm glad I didn't. I think he turned out very well. She did a wonderful job as a single mom, and I'm not sure that I could have contributed anything that would have helped him turn out any better.

It's not that I didn't want to be close to him. But I didn't want George to be confused about his loyalties to Mom versus those to Dad. Whenever I visited, I wouldn't impose any values on him because I didn't want to undercut anything she was teaching. I thought it would be better if Ella called the shots, since she was there with him and I was here.

I remember feeling kind of awkward with the boys during my earliest visits. Even though Garland is not my son, I've always strived to treat the two of them the same. I was so mindful of this when I visited that I purposely tried to avoid situations where I would pull George to me and leave Garland out. In retrospect, I probably overdid it and ended up withholding affection from both of them when they were young. Then, as they grew older, George and Garland seemed to act like macho little men when I would see them. As a result, I didn't reach out to the boys with a hug or a kiss because it seemed they would just shrug it off. I wasn't an affectionate father, not at all. To tell you the truth, I never even contemplated whether I was doing it right or wrong. The question didn't even occur to me. But it wasn't a lack of love. I guess it was just history repeating itself.

I tried to visit the boys regularly at first, and sometimes stayed two to three weeks at a time during those early years, but after a few years I couldn't afford to keep it up. When you operate a general store in the country, you don't earn a lot of money. That's why I had to close the store in 1977 and get a job. I worked a couple of odd jobs around my hometown, but nothing too stable until I got hired in 1991 at Shaw Air Force Base in Sumter, South Carolina. I still work there today, setting up rooms and moving furniture for events. It's part-time work that doesn't pay much, but at least it's steady money.

I never felt that I could afford to pay monthly child support, and Ella didn't hound me for it. The way I handled it was that I wrote out a check to Ella at the end of each year, after I totaled up my business expenses, adding in my share of extra income derived from our family farm. Sometimes I could mail only $300 to her, other times it was $500 or $600. When I got that first notice from the State of New Jersey, it demanded that I pay her $300 a month, but there was no way I could afford it. I wasn't even bringing that much home per month—at the time I was grossing only $300. I had to get a lawyer and pay him to get the amount reduced.

Likewise, I couldn't afford to visit much, and I couldn't send for George and Garland to come see me. After Ella and the kids left, I moved in with my oldest sister and rented out my house. Those were fairly lean years for me, and my work schedule didn't have a lot of give in it. I didn't have anyone who could have watched the boys while I was working, which meant summer visits just weren't feasible. I had dreams of spending time with my son; I had a glove and a softball and baseball that I must have kept twenty years, waiting to play catch with him. But that day never came. The miles between us became a barrier that I couldn't figure out how to surmount.

I admit that I should have done more during his childhood. I should have stayed in better touch. But my dependence on alcohol continued to grow, and as a result, my other priorities seemed to fade into the background.

For twelve years after Ella and the boys left, I used alcohol as my preferred means of escaping reality. But in 1984, God managed to get my attention and break that habit. I developed a life-threatening case of liver cirrhosis. My doctor told me bluntly that I would get better and that my liver would regenerate itself if I would just stop drinking. I was finally ready to hear what I had long known—it was time to give up the booze.

That afternoon, I stopped by the liquor store, bought a half pint of vodka, and I took a good sip of it. When I got home, I did a little soul searching. I sat the bottle on top of a linen closet in the bathroom, and decided to go a week without drinking it. Sure enough, I made it through the whole week, and I felt good about what I had done. So I decided to try to make it through an entire month.

Ten years later, that vodka bottle was still sitting there, untouched, when a friend came by to help me fix my washing machine. He asked about the vodka in the bathroom, and so I gave it to him. I had been alcohol-free for a decade. I've never looked back since that day. I did it cold turkey, just me and the Good Master above.

I haven't conquered every problem, though. I still smoke cigarettes. I will get around to quitting one of these days.

By the time I stopped drinking for good, George was in high school and I had missed out on his early years. I was hopeful, though, that things between us would change as he got older. I envisioned that as he matured, we would be able to talk man-to-man, and I would explain to him the things I was going through. Then he would get to know me better, and I would get to know him, similar to the bond I created with my father in my thirties. I thought I had plenty of time, but I guess I put my money on the wrong horse. I was waiting on a day that so far hasn't materialized.

Once George and Garland reached their teens, I stopped coming for longer visits because it seemed they wanted to be with their little friends and they didn't have a lot of time for me. But I made it a point to be there for the big events in his life. I'm proud that one time when he wrote me and asked for money to buy a car, I was able to send him the full amount that he asked for. I'm proud that I made it to all of George's graduations. But I couldn't help but see signs that I had waited too long to kindle a relationship. I made a four-day trip to Newark for George's dental school graduation, but besides the actual graduation ceremony, I only got to see him one time. He and some friends came by my hotel room and stayed for a while.

I carry beat-up photographs of George, eaten up from twenty years in my wallet. I have framed copies of articles about him on the wall. But there's more to fathering than just being able to display mementos, and I owe it to my son to try to make a change. That's why I've had to teach myself to tell George "I love you" when we talk on the phone. It was hard at first. I've always been introverted when it comes to expressing my feelings. I never got to the point with my mother where I could tell her I loved her, and it was late in my father's life when I bonded with him. This is all new to me, and I'm only feeling my way. The only road map in parenting that we have is what our own parents showed us. You don't know what you're missing until you grow up and become exposed to other ways of doing things. Then the question is, are we able to change ourselves?

Now I'm the one waiting for George's attention. Now I wait on him to return my phone calls. I know that his job and his *Pact* responsibilities are time-consuming. He travels a lot and is incredibly busy. I believe that time will work things out. Things will settle down in George's life one day, and when they do, we will get together. I'm only sorry that when he does get a chance to join me down here in South Carolina, we will have missed out on the opportunity for him to meet so many people in his family tree. All my brothers and sisters have passed on, except for Lanie.

Still, George has many cousins who are excited about all that he's accomplished. They've seen him on TV and collected his write-ups. He's family. That's the way they think of him, although they don't know him.

I continue to invite George to family reunions so he can meet the folks down here who are so proud of him. Perhaps one of these days, he'll make time to come.

Chapter 3

GEORGE

What It Takes

WHEN THERE'S A WALL in the middle of a relationship, you know only what's happening on your side of it. Finding out my father's life story really opened my eyes. Due to the distance between us, I never knew anything about his parents or his upbringing until recently.

Learning about his life explained so much about why he is the way he is. Now I understand better the forces that brought about our separation.

The two of us have been cordial toward each other for years, but the problem is that our relationship feels more virtual than real. I know it's there, like money that's in a bank account. Yet it's not readily accessible where I can hold it, touch it, use it.

It's not that I have negative feelings about my father. I don't. I have a lot of love for him and think he's a really likeable guy. But every time we talk, I feel like we're doomed to stay in our polite "Hi, how you doing?" world forever. We exchange some superficial words and then hang up. Click.

All I need to hear from him are the simple words "I'm sorry that I wasn't there for you."

I think that's the one thing that will tear down the wall I built between us. Then we can start building something together. If he never says that, then we'll just continue to be mouthing words, in our virtual relationship, for the rest of our lives.

I know he didn't mean to disappoint or hurt me. I know he's proud that he made it to all my graduations. And I appreciate that he came. But by showing up for only those moments, he left me alone to fight the everyday battles. All I knew was to keep on swinging.

I only wish he'd been there for me on the first day of school, not just the triumphant last day.

Instead, I rolled a cartful of emotional baggage onto campus when I arrived. And Rameck and Sampson lugged a ton of it, too.

So we traded our strengths. The things we admired about one another, we ended up copying.

Rameck, the most skeptical of the three of us, taught me to be less gullible. Back in those days, if you were selling, I was buying. Sometimes, as a poverty-stricken student, I would buy a submarine sandwich and bring it back to my room with every intention of eating half and saving the rest for the next day. But in our crowded dorms, I often ran into a hungry friend who would take one look at the sandwich and say, "Man, let me get some of that." I never hesitated, even though I was giving away tomorrow's dinner.

Rameck told me that I made it easy for people to take advantage of me. "Come on, man, haven't you ever noticed that when you're hungry, that guy never has anything to share with you?" He was right. Those "friends" never offered me their food, and worse, they looked at me as if I were crazy if I asked for some. It happened over and over, but I never noticed it until Rameck pointed it out to me.

Sometimes we ran into friends from high school who claimed they had high-profile jobs and bragged that they had connections to this or that famous person. It always drove me crazy to hear about all their success while we still had years of being broke college students in front of us. But Rameck always listened with a leery expression, picking up on how things didn't add up. "You believed that?" he would ask me incredulously after some friend fed us a line about his soon-to-take-off career in the music industry. "How come he's still living with his mom if he's producing records?" Rameck would ask. Countless times he gave me that "This is bogus" look that always made me feel ridiculous. He taught me to stop stressing out about other people and focus on making my own way to success.

Watching how Rameck didn't take any crap helped me draw the line. And Rameck will tell you that I taught him to be less confrontational. He continually walked around with his fists clenched, ready to throw down and defend himself even if the situation didn't call for it. Once we got to Seton Hall, Rameck had a hard time adjusting to the new environment. He got into fights constantly. I realized he needed to learn a little finesse. "Why do you get bent out of shape over every little problem?" I used to ask him. "Take a look around here. Does that behavior even fit in here? You don't have to be supermacho every second of the day to get respect." Over time, we seemed to meet in the middle; he became less defensive, and I became more assertive. We balanced each other out.

What Sam brought to the table was his phenomenal work ethic and also his shrewdness with finances. Sam has a strong sense of self-discipline that's at the root of both of these talents. I've always been impressed at how he managed to keep a few dollars in his pocket to bail the three of us out, back when we were penniless students.

With a lot of effort on my part, I taught myself to copy his study skills, but I never could figure out how he had the discipline to save when we had so little income. The real reason Sam made sure to always keep a dollar in his pocket was that he knew he didn't have anyone to fall back on. I had the luxury of being able to rely on my mother for financial help. But for Sam, there was no sense in phoning home: Sam's mom didn't work and she had very little income. She hadn't been able to pay for Sam's monthly bus pass in high school, much less his college application fees, so Sam grew up fending for himself financially. At Seton Hall, he watched over his money like it was his lifeline. His future, he knew, depended on how well he performed in college, and he wasn't going to let his grades or his financial struggle force him out. In his rearview mirror was his old Newark neighborhood, and he was determined not to return to that life.

Although we didn't set out to do it this way, we ended up pooling our best traits and using them to complete ourselves. By accident, we performed the job our fathers had defaulted on. We helped one another become better men. This is what makes Sam and Rameck my real brothers. We pushed one another, carried one another when we were weak, and together we made it to the finish line. By graduation time, the three of us had coached and coaxed one another not to give up countless times. When we put on those caps and gowns, it felt as if we had accomplished an almost impossible dream. I only wish we could identify the exact forces that propelled us to defy the statistics facing fatherless boys so we could load our communities up with this ammunition.

Anyone would think that my brother Garland's life and mine would have turned out identically. We shared the same bedroom, him in the bottom bunk and me on the top. We both slipped and slid, without a father's firm hand at our back. But he slipped toward the streets and I slid toward school. While I filled out my college applications, he was spending more time than he should have hanging out in our old stomping grounds, across the street in the Stella Wright housing projects. As a result, Garland spent a few nights in jail on a minor drug charge. Today my older brother is an unmarried dad, although I have to say he's doing a great job as a father. He and his beautiful two-year-old daughter have a close relationship and they spend a lot of time together.

How did we wind up on such different paths? I'll never know for sure, but I think it's partly because he didn't encounter the same positive messages I found. Our mom never went to college, so understandably she didn't emphasize its importance to her kids. When my third-grade teacher Mrs. Johnson explained to me the financial benefits of higher education, she instantly convinced me that college was the place for me. I could see my future so clearly from that day. That was all I needed to hear. Move off Quitman Street, own a nice car, have an interesting career? I couldn't wait. "College is for me," I told myself. "If I get a degree, I can be in control of my life."

I don't think Garland had that message drummed into him as much as I did.

Mentors make the difference. I trusted Mrs. Johnson's words so whole-heartedly that I turned Rameck and Sam into believers, too. I'm the one who convinced them that we should make a "pact" to go to college together.

For Sampson, his karate teacher Reggie provided the voice that gave him life-changing advice. "If you don't do your one hundred sit-ups, you're not hurting anyone but yourself," Reggie would say, and then walk out of the room. Those words echoed in Sam's ears, and became the foundation for the work ethic that is his trademark. Just as Sam forced himself to do the required sit-ups and some extra ones, too, he became a top student by never giving up until he mastered the tricky concepts in our college classes. Years after Reggie instilled it, that work ethic is now doing triple duty—because Sam taught Rameck and me to use it as our biggest weapon against failure.

I'm not a father yet, by choice. I refuse to bring a child into the world until I'm ready for the responsibility—all of it. And right now I've got a lot on my plate, nurturing the many fatherless kids I meet who are starving for some attention and direction. Ever since high school, I've essentially been trying to brainwash friends I see going down the wrong path. "Look at the other guys from the neighborhood who got involved in drugs or gangs," I tell them. "You see they're in prison, they're not having such a fun time right now. Is that what you want?" I push them to realize that their everyday decisions matter. So make your decisions reflect your dreams, I tell them. Only you can make your life something that you can be proud of.

I didn't have a father to whisper encouraging words like that to me, but I can't hide from the fact that there's a ton of fatherless sons out here like me who are twisting in the wind, seriously in need of a positive role model. I can't fix my past, but I can definitely immerse myself in our next generation so they don't have to go through what I did. I can provide advice so they don't bump their heads on the same wall that I did. Now that I'm older and wiser, I know where the trouble spots are on that wall and where young people are likely to bruise themselves. It's my duty to pass on the knowledge, or else we're walking in place.

I knew instantly, by the time we got to Seton Hall University: *We've got to drop some bread crumbs and show kids like us how to get here. We've got to encourage them.*

I felt a powerful desire to unlock the secret of success, to be the mentor who helps poor youngsters find their way here, as Mrs. Johnson helped me. So did Sam and Rameck. During our freshman year, the three of us made friends with a handful of other minority students and formed a group. We threw some parties to raise funds to expose students from the Newark schools to our campus.

The difference between Newark and Seton Hall is striking. In gray, unfriendly Newark, police sirens shriek constantly and kids hang out under the streetlights all night, but just down the street in orderly South Orange, where Seton Hall is located, everyone's smiling, acting neighborly, and shaking hands. No lie, the grass really *is* greener on the South Orange side. Here, the lawns are fertilized and fussed over until they reach the perfect shade of golf-course green.

On a spring Saturday, we brought some kids in from a nearby Newark elementary school for a tour of the campus, and then put them in a classroom and broke it down in the best way we knew how. "Yo, shorty, this is how it is here. You can have all this," we told them. "I know you hear from your friends that college is corny. But trust us, that's wack. This is where you want to be."

It definitely wasn't your average college tour. But we were youngsters ourselves, doing our best to persuade the grade school kids we'd assembled to think past the quick fix. We wanted them to realize there's more to "making it" than getting a new pair of sneakers, some jeans, a nice watch. We tried to connect with them, playing up the advantages of campus life from our vantage point: "Here, you can eat as much food as you want from the cafeteria. You've got cable television in your room, and air-conditioning, too." This is one place, we told them, where you don't have to worry about fighting every day. And there's not always someone tapping you on the shoulder, trying to recruit you to do something illegal.

Some were open to our talk, others resisted. Can you blame them? At home they didn't have anyone helping with their homework or encouraging them to think about college.

We knew it would be hard undoing the brainwashing that these kids had endured for years. For us, that was just the beginning.

And truthfully, parents who have never been to college can't be expected to supply the advice that will help their child find their way through the testing and application maze. It's funny how so many professionals from the middle class complain about urban youths, instead of realizing that it's up to them to open doors for these kids. We need to treat each child like a diamond, not a future thug. If it hadn't been for Mrs. Johnson's encouragement or that chance encounter with a dentist, I never would have had the guts to dream of a world beyond Quitman Street.

That's why Rameck, Sam, and I are firm believers in the power of role models. We wouldn't be where we are today if we hadn't had them. We only regret that there's such a shameful shortage of mentors.

In Newark, I've seen with my own eyes that there's a tangible rift between older men and younger men when it comes to mentoring. All the politicians and leaders, they'll take care of their sons. But no one's helping poor kids from the ghetto who don't have connections. No one's passing the torch to them, or offering to help them let their light shine.

Mentoring is something that every professional needs to find time to do. It's not that you're training someone to take your place. It's a legacy that you're building. And the payoff is a tremendous investment in our community's future. If you mentor ten guys, then you've created a legacy of ten professionals who can strengthen our community so that you're not doing it alone. The middle class needn't fear us, it should be mentoring us. We need to learn what you know, and in return, we'll enhance and strengthen the groundwork you've laid.

I'll never forget how it felt to be adrift and confused in college. I needed someone to help mentally prepare me, and to tell me simply that they believed in me. And that's why I'm never too busy to offer advice to somebody who's striving. As long as they're trying to get an education and do something positive with their lives, I just can't walk away.

Because I take this part of my mission so seriously, I collect new "mentees" all the time and I'm constantly interacting with them. Sometimes it gets crazy with the e-mails, calls, and text messages I get all day long from my crew. But I love doing it. My two newest mentees are Stanley and Taysha, both ninth-graders I met during the summer of 2006 when they took part in a youth jobs program. They happened to stop by my booth during a seminar at my former workplace, the University of Medicine & Dentistry of New Jersey, and after we got talking, they just wouldn't leave. I took an instant liking to both, especially when I found out they go to my old school, University High. So I just "adopted" them.

Bubbly fifteen-year-old Taysha told me she lives in the projects. She had just finished reading *The Pact* when we met, and she felt so exuberant about meeting one of its authors that a day or so later, she showed up at my office with her latest report card in hand. Not only had she earned straight A's, but every teacher put a check in the "pleasure to teach" comment box. As soon as I learned that, I knew the kind of kid she was. Streetwise and book-smart, too, she's a diamond in the rough who knows her priorities, but she's having a hard time finding support to follow her dreams. I want to do whatever I can to help her stay on course, now that she's entering into the high school whirl of boys and other temptations.

"Are your parents the kind who will stay on top of your grades? If you drop down to a C in one of your classes, will they jump on your behind?" I asked. She said no. Her father didn't live in the home, and her mother stayed busy raising three teenagers. I knew that story well. So I took the leap. "I'm going to be that person for you," I told her.

Within a week, she had dropped by my office at least three times and introduced herself to every staffer in my hallway. "I can't believe you're my mentor," she told me once. "I run into people all the time who *say* they're going to help me but never do it." She's so hyped to get to her future. That's the enthusiasm I love to see. And I hope it never burns out. I want only to help these kids preserve that energy and make it to their goals.

It's amazing to me how hungry these young people are for attention. The positive influence a mentor can have is amazing. Stanley, a short, chocolate-complexioned kid who is much quieter than Taysha, used to tell me he wanted to be a lawyer. "Why not think bigger?" I asked him. "Think about becoming a judge." Now he walks around telling everyone he aspires to be a judge. And I think that's great. Our kids need to open their eyes.

These kids need support. The things they're going through at home might scare a horror film director. Taysha once called me, totally freaked out, to tell me she had seen a dead body in her apartment complex. The same week, another mentee was in my office crying over the combined stress of a dying stepfather and a delay in his financial aid for college.

"Play the hand you're dealt," I tell young people all the time. "I know life is stressful, but you can't let it deter you from your goals. You've got to stay in school. It's the only way to change your life."

Just like the kids I mentor today, Sam, Rameck, and I had our own misconceptions about what college would be like. We thought the hard part was just getting there. We didn't realize how hard it would be to stay.

We learned quickly that college is a business, and there are no free rides at expensive private schools. The school actually threatened to bar us from enrolling because we had unpaid tuition bills from the previous semester.

Each of us made an appointment to plead our case with the bursar.

Rameck even brought his transcript to the meeting, confident that he wouldn't be denied. "Just look at my grades," he said proudly. "Please release my account."

The bursar chuckled. "That's nice, Mr. Hunt, but it really doesn't matter."

He told us all the same thing: He couldn't forgive the debt. If he did it for us, he'd have to do it for everyone.

But we wouldn't leave his office until he relented. We suggested countless compromises. "Put us on a payment plan, anything," we begged. Finally, he agreed to let us make nominal monthly payments and allowed us to register for the next semester.

Whenever it seemed as though our good fortune had hit a dead end, we always found a new path. I've grown to think that God has put us on this mission and helped us along the way. I wasn't a regular churchgoer as a kid and neither were Sam or Rameck. Yet life has taught me that God truly does help those who help themselves. I often preach that message when I speak to young audiences.

I tell them that you can never be too afraid to ask for help. If you need to get from point A to point B and you don't know how, I've found that all you need to do is take the plunge and just set out walking toward your goal. Nothing will change if you just stay put. So start walking. Along the way, don't be afraid to let people know what you need and what you're after. Somehow help will appear. That's what we experienced every time. Whenever people saw us floundering, trying to get to the next step on our own, they helped us.

One guardian angel who became our greatest advocate was Carla Dickson, the director of our pre-medical/pre-dental program at Seton Hall. I can't count the times she intervened when we needed an advocate on campus, helping us to solve our own problems and pushing us when we were on the verge of giving up.

I thank God for the help of angels like Carla and believe that I have been called to pass on the blessings. Every chance I get, I preach the importance of "education, education, education" to these kids, and I try to give them the tools to succeed.

But as long as their dad's missing, their tool kit's incomplete. Studies show that when dads disappear from the household, it heightens a kid's chances that he or she will drop out of school before graduation. Also, students who live with both parents are less likely to get suspended.

These are the reasons that dads need to show up starting on the first day of school, not just graduation day. They're needed on the front lines to support their kids, especially because inside many urban schools, it's a battle just for a kid to receive a decent education.

I'm reminded of another mentee of mine, Kenny, who caught his first glimpse of The Three Doctors at age ten, when his mom called him to the TV to see us on *Oprah*. We didn't make much of an impression on him at first. But a week later, he saw a poster promoting *The Pact,* and something clicked: "These guys are real. And they're from my city," he thought. Kenny and his mother, Monica, made plans to come to our next book signing to meet us.

When the day of the book signing came, his mom had a sore throat and didn't want to go out. "If I don't mention the book signing, he probably won't even remember it," his mother thought.

Wrong. Kenny reminded her of it, and protested loudly when Monica said she didn't feel well enough to take him. An hour later, they were in the car on their way to the bookstore. Monica decided that if Kenny wanted to meet some doctors that much, she wasn't going to stand in the way. At the book signing, Kenny grabbed a pen and started taking notes as we spoke. Monica had never seen him so enthralled. During the Q&A period, she raised her hand and asked what inspiration we could offer to her son to stay in school and not let peer pressure derail him.

She expected only a few words of advice, but since that day, we've appointed ourselves the official mentors of Kenny, who hopes to become a doctor. We've found him to be such a standout that we've made him our guest of honor at many Three Doctors events.

That day at the book signing, I gave Kenny my e-mail address and told him to stay in touch. During the years, we've visited and conversed a lot and I've shared my advice with him. Kenny doesn't see his father often. He's a bright kid hungry for a male role model. Over and over, I encourage Kenny never to be afraid to approach the person holding the knowledge he needs.

Kenny's an eager learner. But seventh grade was a rough year for him. His parents' divorce became finalized and he started a new school. Before long, his math grade dropped to a D. His mom got concerned. And so did I.

I came to his house, sat with him at his desk, and helped him do a few math problems. "What's happening in math?" I asked. "Why is your grade so low?"

I had to probe to find out what really was holding Kenny back in math. It turns out, he was having a hard time trying to learn in an unruly classroom. As soon as the bell rang, chaos erupted. Kenny's classmates did everything but pay attention. They wandered in late, played games on their school-issued laptop computers, sent one another e-mails, threw paper airplanes, and stole stuff from the teacher's desk when he had his back turned. One kid had mastered the prank of making the classroom phone ring, which was a constant disruption. Another student refused to take a seat: "I don't feel like sitting down so I'm gonna stand up," he told the young, inexperienced teacher, who ended up doing more fussing than teaching.

In the midst of it all, Kenny sat in the back of the class trying to learn. Sometimes he gave in and misbehaved, too, drawing pictures of the teacher with stupid faces and playing games on his own laptop.

Together, we made a plan to improve his math grade. "You need to surround yourself with people who will help you and not bring you down," I told him. "Why don't you go to the people who are getting A's all the time and ask if they'll help you? And start by going to see your math teacher so you can catch up on the stuff you missed. Don't be shy, Kenny, go after what you want."

Dutifully, he went to the teacher and they agreed to meet on the following Wednesday.

But when Wednesday arrived, Kenny really didn't want to go. When the bell rang after school, he met up with his friends and started walking home with them. He had gotten three blocks from the school when his conscience got the better of him. "I got to go back and meet with my math teacher," he explained to his friends.

The teacher was still there, waiting.

Although he didn't want to, Kenny stayed for ninety minutes that day, brushing up on his pre-algebra. At the chalkboard, he practiced his number sentences, erasing them over and over until he grasped the concept. He continued to study the material with his tutor.

And by the end of the year, he had brought his D up to a B. Kenny knows he learned an important lesson in seventh grade: that he can conquer any problem.

That's good, because his eighth-grade science class is shaping up to be his next big problem. Although science has always been his favorite class, he's not pulling his usual A's. "I've learned my lesson," Kenny said soberly. "I'm not going to wait till the last minute to get help like last year. My science teacher told me to come for help on Wednesday morning." This time, he made a point to get there early.

Every time I get a report of success from a kid like Kenny, I feel like a proud papa.

This is how I'm building my legacy. I mentor ferociously because I didn't have a cheering dad behind me. That's what pushes me to go above and beyond, to wear myself out being a mentor. We didn't have that fatherly support. Yet I desired it so intensely that now, I provide it with intensity.

I believe in sharing the blessings I have. I've always let friends stay with me, raid my fridge, share whatever I have. If I made it alone to the top with tons of money, I wouldn't enjoy it.

Maybe some people are threatened by the younger generation, but I'm secure. I'm trying to leave this world better off than when I arrived. It's my responsibility to pass knowledge down and pull people up.

When I die, I want ten thousand professionals at my funeral all saying the same thing: "No question, if it wasn't for Dr. Jenkins, I wouldn't be where I am today. He encouraged me to stay in school. He got me on the right track."

I think that's an achievable goal. And if I make it, I'll take great joy in knowing I enabled a fatherless generation to go higher than I did.

Chapter 4

GEORGE

Learning to Be a Man

When you grow up in a poor neighborhood, escaping from
poverty is the ultimate test of your courage.

It isn't easy for a boy to find his way to maturity and manhood without
a father's support.

What helped us is that the three of us created "superordinate goals." It
sounds fancy, but basically it means that we joined together to reach beyond
the self-limiting behaviors we saw in front of us and pushed our way to the
next level.

Simply put, it was our pact that made the difference. That's how we defied the statistics that told us that, as fatherless boys, we were at a higher risk
of dropping out of school, becoming violent, and becoming absentee
dads ourselves.

The best way to overcome the void left by an absentee father, we've
found, is to surround yourself with positive people who can point the way
to success. In the coming chapters, we hope to help out, by sharing the stories of people overcoming the same obstacles you face.

Your first challenge: teaching yourself to become a man without a father's guidance.

Here are a few young brothers we've met who have managed to do just that.

NAJEE

Najee Carter, a senior at Bloomfield High School in New Jersey, reached out to the three of us after he finished reading our first book. In an e-mail, he wrote: "I want to sincerely thank you for writing *The Pact*. This has helped me to succeed, and go for my goals. I was born in Newark to a single mother. I can relate to your story because I know how it feels to be raised by a strong black woman.

"The strength of my mother, however, cannot fill the void and emptiness of not having a father in my household. Through my lifetime, I have chosen role models to fill that emptiness. For example, God, my mother, grandmother, Nelson Mandela, Malcolm X, Tupac, P. Diddy, Martin Luther King, Jr., Denzel Washington, and most recently the Three Doctors. You have become one of my greatest role models because your story hits so close to home."

Najee, we've learned, is a talented poet who confronts the issues of racism, religion, insecurities, and finding one's identity in his writing. He's a grass-roots Shakespeare, breaking it down in poems like this one titled "Voice of the Ghetto":

Single mothers struggling, childhood cut short
Father not ready so she takes him to court
He gives child support but that's not what the child needs
He needs someone to teach him, show him, and lead
He needs someone to trust and to direct him to manhood
She needs a father to love her and to tell her she looks good

Najee obviously knows of what he writes firsthand. His parents never married, and he doesn't see his father often.

Yet he's determined to break the cycle. He intends to go to Hampton University to study journalism. He wants to write for a living, and to keep penning thought-provoking works.

Najee sees the harm in the trend toward single motherhood. "Certain things, my mom can't do alone. It's the whole masculinity factor," Najee said. "She can't teach me certain things. She tried. When we were kids, she took us to play basketball, but she couldn't teach us."

Najee's got a perfectionist streak, his mother told us, and as a result, he's never felt comfortable going out for organized sports because he believes he's not as good as the other kids. "He felt he had nobody to show him those things. He feels vulnerable around other guys. He doesn't want to look less than perfect," she said. "From what I see, a father is irreplaceable. Other people can help fill the void but they never replace it," she added.

Yet Najee has made up his mind that he's going to overcome this handicap. He's adopted a mind-set that we call "Be better, not bitter." He's entering manhood determined not to repeat the cycle of fatherlessness. He is insistent that he will never father a child out of wedlock. No babymamas for him.

Growing up without a father means you have to ask people for help, Najee realizes. One reason he is such an outstanding young man is that he's constantly on the lookout for healthy, inspiring people worthy of being emulated. "I look up to Martin Luther King for his strength. Not his physical strength, but the way he led the nonviolent movement. That was the perfect example of what a man should really be," Najee told us.

He also seeks out role models he knows, too, to answer intimate questions. His uncle, for example, provides advice on girls and grooming. And he's followed our advice and cut loose a few friends who used to lure him into trouble. "Now I don't have that negative energy all around me. I've gained a few friends, too, who have the same goals as me," he said.

"I long ago made the decision to never allow myself to conform to the corruption of the streets. Because of my strength and relationship with God, I have been able to do this. Unfortunately, everyone isn't as blessed," he wrote.

Najee, a good-looking kid with close-cropped hair, refuses to blend in. Even when he puts on the urban gear favored by today's teenagers, he loves wearing attention-getting colors to set himself apart. Ever the questioner, he doesn't hesitate to challenge teen behavior. But he doesn't do it through confrontation—instead, he has found that a more effective way to get his points across is through poetry. For Christmas, he even asked his mom for a guitar so he could teach himself to set his poems to music.

We know that teenagers risk rejection when they don't follow the crowd, but Najee proves it's possible to be both popular and an independent thinker. His class voted him "best personality" and "most likely to succeed" in his senior year. Classmates obviously admire the way he constantly prods them to use their God-given brains and think about their actions. Recently he gently scolded a friend on MySpace who referred to herself as a bitch: "You should never call yourself that," he told her.

It's not your average teenager who writes a mission statement for his life. But Najee has done so—and his unsolicited advice to his MySpace pal reflects the mission he's chosen: "To inspire all people but specifically minorities who are often held in bondage to stereotypes, labels, and expectations. I believe it is up to us to transcend the negativity placed on us."

QUAMEEN

When the three of us visited Cleveland in 2005, we met an impressive group of young men from the Cleveland public schools called the Barbara Byrd Bennett Scholars. These well-dressed guys, all in shirts and ties, had a million questions for us. They were hungry to know the path to success. Deemed promising but at-risk students, they were handpicked for the Scholars program in eighth grade. They've been guaranteed a full college scholarship if they stay in the program and keep their grades up. Nearly all of these young men will be the first in their families to go to college, as long as they stay focused and stay in school. This bold pilot project is named after the chief executive officer of the Cleveland schools who helped spearhead it. In a way, these thirty-three young men carry the hopes of their struggling urban school district on their shoulders. For them, *The Pact* was required reading. And they've made a similar promise to one another, to stick together and help one another over their obstacles.

As you might suspect, it's mainly the mothers who come to the parent meetings and support their sons through the demanding Scholars program. Not too many fathers are that involved.

One young man in the program put his head in his hands and searched his memory when asked about his father. "I know his name, I just can't remember it," he said, screwing up his face in concentration. He is one of a few young men in the program who have never even met their fathers.

Another scholar, Quameen, eighteen, is a beefy 245-pound football player with a confident smile. Yet he didn't used to like what he saw when he looked in the mirror. He resembles his dad, in the round shape of his face and his chocolate skin. For years, he wrestled with the fact that he looked so much like the man he hated.

Quameen didn't see much of his father in his early years. He stayed in school and kept out of trouble, with no help from Dad.

Now the idea of creating a relationship with his father "is like building a house on water. It'll never work. We can never get there," he said.

As a young boy raised in a house of women—a mom and four sisters—Quameen recognized as a teenager that he needed a man's influence. "If you were raised like I was, you might take on women's tendencies: catch an attitude, get moody. It gets hard because you don't have that father to be that extra voice. Point-blank, a woman can't raise a man. She just can't put that killer instinct into you like your father can," he explained.

So he went in search of male role models. He walked up to the corner and sold marijuana for a while. "Only reason I went up there to the corner was I was looking for somebody to be like and that's all there was around. I was a nickel-and-dime hustler. I sold five-dollar and ten-dollar bags. But I found out I was smarter than that. My mother didn't raise a fool. Even the guys on the corner told me I was too smart to be standing out there with them."

He knows now that it was an immature phase. "I didn't realize the seriousness of it. It was like a game to me. Soon as they say a certain word, you gotta run because the police might be coming. It was a game of who could sell out the fastest." Luckily for him, he never ran into any trouble with the law before deciding the street hustle wasn't for him.

Now he hangs with college-bound boys through the Scholars program, and he's found a mentor, his mother's ex-boyfriend, who encourages him to stay focused on his schoolwork. "Education is a small price to pay for a lifetime of pleasure" is one of his mentor's favorite sayings. A high school senior, Quameen hopes to find a career in the communications field, maybe as a radio host.

The hardest lessons to learn without a father, Quameen said, are about sex and love. "A dad is supposed to give you your first condom. My mother attempted to talk to me about sex, but I don't want to talk about it with her. That's what the fathers are there for. When you don't have your father and you don't want to talk about sex with your mother, then who do you talk to? I went to the wrong people about it at first."

He had to undo the messages that urban culture sent him about women, and teach himself right and wrong. "At first, I was under the impression that you ain't no man until you had sex," he said. He had a lot of friends who sought sex constantly and carelessly. Some became fathers before they got out of high school.

Yet he knew that he didn't want to go that route. All four of his sisters became pregnant in high school. He watched each of them repeat his mom's pattern as a single mother. "I've seen the struggles and hard times they have to go through. I wouldn't want to put a woman through that," Quameen says. "My mother and my sisters are the five strongest black women I know today. All of them have raised children without help. That's hard."

So he found a steady girlfriend, and although they're now in a long-distance relationship, he's faithful to her. "I don't do anything to people I don't want them to do to me."

Quameen has navigated his way through the most common pitfalls and is well on his way to college. He's surrounded himself with positive messages—the Scholars program, the football team—and decided to let the distractions alone. He had the good sense to look past the influences on the corner, and kept searching until he found better role models.

WILL

One of Sampson's closest friends while growing up in Newark was a guy named Will, who lived in the projects. Will's parents separated when Will was only a few months old. His dad found time for running the streets, drinking, and heavy drugs, but never had any time for his son. There was nothing unusual in this—that was the pattern in our Newark neighborhoods. But as any little boy knows, it doesn't feel good to be neglected by your father.

When Will was young, he occasionally ran into his father while visiting his paternal grandmother. He got birthday cards faithfully every year from his father, but they were always signed in his grandmother's handwriting.

His mother tried to fill in the gaps and rear him on her own. A strict mom, she set firm rules in hopes of protecting Will from the problems that plague fatherless boys. As a youngster, he was always the one who had to be in the house by nine P.M. when everybody else stayed out until ten or eleven.

She kept him busy with sports, trying to prevent him from having idle time on his hands. "I was always walking through here with a basketball when the other kids were stealing cars," he remembered. It touched him to see how much she sacrificed. She never broke down in front of him, but sometimes he could hear her crying softly in her bedroom when she couldn't afford to buy him new sneakers or something else he needed.

"I give my mother all the credit, she was great," he said. "But she couldn't teach me the toughness of being a man."

While hanging out in the streets as a teenager, he made the typical mistakes. Without a father in his life, he relied on his friends to give him the scoop on women and birth control.

It's such a familiar story that it's easy to predict what happened next: Will conceived a child with his girlfriend before he graduated from high school.

But that's where the predictability ends in this story.

Realizing that it's natural for most men to copy their father's parenting style, whether it was good or bad, Will made a conscious decision not to go down that road. For him, it wasn't difficult. "I never had my dad there for me so I knew I could be a better dad than that." He knew he had to "man up." He told himself, "I created this baby and I need to take care of it, no matter what."

It meant that he had to make some drastic changes. By age seventeen, he had left school, gotten a job at a psychiatric hospital, and rented an apartment, and was supporting his girlfriend and their baby daughter, Asia. He couldn't afford a car so he commuted to work on the train and the bus. He felt alone because his friends were still enjoying their happy-go-lucky teen years. "It was a lot to swallow," he admitted. "When my friends were hanging out, I couldn't go have fun. I had to go buy Pampers and milk."

Breaking out of the unhealthy patterns he sees all around him hasn't been easy. When his daughter was young, he watched how many of his friends with kids neglected their families, and he struggled mightily against the desire to run with his old crowd. It took him a while to realize that what his friends were doing was selfish: "They would rather run the streets and leave the baby in the house with the mother."

For Will, it helped to remember how unloved he felt by his father. "I make sure I see my daughter every day. That's something I didn't have," he said.

Eventually he split up with his daughter's mother, but he has remained a committed father to Asia.

Will, now thirty-three, married two years ago and has three young sons. He is the picture of stability. His wife's father helped him get a good job as a chief chemical operator making antacids and antiperspirants. He still lives in Newark, only five minutes from the housing projects where he grew up, but now Will has a three-bedroom house with a finished basement and a yard.

His successes as a husband and father are huge accomplishments, considering that Will almost never glimpsed any happy marriages when he was growing up. Yet he made up his mind that he wouldn't walk away from his commitments. "I feel like I'm doing good, although there's always room to do better. I'm a Mr. Mom type. I'll do the laundry, pick the kids up from school; I take care of it all, it doesn't matter."

His fourteen-year-old daughter, Asia, is Sam's goddaughter. Will is an affectionate, involved dad who chaperones Asia's field trips and still calls her his "baby girl," although she's now five-foot-nine. Her achievements at school are a testament to the power of having an involved father. She makes good grades, and her teachers speak highly of her. In eighth grade, she headed the school's robotics team. Although she's tall and breathtakingly beautiful, she isn't fixated on her appeal to boys.

Perhaps that self-confidence is the biggest gift that her attentive dad has given her. Will admits it gives him a heart attack when Asia wears what he calls her "where's the rest of it?" outfits—yet he trusts her when she goes out.

"Don't let temptation take you where you don't want to go," he has often told her.

At age seventeen, Will told himself to man up. It's the kind of thing a father should say to his son, but Will didn't have a dad and he didn't allow himself to use that as an excuse, either. Although he didn't have a role model, he's certainly become one by raising sons and a daughter who are emotionally complete and fully equipped for the world.

Chapter 5

GEORGE

What I Know Best

I T'S NO SMALL TASK to teach ourselves to become men without a role model. Sam, Rameck, and I banged our heads against the wall so many times that it's a wonder our ears aren't still ringing. It's important for men who came up this way to pass along their hard-earned knowledge. We asked ourselves, what is the best advice we could offer to those in the same circumstance, forced to navigate their way to manhood without a father? These are the bread crumbs we leave for you. Learn them, live them, and then pass them down to someone else.

Get your education. Yes, how you look is important, but too many kids prize their appearance over more substantive things. Education can let you be in control of your life. Even if nobody else around you is thinking about tomorrow, don't let them dictate your future. Set your goals and achieve them. Look into colleges and find out how to access scholarships and financial aid.

Use the buddy system. Hang with the friends who have solid goals, not with the ones who will steer you in the wrong direction.

Find a mentor. Better yet, find more than one. Identify the people in your community who are doing positive things and ask for their help and advice.

And never let the fear of embarrassment keep you from asking the questions that will help you unlock success.

Think before you act. When you can, walk away from confrontation.

Don't have unprotected sex if you're not ready to be a father. Recognize that when you lay down with a girl, it's a huge responsibility. Young men chasing after an orgasm have brought too many babies into this world that they have no intention of taking care of.

Show respect to women. Never mind what the songs and music videos say. Whenever we see a man mistreating a woman, we need to challenge that.

Be an individual with your own identity. Don't fall victim to negative peer pressure or temptation. Stay away from drugs, alcohol, and cigarettes.

Stay busy. Keep yourself occupied, especially during summer breaks. Sign up at the local boys and girls club, or become a leader in your church youth group. Introduce yourself to someone in a career that interests you, and ask if you can accompany them to work. Find out where the internships are in your community. Your free time isn't something to be thrown away on video games. Take control over it and commit time to shaping your dream into reality. Odds are that you'll be recognized for it. Opportunities naturally seem to come to young people who show some ambition.

Learn how to give back. Instead of complaining about the problems in your community, donate your time to do something about them. Volunteer your time at an after-school program, or help raise funds to buy more basketballs for your local recreation center. The true reward is in the overwhelming good you feel in reaching back and helping others.

SAMPSON

Chapter 1

SAMPSON DAVIS
The Beginning

To THIS DAY, I'm grateful to *The Cosby Show.* When I was a kid, it allowed me to dream.

Back then, I didn't have any personal contact with people who were doctors and lawyers. Families like that lived far away, in the safe suburbs, and kids from my rugged Newark neighborhood couldn't even catch a glimpse of that world. But the Huxtables never turned me away.

I loved looking into the center of this TV family and seeing a father there. Cliff Huxtable always knew what was going on under his roof. He made sure Rudy kept her promise to go to dance rehearsal, he helped Vanessa search frantically for a missing history paper, and he always steered flighty Denise back to reality. He was the kind of dad who passed male traditions on to son Theo, even if they were silly rituals like the Christmas episode where they struggled to put up the holiday lights.

Cliff and Clair fascinated me. They touched tenderly, they laughed. Together, they supported their children's ambitions and pushed them to reach even higher. Their brownstone in Brooklyn seemed like a laboratory for life lessons: they gave their kids advice, then stood aside and let them make it on their own.

Those Thursday nights spent watching *Cosby* on our basement couch opened my eyes. But when the sitcom went off, my brief escape ended.

My world didn't look anything like that.

One of my Christmas memories is the year that my father pulled a gun on my mom. I was about six years old, and I remember it happened on a day when every one of my five siblings was at home. My sisters and mother were in the kitchen fixing a holiday meal. Nobody can remember what started it, but Pop definitely had been drinking. He didn't usually drink heavily, but when he did, you could count on the fact that some sparks would ignite his daily conversations at home.

I remember hearing my parents scuffle in the kitchen, and it spilled out to the living room, where my sisters were peeling potatoes. It got so bad that Pop went upstairs and got a gun. He came downstairs waving it and yelling. Everything happened very fast, but it will always be a frozen moment in my memory. My father stood on the third step, pointing the barrel of the gun at my mother. "I'll shoot you, woman. I will kill you." I stood there with my brothers Carlton and Andre, not believing our eyes. I tried to cry but couldn't. All I could see was Moms dying and my father going to jail.

My mother stood still but taunted him: "Go ahead, shoot me," she said. If you've never heard your mom sound like Clint Eastwood, believe me—it's not a good feeling. I knew this was it. All the previous arguments had built up to this day, the day where it would all come to a climactic end. I didn't want my mom to die. Please, God, don't let him pull the trigger. My older sisters jumped up and stood in the middle of the battle. My little brother Carlton was crying hysterically and my older brother Andre was shouting, "Stop! Why don't y'all stop?" I just stared. Is this how life is supposed to be?

Then it ended. Dad lowered the gun and retreated upstairs.

MINE WASN'T THE KIND of house where you could learn a lot about conflict resolution. My mom picked relentlessly at my father. She'd rag on him for coming home late, for not being able to wake up in the morning. Anybody who knows my mother, Ruthener Davis, knows that she is a self-determined, strong-willed person who follows her own drummer. Moms is a homemaker, and I think a lot of her fights with my dad stemmed from the fact that she felt hemmed in by serving thanklessly all the people crammed into our small house on a trouble-plagued Newark street. Still, my always-supportive Moms is my hero, and I've watched her show superhuman strength in dealing with the tough realities of her life. She is in essence a country girl, raised on a South Carolina farm and transplanted (with some difficulty) to Newark. She's been an early riser since girlhood, when she had to feed chickens, and to this day, she rises at four A.M. to sweep clean the streets of her neighborhood. "I've just got to keep busy," she says. For decades after she left the South, she insisted on using a washboard to do our laundry by hand and hanging our clothes outside to dry. My dad found some of this behavior annoying and sometimes shouted at her, "You still got those old ways!"

It's not hard for me to put myself in my father's shoes. His daily life had to be hard, supporting a family of eight on one small salary. My father, Kenneth Davis, grew up in South Carolina, served in the army during World War II, and probably had every intention of taking part in the American Dream when he returned home and married my mother. She was a pretty and petite fifteen-year-old he met at a country carnival. "Breathtaking" is what my father said the first time he laid eyes on my mother. From the moment they said "Hi," he knew she was the one he would marry.

They lived in a small South Carolina town called Hemingway for about ten years and had two kids together—my brother Kenneth Jr. and my sister Roselene—before deciding to join the great migration north in the early 1950s. In Newark, Pop found steady employment fueling planes at Butler Aviation, where he worked for thirty-five years until he retired. Moms played the role of housewife and nurturer for our family, which was expanding rapidly. Four more children arrived after the move to Newark: Fellease, Andre, me, and then Carlton. In 1968, five years before I was born, Dad used the

GI bill to purchase our wood-frame house on Ludlow Street, a nice area at the time. But once crack entered the scene in the 1980s like a thunder-clap explosion, our neighborhood seemed to sink into despair, under attack from within. Crack pulled apart many of the families living near us. Women, who traditionally served as our community's backbone, lost their maternal instincts once they fell under the spell of the white powder. Not since the riots destroyed Newark in the 1960s had we witnessed such vast devastation.

Disappearing into his bedroom every night was Pop's way of coping, after working a full day, then coming home to face everyday hassles from collection notices to corner winos to family squabbles. I don't think Pop intentionally planned to wall himself off emotionally, and he probably never realized that over time he became a distant and hands-off dad. I suspect that he was just repeating his silent past. He left most of the parental duties to my mom, which was common for men of the time.

I'm sure he raised us in the same stoic Southern way that defined his own upbringing. To his credit, he never walked away from his family. He wrote the monthly mortgage check until the house was fully paid off. He gave his children the essentials—food, shelter, clothing, the occasional spanking when we got out of line. He came from a time and place where that was all that was expected of a father. In many ways, he did the best he could, and I recognize that. Many of my childhood friends considered me lucky to even have had a father, which was a nearly extinct species in our Newark neighborhood. I have to admit they were right. Had my family ever gotten together to sit for a portrait when I was young, at least my Pop would have been in the picture. It would have been a nice-looking moment captured in time, with Pop, the breadwinner, seated in a chair, and his wife and six kids clustered around him. And we would have cherished such a photograph because, for that one moment, we would have looked every inch the healthy nuclear family, one that could have given the Huxtable crew a run for its money.

But the camera would have missed the unspoken stories, those disappointments and broken dreams that seemed to overwhelm my parents. Since they couldn't lift themselves out of our poor working-class ghetto, they resorted to blaming each other. "You got all these mouths to feed and can't even pay the bills," my mother would sometimes fling at him.

As children, we used to witness more volatility and fireworks than we thought our tiny two-bedroom house could withstand.

"Oh no, here it comes," I used to think when I'd see an argument between my parents starting to shape up, like storm clouds blowing in to ruin a sunny day. My parents' fights used to make me quake inside, my heart trembling so hard that it seemed the whole house was shaking. I might be sitting in the kitchen, just chilling with my mom, and then we'd hear Pop's car in the driveway. Almost without realizing it, I'd brace myself. A fight could start in a flash and was almost always prompted by something laughably trivial.

"Don't put that water in the refrigerator."

"Woman, shut the hell up."

"Dammit, I told you not to put that water there."

And next thing you know, it'd be on.

Little temper flare-ups were common, and I could easily shake those off. Moms and Pop would spar verbally or lightly shove each other around, then brush themselves off and retreat to their separate rooms. But sometimes there were roaring fights, seismograph-needle-shaking brawls that would pop off at a moment's notice. Like the time when they were shoving each other around in the kitchen and Moms pushed my father out the door and locked it. This sent Pop into a rage, so he smashed his hand through the kitchen window, cutting his arm pretty badly.

They argued about the same things over and over. Neither one ever cared or dared to change the way they interacted. Sometimes I wondered if they even knew how. As a young boy, I could often see the disconnect between the two of them. We were reminded constantly that it was only because of the kids that they were still together. I used to pray that through some act of nature or an outright miracle, they would somehow find their lost love for each other. But as the years passed and our home became a boxing ring for jabs and uppercuts, it became obvious that I wasn't going to get my wish.

Both my parents wear permanent reminders of their stormy marriage. Pop has a gash across his forehead, and my mom's smooth brown cheek is marred by slash marks. Both wounds were suffered during the same fight, which happened before I was born, but my sister Fellease was always happy to fill me in on the drama that preceded me. This particular argument was about her: Moms told Pop that Fellease should have gone to school that day, and he apparently disagreed. Moms grabbed a bottle and broke it on his forehead. Pop retaliated by grabbing an ashtray and using it like a razor to slice Moms's left cheek.

The police came and made sure that Moms and Pop were taken to the hospital since both were bleeding profusely. Both had stitches and came home from the hospital with bandages on their faces. According to Fellease, they actually had the nerve to be lovey-dovey after that. For Fellease, it was proof of our family's looniness that after the episode was over, our parents were at each other's side, all cuddled up, taking care of each other's wounds.

I didn't see much of this kind of affection between my parents. I never witnessed them hugging or treating each other in a caring way. I'm the fifth of six children, and by the time I reached school age, they weren't even bothering to create the illusion of love. The master bedroom belonged to Pop, and he would retreat up there as soon as he got home from work, to play his guitar and listen to music. He'd come down for dinner and that was it. Moms created a space for herself in the basement. This arrangement didn't seem right to me. From what I gathered from watching shows like *Cosby*, parents were supposed to sleep in the same bed. Clair and Cliff, after all, usually shared a laugh or a kiss as they snuggled.

But my parents didn't work together as a team. They went their opposite ways most of the time. Pop went to work and brought the money home, and Moms managed the home front. Pop shopped for the food, and

Moms cooked it. Moms was the affectionate caretaker of the children, and Pop seemed to be worrying about other things when he was at home. One upside to this approach was that Pop wasn't the main disciplinarian. Administering punishments fell to Moms, and she would come after us wielding everything from a belt to an electric cord. But my father hit me only once, when I refused to apologize to my brother Carlton after accidentally hitting him in the eye. Pop's silent demeanor demanded respect and good behavior.

They collaborated best in times of emergency. Then they'd be like Batman and Robin zipping off on a mission, like the day I cut my hand on our white metal blinds. I was about five, and I had been playing with the blinds in our kitchen, running my fingers in and out of the thick slats and cords. I was keeping my mom company while she cooked dinner. Even through the roughest times, she prided herself on having dinner ready when my father came home from work. Minutes before Pop drove up, I grabbed the blinds in my left hand and tore a huge gash in my palm. I was bleeding all over the place when he came in the door. Almost wordlessly, he grabbed me, and Moms grabbed her pocketbook. Andre happened to be walking in the door and nearly had to jump out of the way. Moms and Pop hustled me into the car and backed down the driveway in a huge hurry. "We're taking your brother to the hospital" was all he heard as we screeched out of sight.

It wasn't like there was a fight every night. Sometimes our house was peaceful, especially when Moms and Pop stayed out of each other's way. And on dire occasions, like when I got those ten stitches in my hand after the venetian blinds accident, my parents could be downright nurturing. I noticed that if I hurt myself or got in trouble, Moms and Pop would put their differences aside and rush to help me. Even as a child I began to see a pattern emerging, but I wouldn't fully understand it until later.

It seemed that Pop had erected a force field around him that I couldn't penetrate. I wondered whether, when he turned the doorknob to our house every day, something happened that just sapped the joy out of him. Pop didn't delight in fatherhood. He didn't reach for me when he came in the house. Every day it was the same. He'd say, "Hi," and maybe grab something to eat on the way to his room. He'd close the door, and I'd listen as he gently played his guitar. Sometimes he'd join us in the living room, where he might watch TV with us or play his favorite albums, often something mellow from Nat "King" Cole or, his favorite, the Dixie Hummingbirds. Never did he say "How was your day?" much less "Wanna go fishing or camping?" Perhaps Pop figured he shouldn't be too soft with me because reality was waiting just outside our front door and he felt his sons needed to be as tough as possible to deal with it. But whatever the reason, my father made the boundary lines of our relationship clear: I will not hug you. I will not tell you I love you. I will not have idle conversations with you. I will not let my guard down around you. I will always be your father.

WHAT WAS GOING ON in my house wasn't unusual. All my friends and I scraped by with minimal interaction from our parents. Back then, childhood was a community experience, especially during the summer. We threw our clothes on early in the morning and met one another outside, to hang out all day wherever we wanted. We knew to come back home when the streetlights came on. Our older brothers and sisters, if we had them, were expected to watch us. Our parents were too busy with working and trying to pay the bills and cope with the many hassles of being poor. Frankly, I was grateful I didn't have a more neglectful set of folks. I ran with a lot of guys whose parents found time for everything but their kids: hanging out, partying, getting high, escaping reality. I had one friend whose father frequently came home drunk. Sometimes I looked down the street to see my friend and his father having a violent fistfight in their front yard, duking it out for the world to see. No one ever thought it was strange or out of place to see the two of them go at it.

Our little corner of Newark was wedged between the city's airport and a cemetery, and when I was growing up, I couldn't imagine living in a better place.

We didn't have a lot of money, and it didn't matter to me that I shared a bed with my two brothers or that my parents couldn't afford swimming lessons or vacations. All the people I loved were here, and that was good enough for me.

There's a big age span between the six children in my family. I grew up feeling closest to Andre and Carlton, my brothers who were nearest to my age. Although I looked up to my oldest brother and sister, Kenny and Rose-lene, our relationships were different. They had been born more than twenty years before I was and were often away from the house. I had one more older sister, Fellease, who got married and lived in Hawaii during my preteen days but moved back to the mainland when I was fourteen. It was then that we bonded, staying up late talking and playing spades, Monopoly, and backgam-mon. She and my other older siblings moved out once they grew up, but they often returned to the nest, sometimes with spouses in tow. At one time I counted twelve people living in our two-bedroom house. Although it was always crowded, there was always something fun and exciting going on. To make room for our many houseguests, Carlton and I sometimes shared a sleeper sofa in the basement with my mother.

Across the street from our tidy row of tiny houses stood an eight-story public housing development, with hundreds of low-income people stacked on top of one another. It was chaos right across the street, especially after the crack epidemic hit. As a kid, it was nothing for me to see stripped stolen cars on the street, gun-toting pedestrians, or women selling their bodies for a taste of crack. Suddenly, it became common to hear gunshots or walk down the street and see a crime scene marked off with yellow tape. We kids became so desensitized that even murders ceased to shock us. I remember one day I saw a crowd standing in the street and learned that a neighborhood guy had been shot and his body found under a car. I saw his frame lying in a body bag. It was as common as a ninety-degree day in summer.

I remember that day vividly because the dead person happened to be the older brother of one of my friends. He had just come home from serving time in jail on a drug charge. There had been a party to welcome him home in the recreation center across the street in the projects, featuring good food and lots of dancing. The adults partied all night, smoking weed and getting drunk. I was about nine years old. My little friends and I hung out for a while, then headed outside when the sun went down. In the dark, we had a favorite routine of playing chase games like hide-and-seek, which sometimes evolved into a spin-off that we called Catch a Girl, Kiss a Girl. We always started by putting our feet in a circle and chanting a rhyme to decide who would be the person to find the others: *My mother and your mother were hanging out the clothes, my mother punched your mother right dead in the nose. What color was the blood?* We never gave a thought to the violence depicted in our little rhyme.

I grew used to having friends who stood a few yards away selling drugs while I played baseball with my friend Noody. It was just understood that if the police showed up, they'd grab a bat and pretend to be playing, too—although the streetwise cops usually saw right through it.

Maybe some kids adjust easily to this kind of life, where they're not a bleep on their parents' radar, but I wasn't like that. The older I got, the more I wanted my father's guidance. I yearned for it. Two doors away lived a friend of mine, Mike, who enjoyed what looked like a great relationship with his father. In warm weather, they would shoot hoops and horse around in the backyard. I would stare at them through the fence as if hypnotized, wanting what they had. If only I could have interested my dad in doing the same. I would have loved to burst into their yard to toss out a challenge: "Me and my dad against you guys." But I knew the thought was preposterous. My father often saw me playing basketball with friends on his way home from work and he never bothered to even slow down.

I can't remember a day that Pop glanced at my homework. I built a go-kart by myself. I built a basketball hoop in the driveway by myself. On my own, I developed a love of sports, but my father never encouraged it. It was a kind neighbor, Mr. Brown, who noticed my interest in baseball and took Noody and me to my first Major League Baseball game. His church had organized a bus trip to Shea Stadium to see the Mets. Noody and I sat next to each other on the bus ride and at the game. I'll never forget it. It was a Saturday afternoon in 1986, and the Mets were playing the Dodgers. You should have seen us. Noody and I were thirteen, and we came with our mitts ready to catch a ball off the players' bats. The Mets lost the game, but they went on to win the World Series that year. I loved seeing my favorite players in person: Dwight Gooden, Gary Carter, and Darryl Strawberry. Mr. Brown made sure we were having a good time, supplying us with all the hot dogs and sodas we could consume. It's a memory I'll keep for a lifetime.

Pop rarely talked to me about drugs, sex, women, education, or anything like that. Occasionally he might tell me to stay in school, but he delivered this message more like an order, without much conversation or advice.

This approach didn't meet my needs at all. Being a curious kid, I had a million questions. I was hungry to know how to conduct myself in social situations. What do I say when I meet someone? How should I act? Should I offer a handshake? How much do I reveal about the real me? How much do I keep to myself? I used to mumble and stutter when I was introduced to strangers, not knowing what to say. Nobody ever told me to stand up straight, look someone in the eye, and give them a firm handshake.

I had deeper questions for my dad, but as a child, I didn't know how to voice them. How do I avoid the path that I see my friends going down? I knew I didn't want to be like them. I saw them being driven off in police cars and I knew I didn't want that life. But I couldn't see any other way. You can't aim for what you can't see; I've said that countless times since I first wrote those words in *The Pact*. I firmly believe it's a problem that has choked the hope out of many talented young people.

WITH POP HOLED UP in his room, I couldn't really pull the answers out of him that I needed. Luckily, when I was around eight or nine, I found someone willing to give me his full attention, and I latched onto him so tightly that he could barely turn around without seeing me.

My friends and I would flock to Reggie Brown as soon as we saw his beat-up gold Nova pull up every afternoon and park in the cemetery across the street from my house. To spend some time with him, all I had to do was climb the cemetery's black wrought-iron gate and hoist myself over the top. As soon as I leaped to the other side, it was like landing on a different planet.

Evergreen Cemetery was full of tall trees, peaceful hills, and singing birds. It also employed the baddest mentor anybody could have. Reggie Brown, the cemetery's night watchman, had grown up in the projects. At age eighteen, he somehow managed to sidestep the traps of drugs and violence. He didn't drink; he didn't sling drugs. Still, he commanded respect. Reggie had studied kung fu for years, and nobody pushed him around. He was the role model I craved: smart but cool. Straight as an arrow but not corny. He was vibrant and full of life, especially when I compared him to other guys his age who were nodding on the corner in a drugged stupor.

His paying job, as a security guard for sprawling Evergreen Cemetery, which reaches into three cities, Hillside, Elizabeth, and Newark, was to lock the gates at four-thirty and stay until midnight to chase out unauthorized visitors. Bad guys often sneaked into the vast graveyard after dark to shoot dope and rob folks who often used the cemetery as a shortcut.

It also fell to him to protect the mourners visiting their loved ones. Growing up inside Building 5 of the Dayton Street projects gave him a distinct advantage in this aspect of his job. Give Reggie a description of the guy who robbed you, and he would immediately stride into the projects, knock on just the right door, and yank the missing pocketbook out of a crackhead's hands. Muscled and brown, he was like a real-life superhero.

I was thrilled when he took an interest in me. Reggie called me "Little Man" and eventually started to treat me like I was his deputy, letting me ride alongside him on his nightly patrols. He taught me to drive long before I was old enough, and I'd proudly circle his car around the cemetery's mile-and-a-half-long perimeter road while he kept an eye out for criminal activity. Nobody could tell me I wasn't *the man* when I was at Reggie's side.

Technically, Reggie was being paid to keep neighborhood folks out, but without any permission whatsoever from cemetery management, he secretly was ushering in local kids for what amounted to the best after-school program in our neighborhood. His passion was to rescue kids from the streets by giving them something positive to focus on, so he set up a tae kwon do class in the cemetery's chapel. As a youth, he had studied kung fu under a charismatic master named Frank Melvin, also a hero in our community, and Reggie decided it was time to pass on the skill to an up-and-coming generation. We considered ourselves "in training" with Reggie, and we took it seriously. I was without a doubt his most faithful student. Usually I was the first to arrive and the last to leave.

In winter, Reggie would see my footsteps in the snow and know that, as usual, I had gotten there before him. Within a few seconds, I'd emerge from the shadows below the underpass, shivering in my flimsy kung fu uniform. Our training time together became my favorite part of the week. Reggie worked us out so hard that in a few years he had a small army of preteens strutting around with rock-hard abs. About a dozen of us would meet after school on Mondays, Wednesdays, and Fridays. We'd start with two-mile runs, a hundred jumping jacks, and fifty push-ups. The longer we trained with him, the more sophisticated the tasks became. Eventually, he made us lie across the hood of his car and do a couple hundred sit-ups.

We would do anything he told us, even though we knew Reggie had a prankster side. "You guys are tough, you can take it," he would say before announcing some outlandish physical task. We let him handcuff us to the door handle of his Nova, and he'd make us run laps around the cemetery while he drove in long lazy circles on that endless perimeter road. Sometimes he'd tell spooky stories, then march us up the hill to the darkened mausoleum and send us inside on a made-up mission. Then he'd take off laughing in his car, and we'd have to find our way home in the dark. One night, Reggie had my brother Andre kneel down to hug a tombstone, then handcuffed his wrists together on the other side. Andre thought it was an exercise in patience, so he stayed there fearfully for hours waiting for Reggie to come back. Andre later learned that he had failed the mission miserably. If he had only looked up, he could have easily liberated himself by standing up and lifting his hands over the top of the short tombstone. We would laugh till it hurt about episodes like this, unless we were the butt of that day's joke.

Yet Reggie had strict rules for taking part in the fun: "If you do any drugs, drink alcohol, cut school, or disrespect your parents, you're out."

Once, after a memorial service, he took us inside the chapel where the body was waiting to be cremated. "C'mere, I want to show you guys something," he said, motioning us to him. "See this?" He opened the casket, exposing the face of a lifeless young man in his twenties. "If you go out there and start doing those drugs and hanging out with knuckleheads, this is what's gonna happen to you." I was hungry for fatherly advice, and I certainly got it from Reggie, who delivered it with a dramatic flair that still lingers in my memory.

Most kids probably wouldn't feel comfortable hanging out in a cemetery, but to Reggie's followers, it wasn't a fearful place at all. To my mind, it was a safe haven. My mom used to say, "The dead people, they're not gonna mess with you," and she was right. It was the living, breathing people in my neighborhood who supplied the horror, and compared to them, the cemetery was a calming oasis, a yellow brick road leading to a magical place. The instant I jumped that tall gate every day, I had total peace of mind. I guess that's why I never told Reggie about the stormy fights going on at my house. Kung fu classes were my outlet, and I didn't want to waste a minute thinking about the pressures of home or the street when I was with him.

Over time, I got quite proficient in the martial arts. I know that I impressed Reggie because he'd pair me up with bigger and taller guys for my sparring sessions. Reggie observed me as I progressed from a shy novice fighter to one who could hold his own even in a mismatch. Eventually I started tossing my opponents around instead of being the one getting tossed. Then came the final test, when Reggie himself sparred with me and found that I could block all his moves. I could even execute a perfect "hang leg," a tricky move where you balance on one leg and kick the other one as high as possible while arching the foot. He had to step back that day and give me my respect. I won't forget the pride I saw in his eyes.

Reggie taught us a lot about martial arts philosophy and self-control, and insisted that we clear our mind at the end of every class with meditation. He talked to us constantly about channeling our inner power, or our *chi*, to overcome obstacles. "Never show fear or intimidation," he used to tell us. "It shows that you are weak." A few years later, one of my fellow students got shot six times and survived. Later he said that while lying on the street bleeding, he remembered Reggie's words about *chi*. He focused his thoughts tightly on survival, breathing in through the nose and out through his mouth as he had been taught, until help finally arrived. Reggie's guidance saved his life, he's convinced.

Reggie always preached that using violence to solve a beef is ignorant. He urged us to respect our bodies and to use our brains. "Class, our focus is not on fighting," he would tell us. "I want to build you up mentally, physically, and spiritually." Although he taught us the kicks and punches of kung fu, he made it clear that he didn't want us to use the techniques for street brawling. "Why would you want to hurt your fellow man because you have a disagreement? You're smarter than that. Talk it out. Learn when to walk away. You should only fight to protect your life," he often instructed.

But it rubbed some guys in our 'hood the wrong way to see Reggie developing such a following. Guys were always jumping in our face to challenge us. And there did come a day when Reggie let one trash-talking guy goad him into a fight, and Reggie beat him fair and square. When it was over, Reggie surprised us by apologizing and saying he never should have lost his composure like that. The funny thing is, his challenger was so impressed by Reggie's skills and philosophizing that he eventually joined us in our training sessions.

Reggie, now a lieutenant in the Pennsylvania correctional system as well as a husband and father of three daughters, remains one of my biggest influences and the closest I ever came to the wise, attentive father figure. I reported faithfully to his after-school training sessions until the age of thirteen or fourteen, when I started to lose interest. It was a pattern that Reggie knew too well. "It's like our bar mitzvah, a rite of passage in the most negative sense," he has been known to say, shaking his head, about neighborhood kids when they hit their teen years. "Around here, on their thirteenth birthday, that's when kids get pulled in by the lure of the street and start breaking the law."

I was no different. I was starting to feel that heat of peer pressure. I was entering high school and moving into a new phase. I was now officially into girls and sports, plus dabbling in some other stuff that I knew Reggie would never approve of. So I stopped going.

IN HIGH SCHOOL, I played basketball, football, and baseball during lunch hour, and after school I played varsity baseball for University High. I was a pitcher and shortstop. I even had a few write-ups in the local paper, the Newark *Star-Ledger*, which added to my confidence and convinced me I was a sure shot for the pros.

I was always a smart kid, and good grades came pretty easily to me. My sports ability and demeanor placed me in the cool crowd. I was far from a nerd but I wasn't a dumb jock, either. Through sports and mischief I earned my popularity. Although I wasn't into the drug scene, I started hanging around the older teenagers, staying out late on school nights. Moms warned me to stop hanging out on street corners, but her words didn't penetrate.

I avoided Reggie. I knew he could see into my soul and would know just how much I was compromising myself.

Without a doubt, my teenage hormones were starting to boil. I was starting to look at girls, although I had no clue how to approach them. Kung fu class just didn't seem as important as it used to, once my friends started bragging about how they had kissed or touched a girl. There was a lot of pressure to be sexual, and there was no way I wanted to be left out. At age thirteen, I was already a late bloomer. Many of my friends already had gone all the way, or at least that was the way they told it. We would often gather in a circle and tell one another stories about the girls we had crushes on. I listened carefully, because these sessions served as my main source of information on the opposite sex. In our earlier years, the boys would reveal how they'd touched a girl in a certain part of her body, but with the passing of time, they graduated to discussions of kissing and other acts. Sometimes I thought they were lying, but how would I know? Dayton Street School, just a few blocks from my house, was the backdrop for most of the stories. This was the elementary school I attended through sixth grade: a weathered brick laboratory of tough love with three floors of green hallways, crowded classrooms, and caring teachers who didn't hesitate to spank. Inside our often vandalized bathrooms, hand washing was impossible since the sinks were missing knobs. After the school day ended, many teenaged boys would walk their girlfriends behind the school. As a kid, I often rode my bike past the shadows of teens making out there.

I wasn't in a hurry, but I was curious. It wasn't until my freshman year at University High that I kissed a girl for real. We locked lips in a school phone booth. I closed my eyes and pressed hard, imitating how I had seen it done on TV. I tilted my head different ways, pretending to make it more passionate, although I didn't really feel anything. Then I felt something wet in my mouth and realized the essence of a true kiss from a girl. Instantly, I felt the electricity. I was in shock all day as I roamed the halls. I couldn't tell any of my peers about my new experience, since it came so embarrassingly late. I would have loved to have shared my secret with Pop, since I had no idea what I ought to do next. If I ever needed him to teach me a class in Girls 101, it was at this moment. But we didn't have that kind of relationship. All I had to go on was my mother's direct order: "Don't bring no baby into this house." I'm now thankful that the kiss was as far as this particular episode went, but it would be a few short months later when I progressed to my next course of independent study, Sex 101.

Just like most teenagers, my friends and I were attracted by excitement and hated boredom. In those days, we had to create our own fun. Thirteen is an age when you naturally want to look your best, but for us, finding money to buy clothes was always a challenge. To my parents, wearing the latest gear was not a necessity. My mother would always tell us that a pair of "jeepers" sneakers, as we sneeringly called the no-name brands, was just as cool as a pair of Nikes. Although she was probably right, I didn't know of any teenagers who would agree with her, so I found myself always thinking of ways to find funds. For a while I sold golf balls at the nearby Wee-quahic Park golf course. This job consisted of searching the course for golf balls lost in the bushes and then approaching golfers with a deal to buy them back for a quarter apiece. I would also bag groceries at the neighborhood store. This was my hustle, but the pay wasn't very good.

In the neighborhood there was always an older guy willing to add you to his roster as a junior drug partner. I would watch as many of my friends took the job. They didn't have to announce their new position. One could tell instantly by the sudden change in their demeanor and in their style. They would go downtown on Saturdays to shop, picking up the latest Air Jordans, new two-tone Lee jeans, and a Le Tigre shirt. And they'd accessorize with the most coveted of items: a Kangol hat and a belt buckle that spelled out their name. I always wanted one of the beaver Kangols. They came in different colors and you could brush its soft hairs into certain patterns. My mother always insisted that "clothes don't make a person." Yeah, I'd think, but they could make a person feel a lot better. How could I hang around my friends or even talk to a girl without wearing the latest styles?

At first I resisted the overtures of the guys who tried to recruit me to sell drugs. I depended on my athletic abilities, which were better than average, to keep me popular in the 'hood and at school. During the summer after my eighth-grade year, I played shortstop on a softball team fielded by the housing project across the street. We couldn't afford uniforms but we did have royal blue T-shirts with yellow lettering that read "Kretchmer Homes Softball Team," the official name of the projects on Dayton Street. That year we won our district championship. I remember holding the team trophy high and feeling like a star when we drove around the neighborhood in our coaches' cars, honking the horns and yelling out the windows in an impromptu parade. Sadly, many of the summer programs I took part in don't exist anymore, due to budget cutbacks.

My friends and I played basketball from early morning into the night at the Dayton Street School court. One guy I used to play with there was called Tank-Tank. His father, Frank Melvin, was the guy who taught Reggie kung fu. But by then, his father was dead and all that was a legend. Frank Melvin, who grew up in the Dayton Street projects, had kept many local youngsters off the streets in the 1970s with his inspiring kung fu classes held in the basement of St. Thomas Aquinas Catholic Church, just a few doors from my house. Reggie, his most promising student, served as his personal assistant, opening up the building and taking the class through warm-ups. I was just a little boy then, but I remember that Frank had a black belt in kung fu and a grassroots leader's charisma. On Saturdays, he would organize boxing matches at a nearby school and charge neighborhood folks a few dollars to come in and see the local talent. Then he'd give the winners most of the ticket profits so they'd have some money in their pockets and not have to turn to selling drugs.

Known as Wu-Chi to the students in his Young Kung Fu Association, he taught them to respect and protect their neighborhood. In 1981, he contacted the Guardian Angels to discuss starting a Newark chapter to help keep order near the unruly Dayton Street high-rise. It wasn't long before he became a famous casualty. While on patrol in the projects on the night of December 30, 1981, Frank and a bunch of his newly recruited Angels heard a report of a robbery at a nearby bar, The People's Tavern, and raced to investigate. Reggie remembers that day well because Wu-Chi had begged him to come along on patrol. But Reggie had just moved into an apartment and couldn't make it that night. As it turned out, Reggie narrowly missed out on seeing a tragedy unfold.

At the tavern, Newark police mistakenly assumed Frank was the robbery suspect and fired on him, killing him almost instantly. I was eight at the time, and I knew it was a blow for our whole neighborhood. The strongest leader we'd ever seen had been cut down abruptly, leaving a wife, three sons, and an entire community to mourn their loss.

His sons grew up in the Dayton Street projects, and we often crossed paths. Tank-Tank had a chubby little brother, whom we called Mike-Mike. He was about seven years younger than me, and we used to spend a lot of time shaking him off so he wouldn't follow us around. I used to give him quarters to go to the store and get me juice and chips. He was too little to play with us, but he'd always hang around the court and throw the ball back to us if it bounced his way.

Their home life after Frank's death appeared to be in ruins. Their mom, it was said, couldn't pull her life back together after her husband's death. Her rudderless, fatherless boys got drawn into the drug culture, and Mike-Mike ended up with the longest rap sheet of all. He served time off and on for various assaults and robbery and drug convictions.

In December 2005, the front page of the *Star-Ledger* revisited all these people from my childhood in a chilling way. The headline screamed that "Mike-Mike" Melvin, age twenty-five, had been charged in a grisly quadruple murder at St. Thomas Aquinas Catholic Church—the same site where his father once taught kung fu.

Coincidentally, it may have been my own Moms who was first to walk past the murder scene. As usual, she had been up at the crack of dawn to sweep our block clean. Moms belongs to St. Thomas Aquinas, and she always tidies the sidewalk in front of the church during her morning routine. Engrossed in her work at six that morning, she didn't notice the four bodies a dozen yards away. A deacon arriving to open up the church about an hour later found the bodies and called the police. When Moms glanced outside a short time later, police were swarming everywhere, and the yellow tape they were stringing up stretched all the way to her front yard. She ran down the street, where she watched as police put the four in body bags and drove them away.

Investigators pieced together a story about how the four victims, all of whom had robbery convictions, died. They believed that Mike-Mike, already awaiting trial on a previous murder charge, was a dangerous criminal, and that he was drunk when he walked his four victims down the street and put bullets through their heads.

Seeing Mike-Mike's life story splashed on the front page was a sad testimony to how the streets had gobbled up another fatherless youngster. There's no doubt in my mind that Mike-Mike, who was only seventeen months old when he sat in the front row for his dad's funeral, would have turned out differently if his father hadn't been slain. Reggie has told me stories about how Wu-Chi used to serve as the truant officer for the entire neighborhood, chasing down the boys who missed his kung fu classes. "If you weren't at that class, you better not be outside playing. Kids would hide if they missed practice," he remembers. "We knew if Wu-Chi saw us, we were gonna get it.

"If Wu-Chi had been alive, his boys' lives would have been different," Reggie believes. "If he didn't tolerate that kind of behavior from his students, he definitely wouldn't have tolerated it from his sons."

All I know is that Mike-Mike was once a sweet kid who could have grown up to be somebody important. He didn't have one mean bone in his body. Mike-Mike could have been that beacon of light that his father was to Reggie and that Reggie was to me. Instead, he stands charged with multiple murders. At age twenty-five, he seems all but doomed.

BY THE TIME I hit my teen years, I too knew what it felt like not to have a father in the house.

Our household had survived, barely, an extended period when my father found a girlfriend and everyone knew it—even my mother. It started with phone calls. The phone would ring at a certain time of evening, and Pop would race to pick it up on the first ring. This was out-of-the-ordinary be-havior for him. We soon suspected something was up.

Then Pop started disappearing regularly on weekends. He'd leave on Fri-day night and walk back in the door on Sunday without much of an expla-nation. Moms didn't take kindly to this development. "Go see that other bitch, go ahead!" she would snap at him. I once saw her throw a brick at his car as he drove away.

When I was twelve, he finally moved out for good to live with his girl-friend, Thelma, whom he married a few years later. Although I would miss my father dearly and his departure would send our household into financial chaos, I breathed a sigh of relief that day. The house was finally peaceful.

Moms got served with divorce papers a few days later. When the papers arrived, she called her children in for a serious talk. By then, my three older siblings had moved out, so it was just the three youngest boys, Andre, me, and Carlton. Sitting us down in the living room, she let us know that our lives were going to change drastically. "Your father and I are divorcing. That means we won't have his paycheck to rely on," she warned us. "But we will survive, and I will make a way. I promise you that."

Moms told us that day that we would always be her first priority. "I'm going to stand by you kids, and I will never leave you. You don't ever have to worry about me bringing another man into this house." That had to be a big sacrifice for her, ruling out the very idea of dating, but it gave sooth-ing reassurance to the three of us. Although we had long expected that our parents' fiery marriage would end in divorce, we still felt lost at the idea of life without Pop. Her words that day wiped away my worries that maybe somebody would steal Moms's affections and cause her to run away and leave us behind, the way Pop had done. I don't think I've ever admired Moms more than I did that day.

It was a sink-or-swim moment for Moms, and as time went on, I could see her changing and growing. It seemed as if she finally had a mission, and she was determined to fulfill it. She did whatever she could to make ends meet. She signed up for welfare, and even scoured the streets for cans and sold them to the scrap man. She made sure we had the things we needed, from back-to-school clothes to lunch money. She could have easily rolled over and gotten depressed from all the new worries piled on her, but my tiny mom, five feet tall, responded like a champ. There were plenty of single moms up and down our block who turned to drugs when the going got tough, but for Moms, that's when she showed her inner strength. I loved seeing her bloom. She always let me know during those tough times that I was loved. I owe her so much.

She's not perfect, but no one is. Perhaps her biggest limitation was that she couldn't read. Her mother died when Moms was a little girl, so she dropped out of elementary school to help her father run his farm. As a result, Moms couldn't read the electric bill, the newspaper, or even the divorce papers when they arrived. After Pop left, I helped Moms with everything from reading letters to paying the bills. When a homework paper had to be signed, I just went ahead and signed Moms's name myself.

I'm proud of Moms for finally learning to read, at the age of sixty. She was a grandmother by that time. In fact, being a grandma is what motivated her to do it. When Andre's children began to read, it ate away at Moms that a new generation of children would realize she had never learned to read. So she taught herself to sound out words, and attended literacy classes at the local library. One of the first books she struggled through was *The Pact*. Moms wanted to get inside it and see what I had to say. She bravely tussled with the words on the printed page until their meanings became clear to her. I'm glad she got to read for herself how much I admire her.

Pop stayed in our lives peripherally. After he left, he moved into an apartment about twenty minutes away in Orange, a middle-class area. Andre, Carlton, and I saw him occasionally when he would stop by after work. Our conversations were no-frills Q&As, often with one-word answers on my part.

"How are things?"

"Good."

"How was your day?"

I was tempted to reply, "Man, Pop, my day was awful. My life is pretty bad." But there was no need to bother him with this. Really, what could he have done to change my situation? In order for him to help me, he would have had to step up and help improve my life, and he hadn't done so up to that point. Now he was out of the house, and it didn't seem as if anything good could come of talking about their divorce's ugly aftermath.

Moms and Pop sniped about each other to us kids in a competition to destroy our respect for the other parent. "He ran out on you guys," Moms complained. Pop would say things like "You know your mother's crazy" when we were together. It seemed wrong when they carried on like that. I didn't like it. But with Pop having relocated to a more well-to-do community, leaving us still stranded on Ludlow Street, I tended to side with Moms's viewpoint.

Pop continued to pay the mortgage, but there were plenty of other expenses. At times, the electricity and phone would get cut off. I've seen my mother beg the public works guy to leave our lights on because she needed a few more days to scrape up a payment. Sometimes he would comply, but other times he had no choice but to cut us off. We didn't have a working boiler, so we huddled around the fireplace for warmth and used space heaters in the bedrooms. As a kid, I thought it was normal for mothers to grab an axe and head outside to chop wood for the fireplace.

When Pop left, so did the car—which meant that to get to school, I had to walk ten minutes to the bus stop, catch the number 24 bus, ride six miles to downtown Newark, and then transfer to the number 13. Without a car, we would go grocery shopping and then borrow a shopping cart to transport our food back to the house. We went from quality meats to budget meals, from steaks to liverwurst and bologna (and I'm not talking Oscar Mayer).

My father had extricated himself from our household during a crucial time in my development. It was just in time for the thirteen-year-old-coming-of-age passage that Reggie had learned to dread. My older brothers and sisters were more independent and didn't seem to miss our father's presence so much. Carlton, who was also approaching his teen years, and I probably felt it the most. Carlton adored Pop, and as a child he would wait for Pop after work each day at the bottom of the driveway. It was their ritual. Pop would let Carlton sit on his lap as they motored slowly up the driveway together. During the divorce, Carlton cried through the whole court proceeding. He was eight at the time, and I could see the change in him instantly. His grades began to sink, and my mother got summoned to school regularly about Carlton's behavioral and academic problems. She had so much going on that she depended on Carlton to resolve his own issues, but he was just a child and never truly recovered from the divorce.

At age sixteen, I woke up one summer morning feeling a searing pain in my back and abdomen. When she saw how much agony I was in, Moms called Pop. He arrived quickly and drove me to Irvington General Hospital. I remember the pain being so bad that I couldn't help but moan and scream. At one point, a nurse showed up at my door and told me to hush my noise because I was disturbing other patients. Pop barked at her and told her to leave me alone. As it turned out, I had kidney stones that needed to be removed through surgery. I spent a week in the hospital. Eventually, the pain subsided, and it ended up becoming a blissful week because, for once, I got to bask in my father's attention. Pop visited me every day after work, bringing me ice cream and other surprises. I remember watching the clock to see when he would arrive. Just having him there gave me a sense that everything was going to be okay. Yes, I was a swaggering teenager by then, but I still responded like a little kid to my father's attention. Looking back, I realize that I had the perfect opportunity at that moment to whisper to him, "I wish we could be like this all the time," but I didn't say it. I didn't want to have to request his attention—I just wanted him to give it, unasked.

It's only fair to say that Pop came through whenever I asked for help. He certainly helped pull me through my woes in college, when I was having the worst luck with cars. I had been the embodiment of cool in high school when

I pieced together enough money to buy my first car, a used but fashionable Audi 5000. But it was a lemon, and it does nothing for your image when you have to hop out of your car and push it to the side of the road. So I sold the Audi and bought another car, which my sister Fellease promptly wrecked. Pop stepped in at that point and gave me $2,000 to help me get back on the road. He was proud of me for making it to college, and he knew I needed a car to get from Seton Hall to my part-time job. This time, I didn't worry about driving something dazzling. I bought a used but reliable Honda Accord. That car lasted me from 1991 to 1997 and took me on many road trips to hang out and have fun with college students from different parts of the country. I traveled to Howard University's homecoming and Atlanta's "Freak-Nic," and checked out the Penn Relays and spring break at Virginia Beach.

A few months later, I sent Pop a birthday card.

12/12/91

To Pop: What is the definition of a man? Who is to judge what represents a man? Well, if I was the decision maker, I would surely say you fit the description perfectly. You are there for me on a moment's notice. I can call you anytime and you will do your best to fulfill my requests. I don't take any of this kindness for granted. I truly appreciate all you have done for me in the past few months. You are truly the best father a son could wish for. Sometimes this is hard to say but I truly love you. If given the power to change any of your actions toward me, I wouldn't. You are simply marvelous. Love, your son.

It's hard to explain now why I would write something so flowery on his card. But I reliably sent my father birthday and Father's Day cards, and I always took the time to fill them with long handwritten notes like that. My stepmother, Thelma, saved the cards faithfully and recently shared them with me. Seeing them reminded me how hard I had tried to connect with him, in a way that he could accept. I wanted to let him know I yearned for a deeper relationship, although I didn't know how to ask for it. I guess I believed the best route to open up a dialogue was through flattery. I wanted him to be a Cliff Huxtable kind of dad, even though I didn't know how to come right out and say it. So I wrote out those heartfelt cards to the father I wished I had. Just maybe he'd think more about me and reflect on my words. Maybe he'd see how important he was to me, and I'd see more of him as a result. That was my strategy. But it was too subtle to be successful.

Without a father's full-time presence to rein me in during high school, I was running the streets and coming home whenever I wanted. Moms often told me to "go to school, go to school, go to school," and although I wondered why she would always say it three times, I did what she demanded, keeping a high grade-point average at University High. There, I spent most of my days with George and Rameck. Since we took most of our classes together, it felt natural for us to form a team. The three of us had a lot in common. We got good grades and loved having fun, from cutting class to pulling practical jokes. During our sophomore year, we started asserting ourselves as a group, coming up with a slogan, SKAT, which stood for Sophomores Kooling and Terrorizing. We even had a theme song of sorts; we would beat on the cafeteria tables while singing "Skat, skat, skat, skatadat dat," leading our class in a rhythmic challenge to the juniors. The seniors didn't pay us much mind since they believed themselves to be more mature. Still, we commanded their respect. As George, Rameck, and I spent our free time playing football, baseball, basketball, and blackjack, we carved a friendship that helped us see ourselves in a new light. We were cool, we were smart, we were leaders. My school family provided a marked contrast to my home life.

As I stepped off the bus into my 'hood, I had to change my whole persona. I switched into an exterior rawness, and didn't smile or laugh as much. Back then, it was extremely important for me to be a part of my peer group, and most of my neighborhood friends were using drugs and alcohol by high school. Many of my boys respected the fact that I had long taken a strong stance against drugs, so they didn't push them on me. But I found that the older I got, the more the expectations escalated. All the time, every day, there were decisions I faced, as guys offered me opportunities to make some money by taking part in their drug operations.

Occasionally during high school I took part. The quarters earned from bagging groceries and selling golf balls just weren't cutting it, and neither was the minimum wage I earned at age fifteen when I started working at McDonald's. I had to find a better way to make money. Some of the kids would steal cars and sell the rims and radios. Some had chop shop contacts and would take the vehicle to the factory for their payday. Poverty makes people resort to illegal tactics just to survive, and, now with my father out of the house, I didn't want to be an added burden on Moms. It was tough enough for her. The monthly $400 welfare check didn't go very far. Some can't even imagine how tough it is to have no money in your pocket, an empty belly, and no way to satisfy that hunger.

I don't use the economics I faced as an excuse. Every time I took part in the drug game, I knew I was making a bad decision. I don't like to think of it as caving in as much as I think I failed to take a stand and, by default, got caught up in life-changing dilemmas. True, I didn't initiate any of the illegal operations I took part in, but I didn't say no when I could have. I should have been on alert to defend my values at all times. The same passive behavior I showed leads some to a death sentence.

In the summer between my junior and senior years of high school, I was hanging out with some guys and we came up with the not-so-bright idea of robbing drug dealers to make some quick money. We preyed on young drug salesmen, pulling a gun on them, snatching their money, and driving off. The plan worked ridiculously well for a while. But one day we were in the middle of jacking some dope boys in nearby Montclair when a brown four-door Chevy pulled up with two plainclothed policemen inside. I knew my best bet was to act like I was a bystander. So I coolly started walking away from the scene and tried to calm my frenzied heart when one of my boys sprinted past me with police in hot pursuit. Each step he took, it seemed the cops took two. Their footrace ended a few yards from me. As I saw the police wrestle him to the ground, my face mirrored his as fear took over. I prayed he wouldn't gesture toward me, letting the police know of my involvement. Snitching was frowned on, and I depended on our street credo at this moment. I managed to walk the rest of the short block while maintaining my composure. But as soon as I made the corner, I took off running.

When I got home, I poured out my story to Fellease. I couldn't believe it: I was out of control, officially, and now my poor decision-making had caught up with me. I didn't want to tell my mother; I knew she would be disappointed. Fellease suggested that I turn myself in the next morning.

When the next day dawned, I called the police department and learned that my "friends" who did get arrested had already given them my name. "You need to bring yourself in for questioning or we will come get you," a police officer bluntly told me over the phone. Fellease drove me to the police precinct in Montclair, where the two of us were ushered into an interrogation room. The detective sat me down in the seat across from him. He insisted on calling me by my middle name, Marshall, which was the name I was known by in my neighborhood. Someone had definitely talked, I realized. I sat back as the detective described every detail of our crime. I was caught.

After the questioning, shackles and handcuffs were placed on my ankles and wrists. "He's a juvenile. Can't he be released into my custody?" Fellease protested. The detective let us know that since a gun was involved, I had to be detained and await trial. I asked for my phone call. I could hear the disbelief in Moms's voice as I told her what had happened.

I was loaded into a van and taken to New Jersey's most dangerous and notorious youth detention center, the Essex County youth house. There were eight of us in the van, all chained to one another. All the faces looked like mine: black, young, and confused. I was placed in the A unit, for teenagers accused of violent crimes or likely to be charged as adults. As I walked to my cell, I recognized faces from the Dayton Street high-rises and the nearby Seth Boyden projects. Some guys were shouting my name.

This was my new home, but I knew right away it wasn't for me. Never have I been more miserable. I was shuffled off to my closet-sized room, which featured a urine-stained mattress on top of a rusty twin-bed frame, with a thin sheet and no pillow, and a sliver of a window. Morning couldn't come quick enough. Although it was summer, for some reason my room was cold.

I was stunned to see a lot of guys walking around, seeming comfortable with being there. I couldn't understand that. I met one guy who had been incarcerated three times previously for armed robbery and was familiar with the legal system. When I told him the charges against me, he said he was sure I was going to get off. About a week later, I saw the same guy beaten so badly that he had to be rushed to the hospital. A dude nicknamed Trouble had walked up to him and without any warning punched him in the face. Trouble was known for knocking people out in the facility. He would wait until you weren't looking and blindside you with a punch to the jaw. Everyone just stared that day as blood from his victim's mouth dripped down his shirt and formed a puddle on the floor. His jaw was hanging loosely by the skin, and although I was not a doctor yet, I knew it was broken. I knew it wouldn't be long before someone came after me. In "juvey," you had to show your skills as a fighter or else get victimized. The closest I came to a confrontation was one day in the recreation yard when a guy from another unit snatched the water bucket from me. He was sitting with a guy from Dayton Street who greeted me and quickly intervened to help dissolve the matter. "Chill. That's Marshall, he's cool," he told the guy. I was prepared to fight, but in the end I didn't have to.

I wanted so badly to go home. Four long weeks would go by before that became a possibility. My father visited every day and assured me that everything would be all right. Pop made sure I had a lawyer who worked hard to get the charges against me reduced. We decided that I would plea-bargain in hopes of erasing the threat of a jail sentence. I felt like I fully had my father's attention—just as I had in the hospital. But this time, I didn't respond like an attention-starved little boy. Instead I wrapped myself in the hardened exterior that was helping me survive.

During his visits, Pop attempted to reach me in his own way. "How are they treating you?" he would ask. "Hang in there." I stood emotionless during his visits. None of it mattered because at the end of the visit I had to return to my miserable room. None of it mattered because so much had happened between the divorce and now. What could he say that would help me? He had had ample opportunity to say it years before.

After every visit, I had to go through a strip search. I would be stripped naked, along with the other inmates, in front of correction officers as they searched my body for drugs and weapons. They checked every orifice. I had to bend over and spread my cheeks and lift my testicles to ensure that no illegal products were being transported. The things I experienced at the detention center seemed too heavy to bear. I felt a rage building at my father's long-term, lightweight approach to my problems.

His concern seemed to come too late. After all, by not investing in my life, he had unintentionally assisted in steering me to this outcome.

Originally, prosecutors wanted to charge me as an adult, and if I had accepted the first plea bargain offered, I would have faced ten to twenty-five years in prison. But my lawyer managed to make sure I was charged as a juvenile. When I walked into the courtroom to enter my plea, I looked behind me to see my mother and father standing there, firmly in support of me. The judge suspended my sentence and gave me two years' probation. I was free to go.

I knew I was lucky. If I had been eighteen, my story would have been written differently. I could have spent years in prison. Often, during those awful weeks in detention, I thought over my mistakes. I had to get my life together. I promised myself as I left the juvenile facility that I would never return. And I didn't. From that point on, I stuck with Rameck and George and made my way to college without any more run-ins with the law. Years later, I would serve as a medical expert in that same court building where I once stood accused of robbery. I would also run into the same police detective who questioned me at the police station. He was so touched by my accomplishments that he hugged me.

But as I pushed into the unfamiliar world of college, the first in my family to do so, I started to realize that, although I love my parents dearly, their crisis-management style of child-rearing hadn't prepared me for any aspect of the life ahead of me. I hadn't heard enough advice about self-discipline, study habits, male-female interactions, nothing.

I felt as if I was on my own to make it to manhood and I was set up to fall because I didn't know what I was doing. After my time in the lockup, I suddenly realized that those stumbles were the magic events that prompted my parents finally to look up and give me their full attention. Whenever I got sick or got in trouble, that would bring them running to my side.

But this kind of stepping in after the fact can't possibly produce the best results. In fact, I think it can even cause some kids to decide that if acting up is the only way to get their parents' attention, then that's what they're going to do. I know I felt this way. I sometimes did wrong on purpose, just because I knew my parents tended to react, rather than take action ahead of time.

It never occurred to them to take a stand to keep the violence and crime outside from spilling into our home and becoming a part of our everyday living. They didn't find ways to keep us kids busy, to prevent damaging influences from creeping in and taking over our idle time. I'm sure my father noticed my personality abruptly changed in high school. But he never said a word, only offering the same mundane questions as always.

I've had to learn much of what I know about being a man through trial and error. I'm still struggling to learn how to express my emotions with women. Really, how would I know anything about that? I never saw my dad open up. All I had to go on was the input that friends offered on how to treat women. I've had to be deprogrammed. The guys I hung with drew a lot of their information from music videos and from one another. When they'd say things like "She's a ho" or "I got to hit that," that's how I thought it was supposed to be. As a child, there was no place I could turn to see a healthy example of how a man and woman relate to each other, except if you want to count the fantasy world of TV. I had to figure it out for myself.

My parents' battles affected me for a long time. I'd get in an argument and immediately be ready to fight because I thought that was how you handled it. One of my last fights was in college. About six of us were hanging out in a friend's room when a drunken student, surrounded by friends, walked by and called us all bitches and faggots and tossed in some cheap racial remarks, too. I jumped to my feet and exploded out of the room. No words, just a handful of fingers wrapped into a tight fist. I must have punched three guys, while taking a few punches myself. One guy I hit spurted blood from his mouth and nose as he held his battered face in his hand. The next day I found myself in school court. As I sat in a conference room in the student center, waiting to tell my side of the story, I knew my school career was in danger. I had to face the dean of students who sat behind a long desk, flanked by two other administrators. When I leaped into the fight, I never thought the outcome would be so grave. After all, the other guy had started it. But that didn't matter. I had injured the guy; I was the guilty party. To my relief, I got off with a sentence of probation and one hundred hours of community service.

One of the questions the dean asked me was "How could you have avoided the fight?" I answered truthfully: "I don't know." "Did you ever think of simply being the one to walk away, rather than add fuel to the fire?" he asked.

It was a lightbulb moment for me. Walking away hadn't even entered my mind. Even though Reggie had preached the same message much earlier, I had forgotten the lesson. I had been conditioned to think that if someone disrespects you, then you must make them pay. This school official had no idea what my life had been like. But he helped me reclaim those old memories when Reggie had taught that it's always possible to resolve an argument without fighting.

Kids naturally imitate their parents. But when they don't get any direction at home, it sends them out into the streets to discover how to act. It's who you bump into while you're out there that changes your path, for better or worse. I was luckier than most. I was blessed to have found Reggie, who helped me build up my mental armor. Although I didn't resist all the pressures I encountered, he planted a seed that helped me plot a path to college and out of harm's way. I have no doubt that Reggie's classes gave me the discipline, desire, and determination that helped me get to, and through, medical school. It changed my life that God added him to my stable of influences.

This is a dad's job, but in so many homes, fathers fail to perform it. For some reason, many of them don't realize how important they are. A simple conversation signals to a child that "you're important to me." Other people can say that to you all day long, but if a father hasn't done it, then you're missing something.

Sometimes when men reach the age of fatherhood, they forget how it feels to be a child who is hungry for Dad's attention. And the cycle repeats. But I remember how it feels to be that child. The feelings are still as vivid as the days when I stared across the backyard at Mike and his father playing basketball, wishing my dad and I could have that kind of affectionate interplay.

I don't mean to come down harshly on my parents, and I don't think of their style of child-rearing as a failure. I just don't think they knew any better. They did the best they could. Especially as I started heading toward college, stepping through doors my parents never entered, I understood that they didn't know how to advise me. And I've always tried to let them know that I appreciated what they did do.

My story may sound as if my mother wasn't able to give me much, but I realize in hindsight that when she stood by us through the divorce, she became a role model who taught me to stand strong. I've had teachers and professors tell me I wouldn't make it. Police officers who predicted I would return to jail. A judge who emphatically told me to bring my toothbrush next time because I definitely was going to be sent away. I remember many meetings with teachers or the Seton Hall bursar when I had to challenge my grades or ask for a few more months to pay the tuition. I stood alone, probably looking like an easy target. But having seen Moms stand up to men who would turn off our utilities and pick aluminum cans off the street to help pay my tuition, I knew what fortitude looked like. By being both mother and father to us when Pop left, she showed me the true power of parenting.

A big piece of me is satisfied that I made it past my obstacles, but I can't help but dream about how my success would have been even more undeniable if I had had my father at my side. When I think about Tiger Woods and Michael Jordan, I feel sure that having a supportive father coaching and cheering them on helped them become powerhouses who felt comfortable and confident on top of the world. Their fathers helped turn those boys into men who are unapologetic successes. Only a fraction of children in poor neighborhoods get that kind of hands-on fathering.

And because the problem of absent fathers has become so common, it's also become widely accepted.

And it shouldn't be. Children are precious, and you can't turn them loose on the streets and hope they'll turn out okay. Kids need someone to speak for them. I know from my own experience how tongue-tied a child feels when expressing these heartfelt thoughts. The subtle hints I dropped in my cards to Pop didn't work. "Dad, I need you to spend more time with me" sounds like a simple statement, but when you're a child, it's almost impossible to utter those words. I can attest to that.

After my father left, there were times when he seemed to show that he was sorry by picking me up and taking me out for a bite to eat. Those moments reinvigorated me and let me hope that maybe we could have a bond. But they were few. There is a part of me that will always be missing, a part that is uncompensated by everything else I do in life. It is a sentence that begins and has no end. You have only "My father was _____." What do you do with that? How do you fill in the rest of the sentence? I was always a curious kid and demanded to know things, but these are some questions that don't have answers. My sentence will always be a fragment. Only one person could have completed it. And now it's too late.

Chapter 2

SAMPSON

Kenneth Davis, Sr., as Told by Sampson

WHEN WE ORIGINALLY envisioned this book, we planned for each of our fathers to have his own chapter, to tell his life story in his own words.

By the time we got around to writing it, however, my father wasn't able to tell his own story. Two unforgiving diseases, Alzheimer's and Parkinson's, have overtaken him, stealing his ability to communicate.

So it became obvious that the next best plan would be for me to research my father's life. I knew from the outset that it would be a journey for me. But I never could have predicted how what I learned would shake up my world by illuminating a passionate side I never saw of my silent Pop. Now I know that my father was a puzzling man who could cry out for affection and companionship, and at the same time withhold those same precious things from his children. I've learned that his explosive relationship with my mother caused him to deliberately divert his emotions elsewhere, to another woman, starting when I was a small child. And I'm sobered immeasurably by the knowledge that his "other woman," now my stepmother, worked behind the scenes during my parents' fiery marriage to save our lives from being shattered by a gunshot.

All this was news to me. The Pop I knew was present physically for my early years, but an absentee father nonetheless. We didn't talk much. If we had, I'd probably know the name Friday Davis.

But I didn't recognize the name when an ancestry search led me to it. Friday Davis was my Pop's paternal grandfather. The instant I saw his name for the first time, on the 1900 census, it felt as if I had discovered a box of jewels. Although census documents are pretty sterile, it's clear he was a man to admire.

I wish that I had talked to Pop about Friday Davis, back when I had the chance. Born in 1850, Friday was a child when slavery ended. But he made the kind of strides that showed real grit and character, at a time when it was hard for blacks to find a financial toehold in the South.

The first record of him shows up in the 1880 census. He was living as a widower in South Carolina, rooming with a non-relative and working at a Georgetown County sawmill. By 1900, he had remarried. He and his wife, Hester, had a farm and nine children. Their firstborn son must have been a shining prince in their eyes, because they named him accordingly. Prince Davis grew up to become my grandfather.

Years later, when the 1920 census taker came knocking at his door, Friday Davis was looking back on a long and productive life and didn't mind saying so. Yes, he owned his own property in Johnson, South Carolina, he told the census man. Yes, he was the head of his household, at age seventy. And when the census taker asked if he could read and write, he answered yes both times—something few ex-slaves could say.

I love seeing the strong thread connecting the Davis men in the public record. The 1910 census shows my grandfather and his wife, Anna Pope Davis, living in a house next door to Friday and Hester Davis. It's not hard to imagine the profound impact that the father must have had on the son.

These men, both farm owners, obviously didn't fear hard work. The rhythms, struggles, and unpredictability of farming shaped their lives. Both had large families and were heads of households, not men who shirked their responsibilities.

By 1920, my grandfather, Prince, had ventured out from under his father's wing, relocating to another South Carolina county, perhaps with the idea of duplicating his dad's success. He and his wife, Anna, did well for themselves, establishing a tobacco farm in Hemingway, a piece of property that remains in my family to this day.

This is where my father, Kenneth Davis, was born on December 12, 1926. He was the baby of the family, the last of eight children, although only six survived.

Just like I used to think there was no place on earth better than our house on Ludlow Street while growing up, I know that my Pop felt the same way about his beloved family farm. Everything in his rural, insulated world revolved around the growing, curing, and selling of the all-important tobacco leaf. Behind their house, there was a tobacco barn and a smokehouse and beyond that, a barn. It was a nice-looking farm, dotted with pine and mulberry trees, and yellow plum trees that gave the kids—Leroy, Mildred, Persena, Joe, Olin, and baby Kenneth—something to snack on.

Pop's mom was a brown-skinned woman with a slight build and a sparkling personality. She lived to be almost one hundred, and I got a chance to meet her during my first summer trip down south when I was five. I was too young during that visit to have many memories, but a yellowed newspaper clipping shows that my popular grandmother thoroughly charmed a reporter sent by the *Weekly Observer* in Hemingway to chronicle her ninety-second birthday party in 1974. At the party, my grandmother recited a poem, "There Will Be No Tears in Heaven," which she had learned in school as a child. "She used so much expression, you would think she was a graduate of a school of dramatic art," the captivated reporter wrote. My grandmother was a loyal churchgoer and never spent a day in the hospital. "The diminutive woman, who weighs only 96 pounds, appears ageless," the article said.

My grandma's contented outlook and good looks didn't give a clue to how difficult her life must have been. My grandfather died in 1935, when he was about fifty-three, leaving her widowed with six children. My father wasn't even ten years old at the time. It's a theme that echoes eerily through George's and Rameck's stories, and mine: Not a single one of our fathers got the chance, as a boy, to bond with his own biological father.

My dad, being the baby of the family, soon had everyone in his close-knit family looking out for him, since his widowed mom now had the responsibility of managing the farm by herself. His biggest fan in the household was his new aunt, Amelia, who had just married his older brother Leroy. Pop adored Amelia and loved being the center of her attention, a story that Aunt Amelia, now ninety-five and remarkably lucid, loves to tell. "Take me with you," he'd cry out whenever he saw Leroy and Amelia getting in the car to go shopping or visiting. He especially loved going to Amelia's mother's house, and often begged to be taken there to spend the night.

"No, you're too little," his big brother would say, giving little Kenneth the brush-off so he could spend time alone with his bride. But Amelia was a pushover for Kenneth's whining, and in time she taught him to climb into the car and hide before the couple left. "When we'd get way down the road, Kenneth would stand up," she remembered with a laugh. "My husband would say, 'Oh well, it's no use to turn around.'"

Aunt Amelia said that my father eventually "adopted" his big brother Leroy as his father figure. "All during his life, if he had anything he wanted to talk over with a father, he would call my husband," she said. "Even after he got married, he called my husband to talk about important things."

Pop is a self-taught musician, and Aunt Amelia remembers that his interest in the guitar began in high school when he and a group of teen friends started a band. In the 1940s, they performed throughout the community, going into private homes to play and sing. He loved gentle gospel songs and popular music, so much that sometimes he would cry from the sheer joy of singing, Amelia said.

In 1945, near the end of World War II, he was inducted into the army. He was proud to serve his country. He cherished his photo album, filled with pictures he had snapped overseas in Japan, and I remember him talking happily about his army years. From what I gathered, my father loved the chance the military had provided for him to see the world.

The army first shipped him to Fort Knox, Kentucky, where he underwent eight weeks of basic training. My lonely Pop seemed to really struggle during that period. "Those eight weeks seemed like eight years because I wanted to go home so bad," he once wrote in a neatly typed statement he titled "My Military Career." "Entering the army, I was mostly homesick on Saturdays and Sundays for at least four or five weeks until I was stationed, then things began to get a little better when I began to know the fellows."

In the summer of 1945, Pop was shipped out to the Pacific. Later, the United States dropped atomic bombs on Hiroshima and Nagasaki, bringing a swift end to the war. Pop's antiaircraft unit and many other U.S. military regiments remained behind after Japan surrendered. Their new job was to occupy Japan and oversee the rebuilding of the country in the months following World War II.

On September 13, 1945, Pop sent home a letter:

Dear Mother,

How are you all? I hope, as this leaves me, fine. Well, I'm learning to type a little if I didn't take it in school.

Don't pay any attention to my mistakes because I'm not perfect.

I went to Tokyo last Saturday and that is a wonderful place. I got a letter from Persena last week, and she said they were fine.

I imagine you all are rich off the tobacco, how did it sell? You should see me now, I'm sitting behind a large desk with a typewriter at my disposal. (smile)

    I'm sending some money. Go ahead and spend it if you need it, and for goodness sake, don't work too hard. I guess I will close now.

Your son Kenneth

My father, a private first class, served until July 1947, when he returned home to South Carolina at age twenty-one with an honorable discharge.

When he came back to the family farm, his mother fixed a feast to welcome home the returning soldier. Back in the bosom of the family he had missed, my dad resumed his old social life. And like many black soldiers, he had to readjust to the rigid rules of the segregated South after experiencing more freedom overseas. A budding camera buff with a knapsack full of undeveloped film shot in Japan, he debated whether he should take the rolls to a local photo studio. He was eager to see the pictures he'd taken of Iko, a Japanese woman with a sweet smile whom he'd considered his girlfriend. But eventually he decided it wasn't worth the risk. No sense in identifying himself as an uppity Negro to the white townsfolk, he decided.

My father, a short, wiry man who carried himself with a military bearing, loved to dress in his army uniform for special functions. One day in 1948 he put on his carefully pressed uniform to attend a carnival that had come to town. At the penny-toss booth, a pretty little fifteen-year-old spied the handsome young man in uniform and spoke up about him. "I wouldn't mind talking to him," Ruthener Lawson remarked to her cousin. "I know him, that's my friend. I'm going to connect you up," the cousin replied.

The cousin made the introductions, and shortly after that, Kenneth Davis came calling at the home of Emory Lawson, Ruthener's father. This was a sensitive situation, one that Pop had to finesse. Ruthener was only fifteen, yet she was the backbone of her father's household. Her mother had died when she was a little girl, and her father never remarried, so it fell to

Ruthener to handle all the wifely duties around the farm. Also, Kenneth was seven years her senior.

He courted her carefully, taking her into town on movie dates when he could coax his brother into letting him borrow the car. And when the car was off limits, he didn't hesitate to walk the five miles between their farms just to talk to her. One Wednesday, when they were returning from the movies, he asked Ruthener to marry him. Moms was startled and stammered, "Well, I'll think about it."

About a week later, Pop showed up to check on the status of his proposal. "Have you thought about it?" he inquired. Moms indicated that she was leaning toward saying yes, but she didn't think her father would approve.

The two of them cooked up a plan, and executed it that weekend. As usual, Moms went into town that Saturday with her sister to do the shopping, and Pop met her there. Quietly, they strolled away. Later that day, Pop drove her back to her father's farm and dropped her off. For a year, they kept secret the fact that they had slipped away to Florence, South Carolina, and had gotten married.

They still courted on weekends, and Ruthener continued to care for her father. In time, her father grew fond of Kenneth, who volunteered his time doing chores around the Lawson farm and also helped out by driving Moms into town to pick up items at the store. My Pop, in turn, respected Mr. Lawson and appreciated him for treating him like a member of the family.

The two men's growing affection for each other certainly helped the situation a year later when Ruthener's bouts of morning sickness tipped her father off to the fact that she was pregnant with my brother Kenny. Fearing his response, Moms hastily told her father the truth. To her surprise, he didn't fuss. "I can't do anything about it, you're married now," her father responded.

With the secret unmasked, Kenneth and Ruthener finally could live under the same roof. With his father-in-law's blessing, Pop moved into the Lawson household, where Kenny and Roselene both were born. Sometimes, however, the young couple went to stay at my Pop's family farm to keep his mother company.

Pop got a job pumping gas and changing tires at a filling station. While he went about his day, he began to hear in his mind the same internal debate many Southern blacks were puzzling over during this period. "Stay in the South, where I'll be relegated to menial jobs like this for the rest of my life?" With two babies already and the hope of fathering a larger family, he didn't want to limit his income.

"If we go up north, we can make more money there than we can down here," he told his wife, who agreed.

Most of Pop's brothers and sisters opted to stay put, sticking close to the family's Georgetown County property. His brother Leroy opened up a successful little store right around the corner from the farm that stocked all kinds of necessities, including rows of sweet treats. I remember during our occasional summer trips down south, he would give us candy and cookies when we came in the door.

Studying my family's geography in order to write this chapter helped me to realize how boldly Pop acted when he decided to come north. He faced heavy pressure from aunts and uncles who didn't want him to leave. His South Carolina relatives, the center of his world, fretted about their baby leaving home. "He was too young to go off," Aunt Amelia remembers thinking. And Ruthener was still a teenager! How would they manage with two toddlers? "They're too young to be on their own in the big city," Amelia insisted.

But Pop did have one role model. His sister Persena had moved to New York a few years earlier. A single mom, she probably felt that New York was a place where she could start over and build a new life for herself.

Her little brother Kenneth followed her lead cautiously. He came up north by himself, in 1950, to stay at Persena's apartment and look for a job. He landed one at a New York store and started mailing money home to his family.

As soon as he could, he sent for his wife to join him. Ruthener left little Kenny and Roselene in the care of relatives, and she headed north. They took an apartment in the Newark area after my father landed a job at the airport with Butler Aviation. She took a job at a New Jersey box company, operating a machine that made boxes for stockings, shoes, and candy.

Kenny and Roselene stayed safe in the sheltering South for several more years, bouncing among their parents' relatives. Kenny remembers that at first they lived with Moms's father, Emory Lawson, and got to tag along on many of the farm duties. Soon they were doing their mother's old job feeding the chickens.

After Moms's father died, Kenny and Roselene shifted over to the noisy, child-filled home where Pop's mother and his brother Joe's family lived. To make them feel more comfortable, our grandmother, whom they called Ma-Ma, took them on a walk through the farm. "This is your very own tree," she told them, picking out an apple or pecan tree for each. They could help themselves to its fruit, or just retreat to it when they needed some comfort. Sometimes those personal trees came in handy; Kenny and Roselene missed their parents like crazy. Uncle Joe had a lot of kids, and feelings could get hurt in a house with so many personalities.

As those country months stretched on, my brother Kenny often insisted to his cousins that he hadn't been forgotten. "My mom and dad are going to come and get us," he would tell them while sitting on the porch gazing at the dirt road leading out of the property. "They didn't just leave us." But as he waited for word from his parents, summer came and went.

Then, one morning when Kenny was about seven years old, he woke up and felt his heart rejoice without explanation. A little later, he looked down their country lane and could see a car in the distance, raising dust. "That's Mom and Dad," he confidently told his same-age cousin, Glen. Kenny was correct. "I told you they were coming!" he shrieked when his parents stepped out of the car.

I wish more than anything that I had been born in time to witness those first triumphant years when my family was reunited in Newark. They had to have been the best years of my parents' marriage. Kenny's memories of that period are bliss-filled. He remembers family outings to the park, and Sunday evenings after church when Moms and Pop would embrace on the couch while he and Roselene parked themselves in front of the TV watching *Bonanza*.

He remembers going to Christmas parties at Pop's job, where he'd have a chance to sit on Santa's lap. Christmases were great, he recalls: "I got everything I wanted." After all the presents were unwrapped, Moms and Pop would teasingly blame each other for spoiling their kids rotten.

Even today, Kenny talks with little-boy awe about the day that Pop walked with him into the neighborhood boys' club, where my brother often participated in woodshop classes after school. As the instructor showed Pop some of Kenny's woodworking projects, my brother could hear the other kids whispering, "That's Kenny's father," with envy. "That was the proudest moment of my life," Kenny declared. "He was a whole lot better than a lot of the other dads that are out there."

My parents welcomed four more children after they moved to Newark. My sister Fellease arrived quickly after Moms and Dad reunited. Ten years later, my parents resumed their childbearing streak. My brother Andre was born in 1968, I followed in 1973, and my little brother Carlton showed up in 1977.

As the second set of Davis kids arrived, the economics of raising a big family on a little salary began to take a toll on my parents' relationship. The attentive dad that Kenny and Roselene remember doesn't resemble at all the reclusive guy that Andre, Carlton, and I knew. "To me, he was the greatest father alive. He was my friend as well as my dad," Kenny told me. "Sometimes I feel sorry for you guys because you missed out on the good stuff. Y'all weren't able to see the love that Ma and Dad had for each other."

What happened to change my father's outlook? His dreams must have been limitless when he took that job at Butler Aviation in the 1950s. He must have felt immense gratitude just to be hired, since it was essentially a guarantee that he wouldn't have to return to South Carolina. Pop worked at Butler for thirty-five years. His job was to drive a fuel truck to the planes at the airport to fill the tanks with gasoline. He endured summer's humidity and the biting cold of winter on Newark Bay, reporting to work at six o'clock every morning. He was never promoted to foreman, and to my knowledge he never complained about it. When I think of my father's demeanor at work, I know it's a testament to his upbringing. My Pop was just loyal. Considering that he'd come from the rural South, where logs in the stove heated the house and indoor plumbing was a relatively new advancement, he settled gratefully into his workaday life, happy to have a job.

This was the attitude of many black men of his generation who flocked to the North. They had fled outright racism and had high hopes of being able to raise their families in a place where the chances of prospering were much better. In the 1950s, his generation could feel free to dream. But reality set in during the ensuing years, as black low-income ghettos started taking shape in the major urban centers in the Northeast.

I think one of Pop's main challenges was that the support structure he depended on in the South just didn't exist up north. In the South, the extended family created an important safety net. They'd take in a needy relative and freely share their food, their resources, their values. Couples rarely divorced. Relatives and church members would feel free to intervene if a philandering husband needed someone to shake him up and tell him to act right. In the rural South, the community shaped the values of its people.

But in Newark, the community was turning Pop's world topsy-turvy by its relentless barrage of drugs, violence, and negativity, and I suspect that he didn't know how to fight it.

When Pop came in at night, he'd seal the world out, never even glancing across the street at the Dayton Street projects. Although my brothers and I knew all the faces and haunts in our neighborhood, Pop rarely socialized with any of the neighbors. The one day that he did stride across the street and walk into the projects sticks out in my memory because it was so out of the ordinary for him. On that particular day, Andre had taken the bus to school, something he typically avoided doing because rowdy boys from the projects usually started some mischief on it. And sure enough, before the bus ride was over, Andre got pulled into a slapboxing fight with some of the boys from the projects. Andre not only got a reprimand from the principal when he got to school, he was assaulted again on his way home by the same boys, who saw him alone and surrounded him.

When our father got home and heard the story, he grabbed some friends to back him up and walked into the projects. He didn't leave until he found out who had attacked his son. He left behind a warning not to do it again.

But every day, in dozens of ways, his children were under fire from unhealthy influences, and Pop couldn't possibly fight them all. He had worked hard to save enough money to buy our house in what was originally a stable area, but the neighborhood decayed around us. There was no safety net that could help him shield his kids from the violence and crime in our environment. In time, my fun-loving, down-to-earth sister Fellease, whom I adored, got hooked on drugs and resorted to a lot of risky behaviors. Several times, Moms had to find the money to bail Fellease out of jail. And my popular brother Kenny became a terror in his teens and twenties. Kenny drank heavily, acted abusively toward his girlfriend, and raised all kinds of hell at home. During my college years, Kenny suffered a traumatic head injury in a fight, ending up with permanent brain damage.

After the accident, Pop stayed at Kenny's side in the hospital and helped him through those angry months of rehabilitation when Kenny questioned why his life had turned out this way. Doctors told Kenny to prepare for life in a wheelchair. This was one time when the emotionless Pop I knew showed another face. He didn't flinch from the tough job of being there to help Kenny deal with the fact that he couldn't walk. He provided the shoulder that Kenny needed to cry on, and they forged a special bond during that time.

Today, my brother has made peace with the events that robbed him of his independence and put him in a nursing home. When I interviewed him for this book, he had much to say. If through some miracle he could rewrite history, Kenny said he would toy with the idea of erasing our family's decision to migrate to the big city. "I wish at times I had been brought up like Pop. I would have appreciated things more. I figure if I had been left down there [in the South], I wouldn't be in this wheelchair right now. I didn't listen. I had to find out the hard way," he said.

"If I had stayed in the South, things wouldn't have turned out like this, I wouldn't have tried all that crazy stuff. Down there, I wouldn't have been messing around. You didn't have that free time on your hands. You had to help out. Me and Roselene, we had chores. 'Finish your work, learn the Twenty-third Psalm, go to bed,' that's what Ma-Ma would have said."

Coming of age in Newark was a totally different story, Kenny said. He remembered feeling forced by his peers to demonstrate his manhood through violence and drinking. "It's the city life," Kenny believes. "When in Rome, do as the Romans do. If I hadn't conformed, I would have perished. I wanted to be one of the boys."

In the 1960s and 1970s, when my parents were struggling to keep their kids off the streets, the concept of "quality time" hadn't come into the nation's vocabulary yet. Steering his kids past inner-city Newark's land mines required skills and fortitude that Pop just couldn't manufacture.

Retreating behind a closed door was Pop's method of coping, and without a doubt, it takes amazing coping skills to survive in a poor neighborhood. Sometimes I think that middle-class folks who frown on the behavior of poor people need to see for themselves what it's like. It would be an interesting experiment to drop someone like that off in the 'hood for a few months and see how they survive with no job prospects, no source of income, a houseful of mouths to feed, and a neighborhood bulging with addicts and criminals. How would they find someone suitable to marry when all the potential mates are addicted to drugs and alcohol?

How would they combat the experiences their children receive at substandard schools where their brains get stuffed with profanity and hallway violence instead of math and reading? Pop certainly couldn't figure that one out.

When I was young, I heard him many times warn my older siblings away from the bad influences. I guess he wished his children could shut the world out, as he eventually taught himself to do. But like the hardheaded teenagers they were, they stubbornly defied him. My brother Andre remembers Pop urging him to be in by midnight. "Nothing good happens in Newark after twelve o'clock at night," Pop would warn him. My brother admits that he didn't listen. He thought he had the right to hang out in the streets with his friends until morning if he wanted to.

By the time I was approaching my teen years, Pop seemed to admit defeat. For him, life in our house appeared to be torture. In the waning years of their marriage, my parents attempted to curb the altercations by moving to different areas of the house. I long believed that the way they carved out their domains contributed to the way that Pop sequestered himself. He was the breadwinner, and the house was Moms's responsibility. That sharp division of duties ended up contributing to the emotional distance between the kids and Pop. When my dad was in my mother's territory, he walled himself off.

Music served as his emotional getaway. Although he couldn't read music, he had a load of natural talent and would sit in the living room and play his favorite songs on his guitar. He loved spirituals and down-home rhythm and blues. He has a beloved collection of albums, some of which are older than me, from his favorite artists including Glenn Miller, Nat "King" Cole, the Mills Brother, and his beloved Dixie Hummingbirds. For him, music was a gift and he loved every moment of it. He could drift for hours, playing his guitar and singing his favorite tunes.

When I was little, he joined with some other gospel musicians to form the Holy Righteous Gospel Singers. Dressed formally in matching black suits, they performed at gigs throughout the Newark area. I saw him perform once at a local Baptist church. He was the lead bass guitar player. He stood tall and dignified, and I remember feeling so proud of him. My father dreamed of one day earning his living as a performer.

Even as a youngster, I could tell from Pop's unhappiness that he envisioned another life for himself. But what I didn't know was that from the time I was a little boy, he had begun to shape a secret life, chasing after the satisfaction he thought he was lacking. I learned this only recently from my stepmother, Thelma. When I asked Thelma to help me construct Pop's biography, she filled in many of the details of Pop's life that I never knew about.

Pop met Thelma in the summer of 1977, when I was four and Carlton was only a baby. They were introduced by a neighbor of ours who asked Dad to give Thelma a ride back to her place in Queens. From the beginning of their relationship, Pop never hid the fact that he was a husband and father. But he and his wife were so incompatible that they lived in different parts of the house, he told Thelma, and his house was too chaotic for him to be happy.

He asked for her phone number. Though unsure, she gave it to him. "I'm not interested in a married man," Thelma told him at first. "With what I'm going through right now, I'm not interested in anyone." At that time, Thelma was helping her family cope with the ordeal caused several years earlier when her husband killed a seventeen-year-old, her oldest son's best friend, in the lobby of a Brooklyn housing project. By then, her husband was in prison, serving five to sixteen years, and she was in the process of getting a divorce. Thelma, who was twelve years younger than Pop, simply wanted to focus on healing herself and her family.

But Pop put his mind to pursuing her, and for Thelma, it felt good to be treated with dignity and sweetness. Although they didn't see each other often, since they lived an hour apart, he never stopped calling and telling her how lonely he was for her. He had been praying for someone to come into his life who would appreciate him for him, he told her.

As Pop began to open up and let his feelings out, Thelma began to let her guard down a bit. "It's not your average man who prays to God for someone to come into his life," she told herself. She could sympathize with how he had struggled with marital problems but hadn't yet left the relationship. Her husband had been a drug user and a womanizer, but with six kids to support, she never seriously considered leaving him. When Pop told her that all he wanted was some peace and happiness in a relationship, it struck a chord with Thelma. It was something she, too, craved.

The two started an experimental courtship, although Thelma continued to be unsure of whether she was doing the right thing. Thelma even remembered a day when she got to meet Pop's youngest boys. Pop, she said, one day put me, Andre, and Carlton into the car and took us to a mall to meet her, although of course we were too young to understand what was going on.

Their budding relationship wasn't so much sexual as it was a source of comfort for the two of them, Thelma said. It wasn't long before my father told her he loved her. But on one point, Thelma remained firm: If Kenneth Davis wanted her, he was going to have to wait. "I'm not even going to think about marriage until my youngest daughter graduates from high school," she told Pop.

So my father settled in for a ten-year wait, always wooing Thelma back whenever she attempted to break it off. "If you end our relationship, I have nothing to live for," he told her once. "I love you and I don't want to lose you."

I must admit, learning these raw facts about my father's infidelity has been painful for me. Yet it makes sense. Now I finally know where my father's love and attention were going. In essence, he left me to fend for myself after his soured marriage caused him to head off in search of love.

For years I felt alone. That doesn't even sound logical—I had both parents living with me, yet I was alone. But my mom and dad were busy battling their issues and going through their challenges. I learned to stay quiet and not add any fuel to the fire. Their volatility shaped me. I would stay away from the house for hours when I was a boy, simply because I didn't want to go home and say something that might cause a fight. I spent those years wishing for my ideal dad. I yearned for my parents to be in love. What child doesn't? As I grew older, I stopped fantasizing and realized it wasn't going to happen. I blamed myself at first and thought it was a mistake that I had been born. Then I forced myself to move on and learned to depend on myself. Yet there is a piece of me that will always be empty.

As I learn the story of my father and Thelma, a side of me is happy for Pop. Everyone needs happiness to sustain them, and obviously he wasn't getting the love he desired at home. He needed it and Thelma was there. I understand. Yet I wish that my father had been there for us in the same way that he was there for Thelma. It baffles me that Pop put his needs ahead of ours, not recognizing that his children had the same needs and desires he did.

I also learned from Thelma that she played a key role in helping Pop learn to cool his head and quell some of the violence in our home. In fact, she may have been the angel who indirectly saved our lives. Pop, she said, had told her how my mother's hot temper could provoke him to rage. He confided to her about an episode when he had held a gun to my mother's head and had to force himself not to pull the trigger.

Thelma, who still lived with the memory of the violent rampage of the man she divorced in 1980, detected the danger in Pop's words. She worked hard, she told me, to counsel my father through those urges. "Get rid of the gun," she insisted to Pop. "Don't even think of hurting her." It was Thelma who suggested that Pop go to a quiet room or leave the house altogether. Again, her story fit like a missing piece into the puzzle of my childhood, seeming to explain why my parents' arguments became less explosive in the later years as we saw less and less of Pop.

Pop finally moved into to an apartment in 1985. Two years later, Thelma moved in with him. She had kept her promise, waiting until her youngest daughter graduated from high school. A few months later, they had a small church wedding and a reception at the home of one of Thelma's relatives.

I was fourteen at the time, and ambivalent about going to the wedding. Who wants to see their father get remarried? I didn't know what I would say or do at a wedding where my father would be marrying another woman. But I got dressed and waited with my brothers for my uncle Buddy to come get us. He never showed up. I never found out why. Years later, I would see the pictures of their wedding day. Thelma wore an off-white dress and headpiece; Pop looked happy in a black tuxedo.

I remember seeing my older cousin Anthony in the pictures. As a kid, I wasn't privy to "grown folks' business," but I now know from Thelma that she had traveled with Pop on several occasions to meet his family in South Carolina, even while my parents were married. Anthony, my father's nephew, was one of many relatives who had known about their relationship for years and cheered them on. It was Anthony who drove my dad to his wedding that day and stood at his side. "This is long overdue and I want you to have some happiness and peace in life," Anthony told my dad.

In talking to some of my dad's relatives, I've learned that they knew how tumultuous my parents' relationship was. Pop apparently had shared his side of the story regarding the turmoil going on inside our house. They knew about the fights and violence and seemed to think my mother was at fault and that my father deserved better. They admired him for sticking it out as long as he did.

Pop retired in 1991 and set about making his long-deferred dreams a reality in the years that followed. He and Thelma bought some land in Raleigh, North Carolina, and in the late 1990s, moved back to the South that my father had missed so much. When the property sales manager asked him what amenities he wanted in his new home, Pop replied only that he wanted "a refrigerator with an ice maker." And when he opened the door of his modest but gleaming new home for the first time, freshly made cubes were waiting for him.

With Thelma, Pop started indulging his love of travel. They signed up for bus tours of nearby sights, and he took his camera along to snap moments that he wanted to remember.

He enjoyed spending hours at a local bookstore, buying discount books about different countries of the world and their history. He loved shopping for CD versions of his favorite music. In his later years, he pursued the things that brought him joy.

In October 2001, he had to make a sad return trip to Newark. My sister Fellease had died, at age forty-three, of complications related to HIV. Andre and I handled the funeral arrangements, and I paid for the funeral. By then I was a full-fledged physician. I had noticed earlier that Fellease was showing some symptoms of HIV. Unable to kick her drug habit, Fellease had gotten lost in the culture of drugs and contracted the disease through unprotected sex. It devastated me to be called to the hospital to identify my sister's body. The heartbreak I felt over her death is only intensified today, as the number of black females with HIV has mushroomed into a deadly epidemic.

Pop was at the wake, and he gave me the kind of half-hug that I had grown used to. I don't remember him crying. But that would have been out of character for him. In earlier years he had made it clear to Fellease that he disapproved of her drug arrests, the way she begged for money, and how she disappeared for days at a time. I think he was silently heartbroken that he had lost a child, like so many families had around us. But, as usual, it went against his personal code to express his feelings to us.

I made sure that my mom, Pop, and Thelma got tickets to attend the Essence Awards at Radio City Music Hall in New York in 2000, when George, Rameck, and I received an award from the magazine. It was a glittering night, with Bill Cosby, Oprah Winfrey, and Hillary Clinton in attendance. It felt great to be included with stars like Danny Glover and Michael Jordan as award recipients. The standing ovation we received felt so intoxicatingly fabulous that I promised myself the Three Doctors would be back real soon. Pop was quiet that night, but all smiles. He didn't say much, but I could tell that he was proud.

I could also tell the event was a moment of reflection for him. Maybe he was questioning his absence in my life? We never spoke about it, but his face gave away the fact that he was thinking about something serious.

That was one of the last times I saw him in good health. As I said my goodbyes and the limousine I had booked for my family took them back to New Jersey, I couldn't predict the battles my father would face over the next few years. He was diagnosed first with prostate cancer, and successfully underwent radiation therapy. Then diabetes started to destroy his eyesight, which he took extremely hard. Slowly, he found himself unable to read or play the guitar.

But the cruelest diagnosis was yet to come. Pop now suffers from Parkinson's and Alzheimer's, two diseases of the brain that lead to dementia with loss of memory. Slowly, he has become detached and unable to process the details of his world.

Pop fractured his hip in April 2005, and hasn't walked since. When I visited him in North Carolina in March 2006, I saw that Parkinson's and Alzheimer's had conspired to take away his awareness and ability to communicate. Earlier that month, Thelma had made the difficult decision to place him in a nursing home in Garner, North Carolina, just a few miles from the retirement nest they had shared.

I've never held any resentment toward Thelma. She made my father happy. As I've watched her care unselfishly for Pop, I've grown to admire her even more. She stays in touch with me and keeps me abreast of my father's health. "You've got to take care of your people when they're in a place like this," Thelma said matter-of-factly, as she arrived at The Laurels of Forest Glenn for her daily visit with my father. She has made sure his room is neat and color-coordinated in blue and white.

I visited him not long after he moved to the nursing home, and was surprised to see how painfully thin and fragile he looked. Even before I arrived, I had pretty much given up on the idea of posing any questions for this book to him, knowing his physical state. His gaunt, weakened appearance let me know that my hunch was right.

But Pop surprised everybody by talking a little.

Do you remember the 2000 Essence Awards? we asked.

"I was on cloud nine," Pop responded.

What do you remember about your mother, Anna?

"She would whip me," he wisecracked.

To break through the haziness of Alzheimer's, we brought pictures and music in hopes that Pop would respond to them. He seemed to enjoy listening to a CD, *An Anthology of Big Band Swing, 1930–1955,* with some of his favorites: Duke Ellington, Count Basie, Benny Goodman, Tommy Dorsey, Lionel Hampton, and Louis Armstrong.

He was most enthralled to see an old publicity photograph of himself and the Holy Righteous Gospel Singers. He gazed at it for a long time and murmured to himself, lost in his own world. It was an oddly familiar feeling for me to be back on the outside, on the other side of the door.

But music, once his escape, is now Pop's doorway back to lucidity. He talks in fuller sentences when he's discussing music. The gospel group picture seemed to open up a speeding train of clear thought for him. He sang a few lines of an old song, "Cotton needed picking so bad," in a voice that was clear and strong.

But as the hour drew later, Pop began pulling away. It's what typically happens in the evening, Thelma said. I watched as he fiddled constantly with his hands, buttoning and unbuttoning his shirt, becoming increasingly disoriented. I recognized from experience that what Pop was doing was called "sundowning," the term for when a patient becomes increasingly restless and agitated at the end of the day.

Eventually he held his head in his hands sadly, as if disappointed he couldn't make sense of things anymore. I lifted my once strong father in my arms and put him to bed. He couldn't have weighed much more than a hundred pounds.

When I visited the next morning, I rolled Pop in his wheelchair down the hall to a large airy room where a few volunteers were holding a devotional service, singing spirituals. Pop looked frail that morning, with a faraway look in his eyes. He seemed unable to comprehend who I was or what was going on. But he tapped his foot in time to the music and inclined his head silently toward me, as if I was the sunshine and he was just drinking it in.

As the vocalist sang, "Lord, I can't even walk without you holding my hand," tears quietly dropped from Pop's eyes. Aunt Amelia had said that he used to cry, as a boy, at the heart-tugging beauty of a gospel song. I could see in that pure moment that her memory was true.

I took Pop back to his room and kissed him goodbye.

As much as I wish our story had been written differently, I still feel the need to spend time at my father's side during his declining days.

I'm still collecting information as I continue my conversations with my family about my father. My brother Andre doesn't dispute the fact that Pop struggled with affection. He rarely heard Pop say "I love you." Yet as the years have passed, Andre has become a father himself, which helped him arrive at a new appreciation for Pop. "I see the love now," Andre said.

Andre pointed out to me that our father was nearing sixty when we became teenagers. Just like me, Andre looked wistfully at the backyard two doors down from us when our neighbor Mike was out there playing with his father—but later he realized the two men weren't the same. "As I got older, I realized that Pop can't do that. He's a much more senior, mature man," he said. Pop, he realized, had other strengths. "He gave us that hardwork ethic. He taught us to be honest and hardworking. Just get out there and do the right thing, even though it's hard."

Today, Andre finds a lot in Pop's fathering style that is worth copying. With a laugh, he even admits that he's been known to borrow that same "Nothing good happens in Newark after twelve o'clock at night" line that Pop used with him. "I'm trying to use the example he set. I'm trying to hold up that bar by being the man of the house," Andre said.

"I remember that he would come home and we'd have to be quiet if he was really tired," Andre continued. "But now that I'm a father, I get it. I know exactly how he felt. Sometimes you go to work and you're bombarded by life's everyday hassles and you get home and you don't intentionally mean to alienate your kids and you're not trying to—but you're really dog-tired.

"I get it," he repeated.

In August 2006, Andre, Carlton, and I took a trip together to Raleigh to see my ailing father. Thelma prompted our visit by telling us that our father often asked when he would see his sons.

I arrived in North Carolina on a Friday evening. Andre and Carlton had taken the morning flight from Newark to Raleigh and already were at Thelma and Pop's home. When I landed, I called Andre to let him know that I had made it in. He told me that they were at my father's house and had brought Pop from the nursing home to spend some time there. This was a surprise. It was the first time my father had left the nursing home since being placed there after his hip fracture. I quickly gathered my bags and made my way to the house, fifteen miles away.

The door was open and through the screen door I could see everyone laughing and talking in the living room. Any outsider would have thought this was the perfect family.

I opened the door and took in the scene. Sitting in the living room were Thelma and my brothers; my stepsister Clarise; Andre's twelve-year-old daughter, Angela; and Andre's fiancée, Makeba. And then there was my father, sitting in his recliner, looking more peaceful and at ease than the last time I saw him five months before. The scent of a good meal was in the air.

They had stirred up some black beans, rice, and fish. I was starving and sent my niece on the mission of preparing a plate for me. I ran around the room giving everyone a hug.

Finally, I found myself in front of my father. I reached down and embraced him. He was sleeping but quickly woke up. Looking at me, he began to smile. "You got your boys here," Thelma told him happily. He replied with an affirmative, "Yeah, my boys." I sat down next to him and we all talked for hours, trying our best to draw in Pop when we could.

As the night came to a close, we had to take my father back to the nursing home. Given his condition and the need for round-the-clock care, it was impossible to keep him home for the night. As we moved him from his chair to the car, he let us know with all his might that he disapproved of leaving. Looking up with all the energy he could muster, he began to repeat one word. "Why? Why? Why?" I took this to mean that he didn't want to go back and he wondered why we were making him go. After all, it had been years since we had come together as a family. It felt so complete for us to gather in one place. This, I thought, is what we missed out on, that feeling of completeness. That wholeness where you know everything is okay because you have the most important thing within your reach—your family.

The weekend sped by as we barbecued, played cards, listened to music, and on TV watched football and saw Tiger Woods win his fourth championship in a row. It was a great mini–family reunion in so many ways, and yet a rare event for the splintered Davis clan.

Surrounded by my family, enriched by the newfound ancestors I had uncovered, I realized there was no sense in holding on to cancerous feelings. Pop's lack of involvement through the years had caused our family to disconnect, but there was nothing stopping us, his sons, from changing that legacy.

Thelma told us that through his haze and pain, Pop often asks, "Where are my boys?" Wasn't that the exact response I had craved from him as a child, when I wished my dad would reach for me when he walked through the door?

More then ever, time together matters, I thought. If it feels good to be together now, then is rehashing the past worth it? Silently, I let go of my resentment and pain and let them float away.

Like Rameck and George, I wanted this book to address my unanswered questions. Yet I knew in my heart that my Pop wouldn't be able to answer them. Even if he had been healthy and whole, I don't think he could have handled a heart-to-heart discussion about being a tuned-in parent who is fully involved in his child's life. That wasn't the way his generation was raised and I knew it.

But if I've learned anything from my father's life, it's that he was a product of his environment and yet he was determined to follow his dreams.

I think that gives me permission to pursue my own dreams. That's the reason I have dared to share my story: in the hope that it will lift today's fathers to a new awareness of how the simple gifts of their attention and affection affect a child for a lifetime.

Chapter 3

SAMPSON

What It Takes

I VISIT CLASSROOMS ALL THE TIME, and I've been keeping an unscientific poll of the kids I meet there.

"How many of you don't live with your fathers?" I ask bluntly.

Inevitably, more than half raise their hands. Sometimes it's nearly everyone. Often a student will pull me aside to share every detail of his or her father's last visit, holding on to the memories tightly.

It's obvious to me even before I ask the question which ones will raise their hands. They're the ones not-so-silently screaming for attention. The ones who interrupt my anti-violence presentation with outbursts, the ones slouching in their chairs, the ones who can't keep their hands off the kid next to them. The undisciplined ones who remind me of myself when I was a little boy in the same boat, hungry for guidance.

On one particular spring morning, I was at Peshine Avenue School in Newark, talking to sixth-, seventh-, and eighth-graders about making smart decisions.

"I practice emergency medicine, like on the show *ER*," I explained. "I'm born and raised here in Newark. I went to Dayton Street School and University High School, right around the corner."

Every day that I report to the hospital for work, I tell them, I have to treat someone who ended up hurt and bleeding because he didn't know how to work out a disagreement.

Then I launch into my presentation, starting with the story of a nineteen-year-old arguing with his eighteen-year-old wife about the care of their child. The disagreement ended when she pulled out a shotgun and shot him in the chest. On a slide projector, I show a picture of a surgeon with his fingers in the husband's chest, attempting to save his life.

I figure I might as well start out with a domestic violence scene. It's something I witnessed as a child and I'm sure many of these kids have, too. To stop the cycle, somebody's got to speak up, even if it means pushing into the private world of these schoolchildren. So I do.

My presentation is part of a program called Cops & Docs, created a few years ago by Dr. Duane Dyson, a physician who was born and raised in East Orange, New Jersey. He wanted to shake kids up by sharing the grim realities from emergency rooms and urging them to take a moment to think before they act violently. He thought of this outreach program and gave me a call. How could I refuse? I jumped at the chance and have been a speaker for the Violence Prevention Institute for several years. I deliver the majority of my lectures with my friend Hashim Garrett, a victim of gun violence. At fifteen, he was paralyzed after being gunned down by boys he thought were his friends. We believe in preventing violence before it happens. One good reason is that it saves money; it can cost $34,000 to incarcerate someone for a year, and as much as $322,000 for a hospital to treat a gunshot wound to the torso. Although many students have told me at the end of my presentation that they will never get involved in gun violence, our in-school prevention program still battles for funding every day.

I have only two sessions to get my point across to each group of young people. So I go for the full shock treatment, bringing along a bag of surgical and emergency equipment. While we're talking about the nineteen-year-old with the bullet in his chest, I show the kids the scalpel I would use to make an incision between his ribs, and then the intimidatingly huge rib spreader that lets me gain access to the heart and major blood vessels.

"You can hear the ribs as they dislocate. It sounds like Rice Krispies—snap, crackle, pop," I tell them. Some kids act disgusted. Good, that lets me know they're listening.

I tell them that the first organ a doctor would see is the patient's lung. By quickly moving it aside, I can see the heart. My job is to find the hole in the heart, or in the vessels coming off the heart, and determine whether it can be repaired. Although this technique worked on the patient in the slide show, too much time had elapsed since the gunshot blast occurred. By the time we restored his heartbeat in the ER, he was brain-dead due to lack of oxygen. My final slide shows the husband in a hospital bed on life support. This is the picture I use to drive home my point that, ultimately, his relatives were faced with the hardest decision a family can make. They chose to pull the plug and end his life.

"It was all the result of domestic violence. All because he and his wife were not able to resolve their differences." Now with them fully drawn in, I drive home the facts: Two lives are lost in the United States every hour because of gun violence. By the time I finish my presentation, two people will have been murdered. Most of the gun and knife injuries are split-second decisions stemming from anger, hatred, and an inability to resolve disagreements. I deliver the next point with a stern face: "Do you think this young father would have chosen death?" I've yet to see the toughest, biggest, strongest patient look me in the eye and say, "Doc, let me die! I've done wrong in life and deserve to die." Instead, the patients of violence cry out in pain, despair, and fear.

My patients' cries, along with my own life's journey, have inspired me to travel from one school to the next with a simple goal: to reach young people before they reach me.

Another one of my slides is of a teenager who took part in a fight that resulted in gunfire. I don't show his face. Instead, I show the eighteen inches of intestines and the kidney he lost when he got shot by a bullet.

"This is the stuff they don't tell you when you join a gang," I tell the class. "They don't throw their arms around you and say, 'Listen, dawg, this could be you. You could be wearing a colostomy bag and not be able to go to the bathroom anymore.' "

By now, I've got everybody's attention, even the squirmy ones. "You want to be a gangster? This is it," I say, holding a catheter high and explaining that it goes into your private parts while you're in the hospital recovering from gang-related gunshot wounds. "This is true G right here."

When I am done with the theatrics, I bring the message home. "The key thing I want you to remember is this: Just like your mouth can get you shot, your mouth can save your life. Be mature enough to say, 'I don't want the problems. You go your way, I'll go mine. It's all just a big misunderstanding.' "

This is the stuff that fathers need to be saying to their children.

That's what I think to myself as I pack up my laptop and equipment and head to my next school. These kids need to hear these messages—over and over until they truly sink in.

Fathers used to be expected to share the load of child-rearing. But no more. Now the idea that a dad should be accountable to his children seems as optional as having a burger without cheese. When I listen to the radio on Father's Day, I hear countless people call in to shout out their mothers: "My mom had to be my father, too, because my daddy wasn't there to raise me" is the story told by caller after caller.

The three of us see evidence of the absentee dad trend everywhere—on the job and in our work with the Three Doctors Foundation. For me, it's so rare to see a child show up in the emergency room accompanied by both parents that I'm tempted to snap a picture whenever it does happen.

When he speaks to students, Rameck often mentions the comic books he used to read in which superheroes lived in the Hall of Justice and the supervillains had an alternate universe. In their underworld, bad behavior was rewarded and good works were despised. Rameck sees a real parallel with poor urban neighborhoods, where smart students can be criticized for "acting white" and ex-felons get honored with a welcome-home party when they get out of prison. "Why do we celebrate the bad in our community?" Rameck asks his audiences.

He might as well add "nuclear families" to his list of things that we've rejected. Parenting has gone through its own mutation, and we've arrived at a point where it's normal for a mother and father to view themselves as adversaries rather than members of a unified team.

I remember taking part in this mistaken way of thinking when I was a boy. After Pop left, when I was in middle school, I remember that my friends and I sometimes ganged up on a kid who stood out simply because he had two parents at home. We would ridicule him and call him a "daddy's boy." He had what we didn't have—a father. And for some reason, we felt the need to tease him about it. It was our way of dealing with our discomfort from coming from single-parent households.

As we got older, we became even more vicious. "You think you better than us?" we'd taunt him. It's the way we coped, to soften the blow of fatherlessness. Eventually, we convinced ourselves that there were advantages to living with just a mom. If our mothers worked outside the home, it gave us freedom to run the streets. Having a dad at home would be a drag, curtailing our ability to hang out at will.

Imitating my friends, I became full of bravado, standing on the corner acting like a gangster because it was expected of me. But that supertough exterior, I've learned, is a defense that ends up stripping young men of their ability to feel emotion. I've come to believe it's just another factor that keeps us from creating close relationships, with women and even with our own children.

Rameck, too, grew up with what he now realizes was a warped view of fatherhood. Taking care of children was women's work, he believed, and fathers didn't need to be involved on a daily basis. He rarely saw any exceptions to that rule. It shocked him when he heard, while we were in college, about a childhood friend who had taken his four children on a vacation to Florida. Somehow, Rameck just couldn't picture this friend, a tough guy with plenty of street cred, splashing in the pool and having a great time with his kids. "Wow, he's not as macho as I thought he was," Rameck remembers thinking.

But as time went on, more of Rameck's friends became dads. And he couldn't help but notice that not all of them chose to neglect their children. Several of his longtime friends, guys he truly respected, were changing diapers, making funny cooing noises to their son or daughter, and generally acting as if being a father was the greatest thing ever to happen to them. Seeing these friends transform themselves into doting dads jolted Rameck into realizing he'd been brainwashed from an early age.

Unless you have your eyes shut to reality, it's not hard to see why kids in poor communities are programmed from birth to accept the single-mom phenomenon. It's no wonder so many of us grow up with no idea of how to collaborate with a partner to raise a child.

I have a friend who managed to unlearn a lot of that kind of thinking. Let's call him Tyrone. Like a lot of my friends who grew up in Newark, he let the streets select his values instead of choosing them for himself. He sold drugs, got arrested, survived being shot, and became an unwed father, all at an early age. He broke up with his longtime girlfriend when their daughter, Angel, was just three.

Yet it was easy to see that underneath Tyrone's street swagger and thug exterior was an affectionate father who absolutely doted on Angel. At first, the stories he shared with me reflected how hard it was for him to be apart from her. During one of their visits when she was very little, she stunned him by clearly pronouncing the word "refrigerator." He had never heard her say a word that big before. Tyrone got so excited, he carried her through the house pointing at things to see what other words had been added to her vocabulary. I could tell that it devastated my friend to miss out on his daughter's everyday discoveries and growth.

But later, as she entered her "tween" years, Tyrone started complaining about his daughter's behavior. One day, when she was eleven, he got a call at work saying she had run away. He gathered a posse of family and friends to search the neighborhood. Police found her in a park eighteen hours later, still angry after a disagreement with her mother.

Tyrone blamed Angel's problems on her mother, who had moved them two hours away from Newark, to Pennsylvania. They had an old familiar routine of baiting each other constantly when they spoke on the phone. "Bring Angel down here so I can see her," he would demand. "I can't," she would respond, without explanation. "You're just stupid," he'd yell. Sometimes the two argued so violently that he would slam down the phone and not call back or see his daughter for weeks.

But then Tyrone woke up. Part of Angel's behavior problems, he realized, stemmed from the fact that her mother was so drained by the responsibility of serving as Angel's sole caretaker that she was acting more like her daughter's friend than a disciplinarian. Although he believed his ex-girlfriend was making a big mistake by not setting firm rules for Angel, he sympathized with how easy it was for an exhausted single parent to fall into that trap. When Angel was seven, he spent a year as her custodial parent, and he'll never forget how hard it was to manage everything from her hair to her meals to her homework.

It's time to make some changes, he told himself. It's time to step up and become a bigger presence in Angel's life. Her mother, he could see, needed some backup. "As a father, I think there are things you can do to make the mother's life a lot easier—even if you don't live together," he told me. "You don't know what she's going through on a daily basis."

He also knew that he needed to convince Angel that he would listen to her problems and help her solve them. Hitting the roof about her running away wouldn't help, he realized, biting back the urge to be angry in those first moments after the police reunited them. "I needed to make her understand that she doesn't have to spaz out and run off," he told me.

Tyrone vowed to end the bickering with his ex-girlfriend. No more personal attacks, no more monthlong beefs, no more slammed-down phones. "Now I make my decisions based on logic, not emotions," he told me. "I don't want my kid to think that being volatile and crazy is the way to solve problems. I want her to learn good habits from me. Everything you do affects the child. It took a long time for me to figure that out."

It's inspiring to see my friend today. Tyrone is spending more time with Angel and has become much more patient with her. Not only has he become a better father, he is sharing with friends his awakening to the importance of committed fathering. At this point, that's what it's going to take to fix this problem because it's become so ingrained. Just glance at the cultural images our kids worship. Soft-porn videos and pimp glorification are big reasons we see reckless sexual behavior among young people without concern for the child they may be creating. If we face facts, we need to realize that it's asking a lot of urban fathers to stand up and resist an avalanche of negative influences, from the brainwashing encoded in their popular music to a family heritage that more than likely reflects generations of absentee fathers.

In his chapters, George discusses the many drawbacks of growing up fatherless. As for me, I'm fascinated by the effects of what's been termed "fatherfullness" by psychologists. Although today's fathers have allowed themselves to think that they're not important in a child's life, studies show that dads do matter:

- Father-child interaction has been shown to promote a child's well-being and ability to relate to others.

- Fathers who spend time alone with their kids performing routine child care raise children who become more compassionate adults.

- Children who live with both parents are more likely to finish high school, be economically self-sufficient, and have healthier lifestyles.

- Children whose fathers are involved in their education are more likely to get A's, enjoy school, and participate in extracurricular activities.

What these studies illustrate is that fathers aren't the dispensable beings we've been conditioned to believe. Their presence can open up opportunities that kids are starving for. Children in poor urban communities need as many champions as they can get in their lives. Interacting with the boisterous middle schoolers I meet during the Cops & Docs program, it's easy to see they're eager for attention and starving for healthy role models. Their talents are being overlooked and their enthusiasm for learning is slowly being extinguished. A chance meeting with me doesn't have a fraction of the influence that a father can have.

I'm particularly intrigued by the finding that an involved father improves the likelihood that a child will participate in extracurricular activities. Whether children grow up on a country road, a suburban cul-de-sac, or a crowded city block, getting to develop their talents, abilities, and desires has a tremendous impact on their lives. These opportunities give children a platform, a stage on which to express themselves and build their confidence. Yet urban kids don't get shuttled to soccer practice, piano lessons, and drama classes the way suburban children do, because these enrichment opportunities are hard to find in poor communities and many parents lack the money for them. And there's often no history of low-income parents getting lessons or trips when they were young, so they aren't aware of the value.

To me, it's just another opportunity in which missing fathers could help provide for their children. What if, instead of seeking their gratification elsewhere, fathers poured their time and energy into exposing their children to something beyond the limited thinking of our urban neighborhoods? Think of the revolution it would spark.

It stunts children's development when they aren't exposed to the world around them. I never understood that more than when I got to Seton Hall and found that pre-med majors had to take a class in the arts in order to graduate. In my junior year, I grudgingly signed up for "Art of the Western World," moaning about how boring it was going to be. As a kid from the inner city, I dreaded the thought of staring at paintings for a whole semester.

But the teacher, Professor Cate, grabbed my attention from the first day and never let go. She loved European art so much that it became infectious. Her cool, breezy delivery captured me. One memorable day, she sipped from a wineglass as we reviewed slides of paintings from France's fourteenth-century masters. It wasn't wine, of course, but I like to think that it was. In her own unique way, she toasted the spirit of the French painters.

She made art come alive to me. I signed up for the second semester of the class because it was so cool.

Professor Cate shared memories of dashing into museums in London and Paris. Although she must have been in her sixties, she didn't act like anybody's granny. Always stylishly dressed, she dared to live life in a way I had never seen before. Once she showed us pictures of herself and her husband riding their Harley-Davidsons cross-country. She had a sense of freedom, a personal philosophy that just stunned me.

What kind of environment had she sprung from? I wondered. My upbringing, I reflected, had produced just the opposite kind of person. I had never felt free to pursue anything that wasn't sanctioned in the 'hood. I had no cultural training at all. I hated history. I hated the arts. Or maybe I just thought I was supposed to hate them.

In my house, music was looked upon as a bad thing. It was my dad's way of escaping, and my mom knew that. "Stop making all that noise in the house," she'd say if I attempted a few notes on his guitar. And I don't remember my father ever offering me a music lesson.

I was reared in a world where a father could take pride in doing the minimum because it was a lot more than some other men were doing. All my life, my dad received kudos just for providing the basics of life—food and shelter—for his children. But I wanted so much more.

Today, it strikes a chord when I hear single mothers say how they sometimes feel taken for granted when their child's father stops by after years of being absent and makes his child deliriously happy by taking him out for ice cream. The mothers are astonished at how a simple ice cream cone is burned into a child's memory bank forever. This is called the "ice cream theory," and it reminds me of when I used to light up with joy whenever my Pop would stop by our house after the divorce. I had learned much earlier that my father was a man of few words, and I gave up on ever hearing him say "I love you." But just to have him walk through the door periodically served as the highlight of my day. I used to fantasize that my father and I would one day develop that special bond I saw between Tiger Woods and his father. It would never be.

There are two obvious ways to react if you grow up with your father missing. The first is to fall victim to the influence of your father and the negative images in the communities and become an absentee dad yourself.

The other is to resolve not to pass on those mistakes to another generation. That's the path that George, Rameck, and I have chosen. We're not fathers yet, by choice. As we carried out our pact, concentrating first on school and then on our demanding careers and the Three Doctors Foundation, we knew there was no way we were ready for children. We don't want to become dads until we're able to give our kids certain advantages: a mother and father who are committed to them, a stable home, and our attention.

We learned through researching this book that a menacing intergenerational legacy of fatherlessness seemed to wrap itself around our fathers, snuffing out their ability to be devoted dads. Just as our fathers weren't in our lives, their fathers weren't in their lives, either. Like so many other men without a role model to show them how to be a strong co-parent, our fathers weren't able to figure the puzzle out on their own.

This would be a gloomy forecast for the future, save for the fact that today we've had the good fortune to meet plenty of good brothers with amazing fathering skills. They've fought off the negative images they were surrounded by during their childhood. They observed the womanizers, the alcohol and drug abusers, the absentee dads, and resolved not to be like them.

How did they do it? When we asked them, they all had the same answer: They refused to forget how much it hurt to be a boy wishing for a dad. So they vowed never to repeat the mistakes their fathers made. Every day, they use their own experience as motivation and inspiration to steer clear of their fathers' behavior. I admire them for allowing themselves to grow. These guys may have been consumed with fears about child-rearing, since they didn't have strong fathers in their own homes, but they didn't run away.

Instead, they faced up to the challenge, and now they're reaping the rewards. For my friend Darrell, a hospital vice president, nothing can equal the glow he gets when he checks his e-mail on his BlackBerry to find an "I love you, Daddy" text message from Gabrielle, his teenage daughter. "You miss out on that, you can't get it back" are the cautionary words he offers fathers who find time to run the streets, hang with their friends, or parent a new girlfriend's kids instead of taking care of their own children. To me, these absentee dads are lost. They're in search of healing or finding something they missed out on. Who knows, maybe the son or daughter they abandoned could be the solution to their inner battles. It's heartbreaking that they've never been exposed to the soul-stirring rewards of good fathering.

I think about all the years that Earl Woods spent nurturing his son into a golf whiz, back before Tiger Woods became a household name. This man absolutely loved sharing time with his son and teaching him the art of golf. They forged a relationship that's one of the healthiest father-son bonds I've witnessed. Earl Woods, a former Green Beret, taught his son to have mental toughness, even jingling change in his pockets while Tiger putted to help hone his focus. And just look at the fruit of the father's labor: his son is more than a dedicated athlete, he's a phenomenal person. Through his Tiger

Woods Foundation, he teaches young people to excel not only at golf but in life. From the time he turned pro, Tiger has carefully maintained his image, demonstrating a charisma and professionalism that I certainly didn't possess in my twenties. I've long felt that Tiger's extraordinary faith in himself stems from having his dad as his biggest cheerleader.

On Father's Day 2006, not long after Earl Woods's death, I was watching the U.S. Open when Nike aired a commercial in tribute to him. For the average viewer, it was easy to get caught up in the engaging video clips of Tiger as a little boy. The ad featured footage of him jumping around as a kid, leaping for joy after a successful putt. But I concentrated on the expression on Earl's face. I saw unmitigated joy there, too. Here was a father who had been unafraid to invest his time and love in his son. I saw the unselfish gaze of a father who drew his rewards from seeing his son's triumphs. Those few seconds captured it all.

Then the TV screen flashed the words "To Dad. And Fathers Everywhere."

Nike may never know how desperately fatherhood needed that commercial plug. Truly, a repackaging of fatherhood needs to happen in our communities to reverse the slide of the responsible father figure. As we look into today's society, more parents than ever are unmarried. It's going to take more than fathers privately resolving to do right by their children to change the trend. It's going to take an each-one-teach-one movement.

I have a friend, Sabu, who has started a small-scale movement, although he probably doesn't realize it. He's honored me by inviting me to be part of a circle of mentors he's constructed for his seven-year-old son, Mekhi.

Sabu and Mekhi's mother never married, but the way that Sabu conducts his life as a single parent has taught me much. There have been times I've called Sabu to see if he wants to go with me to an event, and he's been quick to decline because he's taking care of Mekhi that night. I'm in awe of the way he treats his son. "I'm his dad. I want to be the first person you call if you need a babysitter," he has told Mekhi's mother. His son comes first—always.

I'm part of a cluster of men Mekhi has been taught to refer to as his uncles. We've been in his life since his baby shower. As a result, he's so comfortable with me that he can't wait to let me know when he hits the game-winning run for his baseball team. We're his support team. As Mekhi gets older, he knows that if he's interested in a medical career, he can talk to me. If he's interested in banking or money management, he can go to work with another one of Sabu's friends, Uncle Hassan.

Sabu has done this deliberately. It reflects the way he was raised. Born in South Africa, Sabu grew up in a communal environment where his uncles and other relatives spent time with him and shared in the responsibility of rearing him. "They could discipline me, advise me, tell me what to do, no questions asked," he explains.

Sabu's parents divorced when he was young. He migrated to the United States with his mother and siblings when he was eleven, leaving his father behind. But when he was twenty-one, Sabu went back to South Africa, at his father's insistence, to take part in the rite of passage that is traditional for men in his Xhosa tribe. For a month, he exchanged his sensibilities as a kid who came of age amid Newark's hip-hop culture for a rigorous ancestral experience created by the men of his family and his tribe.

Dressed in only a blanket and carrying a walking stick, Sabu was led into the mountains by a male guide. For the next four weeks, he slept in a tiny shelter and was given little food. His sustenance was spiritual. Men from his tribe, of all ages and walks of life, came to share wisdom with him. Throughout those conversations, which could take hours, important lessons were imparted. The men told Sabu how important it is to be a hard worker and a good father. "You must always keep your word, be a man of honor, and represent your community with dignity," he was told. "You must always conduct yourself as a leader, so that those coming after you will have a model to follow." Another piece of wisdom he'll always remember is "You have a responsibility to improve the world. You must leave your mark on this earth."

The men made sure he learned the history of the Xhosa tribe and shared stories about his family. In fact, Sabu found himself a bit of a celebrity during the rite of passage because the tribe was proud that a son had traveled all the way from the United States to take part in his tribal ritual.

There were nights when, as Sabu slept, the men would come to talk to him, approaching by calling out a phrase. If Sabu failed to wake up, he'd be punished. "I called you," his visitor would say, disappointed. "What are you going to do if somebody's approaching your home? If anyone's coming to your house, you should be aware, so you can protect your family." Sabu became a light sleeper after that. To this day, he sleeps with an awareness of his surroundings.

Sabu never knew when the final day of the ceremony would come. But he knew what to watch out for. If he ever saw a crowd of younger boys strolling by, that would be a sure sign. The day it happened, he was ready. He saw a bunch of young males slowly moving in his direction. Suddenly the boys started chasing him. But Sabu outran them, speeding as fast as he could in the direction of a nearby river, as he had been instructed.

There, Sabu stripped off his blanket and jumped in the water, symbolically washing away his immaturity and boyish tendencies. The children turned and walked away. They had played their part, helping Sabu to prove that he had left his boyhood far in the dust.

When he finished purifying himself in the river and stepped out on the other side, his father, his oldest male relative, and his guide were waiting proudly. He walked to them, and they covered his nakedness with a new ceremonial blanket. "My son, I embrace you as a man," his father told him. Together, they escorted him back to his father's community, where relatives waited to welcome Sabu. He felt like a changed man when he returned to the States.

Sabu believes his rite of passage shaped him into the attentive father he would soon become. It's what propelled him to create a kind of "council of elders" for his son—not just to provide Mekhi with role models but to help him grow up with a sense of accountability to a larger community. It resonates so much more with a child when he has to take responsibility for his actions. "When Mekhi does something good, he gets accolades from his uncles. And when he gets in trouble, it forces him to think, 'What will my father and my uncles think of me?' "

The circle that Sabu has woven around his son has also educated the men taking part in it.

When I see Mekhi copying his father's stride or asking his dad to help him master a video game, I think to myself, "I get it. I see how this is supposed to work." Clearly, this boy sees his father as his advisor and protector. It's been that way since he was a small boy. Years ago, when Mekhi would go with his mom to get his immunizations, he would cry and get very agitated in the doctor's office. So his parents decided to change their approach. Sabu took Mekhi to the doctor the next time, and it made all the difference in the world. Mekhi sat in his dad's lap contentedly and took the shot without a whimper. "If my dad's here, then it's all going to be okay," he seemed to say.

So much of what Sabu accomplished during his rites of passage inspires me because it sounds like the antidote for many of the problems plaguing single fathers here. I firmly believe you can't expect anyone to know instinctively how to be a good father, especially if he's lost in the turmoil of a bad relationship and hasn't had any healthy father figures in his own life. I've said it so many times it's impossible to count: *You can't aim for what you can't see.*

But bad images can be replaced with good ones. The positive influence that Sabu has exerted on the members of his son's "circle of men" is so electrifying that I wish it could be contagious. Who's to say that it can't be? In formal and informal ways, we need more examples of these kinds of circles, this kind of manhood training in our community. Just imagine what would happen if we started educating our fathers, instead of accepting the common excuses that we hear: "My baby's mother, she's crazy. I just can't get along with her." "I don't know how to be a dad. I didn't have one." "I'm in another relationship, I got my hands full with my other kids." What if we demanded more of today's fathers while at the same time understanding they don't all possess the tools to figure it out on their own? What if our communities could recognize that our young men need to be focused and trained in a healthy way, as Sabu's tribe did for him? Although it's common for men to gather to watch football games or to talk about women, we lack a healthy atmosphere where men can talk therapeutically about their experiences with fatherhood or the other things in life that really matter. Imagine an environment where men explain responsible sexual behavior to the next generation, letting them know it's not right to chase after an orgasm without being prepared to face up to the consequences of that orgasm. Wouldn't things improve?

It's sad but in our communities, it's not just children who need role models. Fathers do, too.

Chapter 4

SAMPSON

Learning to Be a Man

I F WE ARE TO BELIEVE society's stereotypes, it's highly uncommon to find a black man taking care of his children. It's as if such men are a rarity, an animal on the brink of extinction. "Oh my God!" we're trained to think when we happen upon a brother at the library with his kids or at the supermarket buying groceries with a baby in the cart. "There's that rare species, the black man taking care of his children!"

But George, Rameck, and I know many men who are loving, attentive fathers. Many of these men lacked a father's guidance in their own lives, but they're diving in and trying to figure out the puzzle for their own children. I respect them deeply for serving as role models to me, and for sharing here the joy and rewards they find in being there for their child.

REGGIE

Although I still look up to my mentor from the cemetery, Reggie Brown, I don't get to spend much time with him anymore. He no longer lives in New Jersey.

In 1988, Reggie had a tough situation on his plate. He and his wife appeared to be heading for divorce, and her employer wanted to relocate her to Pennsylvania.

As a father of two little girls, he weighed his options. He could stay in the Newark area with his lifelong friends and family. There, he had two security-guard jobs that paid decent wages, and he also ran a martial arts school in our Dayton Street neighborhood that he was devoted to keeping alive after Wu-Chi's death. Or he could move to Pennsylvania, where he knew no one and had no job prospects. He didn't think his troubled marriage would last much longer. Still, "I had two daughters and I couldn't leave them fatherless. That was out of the question," he said. "So I decided to drop everything and start over."

To Reggie, it seemed as if God rewarded him, helping him find a job the day after he arrived in Pennsylvania. Reggie got hired at the Montgomery County Correctional Facility in suburban Philadelphia, and since then he has moved up the ladder. "I kept getting blessed. I was an officer at the prison for only a little over a year when I got promoted to a corporal," he said. His martial arts training paid off. Reggie became a defensive tactics instructor and physical fitness coordinator for the prison system. Today he supervises the prison's canine unit, and the job has provided a level of financial stability that Reggie, who didn't go to college, never envisioned for himself in Newark.

He and his wife split up soon after the move. "Even today, it brings tears to my eyes to remember that day when I left. The look on my daughters' faces was like, 'We're not going to see you again?' I reassured them that wasn't going to happen. I was going to be there. I made that commitment," he said. "I didn't run from my responsibility. I paid child support. The girls spent summers with me, and every year I took them with me on vacation. Even today at every holiday family function, they're there."

His older daughter, Aliyya, now twenty-three, said her father's constant attention helped boost her self-esteem as a little girl, and strengthens her today as a single parent. She won't forget how Reggie used to move aside the living room table so he could teach his girls how to punch and kick in self-defense. "Most of my friends can't stand to be around their fathers. I've always known that my dad's kind of special. To this day, he still makes sure we have everything we need," she said.

To Aliyya, it's been a disappointment to grow up and find that all men aren't cut from the same cloth as her dad. Her two children don't see much of their father, who lives in another state. But Reggie keeps two car seats in his garage for outings with his grandkids and has stocked his house with toys and clothes for them. "My kids have fallen in love with their Pop-Pop. I knew they would," Aliyya said.

Reggie remarried and now has a preteen daughter. He's very popular at her school, not only because he regularly chaperones field trips but also because he brings the canine unit in on Career Day and lets the dogs entertain the kids. He believes firmly that "young people shouldn't just see Mom going on these school trips, or only moms volunteering. They need to see fathers in there, too."

Part of what gave Reggie a sense of how to perform as a parent is the great memories he has of time spent with his father when he was a boy. He remembers coming home from school to find notes from Dad, telling him and his brothers to meet him at nearby Weequahic Park. There, he'd happily lie on a blanket and do his homework, while Dad grilled hot dogs. Sometimes they'd spend long, quiet hours fishing at Asbury Park.

But his parents didn't get along, and they fought stormily whenever they drank. One day, completely out of the blue, his father walked out on his wife and seven children, and didn't come back. His mother stayed in bed and cried for four days straight without getting up. Reggie, whose family for years had squeezed into a three-bedroom apartment in the projects, remembers feeling hopeless. "We're never going to get out of this hellhole," he thought to himself. Reggie's dad paid child support and stayed in touch, but his day-to-day absence was hard on his kids.

The way Reggie's parents handled their conflict taught him that there had to be a better way. "I didn't want to be like that," he said. "The important thing is you can't put the kids in the middle. If you and your spouse are having problems, you still have that responsibility to stay in tune with your children because it's not their fault."

That's why Reggie has never lived farther than a half hour from his children, and why he makes it a priority to spend time with them and to be openly affectionate. "I'm in a business where anything can happen. In prison, people get killed for no reason at all," Reggie explained. "I never leave my family without kissing them and saying 'I love you.' "

MAURICE

With sex being one of the main things we were taught to pursue as teens, it's not surprising that many of our childhood friends became fathers. Some are responsible dads, some are not. One of Rameck's longtime friends is a guy we'll call Maurice, who has a dedication to fatherhood we all admire.

Rameck remembers envying Maurice when they were kids because he had an intact family: three brothers, a mom, and a father who came home after work every night. But Maurice insists that the grass wasn't any greener over at his house.

Maurice's father was one of those distant dads who didn't interact with his kids when he got home. He drank heavily, smoked cigarettes, and cursed in front of his sons. And he had a short fuse, as evidenced by the day Maurice got in trouble in kindergarten for saying a curse word. When his father found out, he backhanded his son so hard that Maurice fell backward off the bed, rolled across the floor, and hit his head hard against the closet door.

"You shouldn't be hitting me for what you're teaching me," Maurice thought to himself. Although it's a boy's first instinct to imitate his dad, Maurice realized at an early age that in more ways than one, he wouldn't be copying his dad's behavior anymore.

Maurice's parents separated when he was a teenager, and his mother took his father to court for child support. His dad had always been very critical of his boys and quick to tell them when they weren't acting manly enough. So it came as a big surprise to Maurice when his father quit his job to avoid paying child support, and moved from New Jersey down south. Maurice couldn't believe his father's behavior. "For all those years he was so hard on us, at the end of the day, he was a coward," he said incredulously. The two haven't spoken in more than six years.

Maurice was a bright kid. He excelled in math and wanted to go to college, but he couldn't solve the puzzle of how to pay for it. Dejected, he resorted to joining the largest industry recruiting black youths in our neighborhood at the time. "When I didn't go straight to college at age eighteen, I started selling drugs instead. I always carried a gun. What are you gonna do? It's a cycle," Maurice said. He got in a shoot-out over a drug deal and got arrested for shooting a guy in the foot.

Today, Maurice views the year he spent in jail as a blessing. "I believe in God and where he leads me is where I'm supposed to go," he said. "Most people think jail is a negative thing, but I was very reckless when I was younger. Thank God I only shot the guy in the foot. I didn't kill him. God gave me a slap on the hand and said change your ways, and that's what I did."

When he got out, he got a student loan and went to a technical school. From there, recruiters helped him find a job that paid for his associate's degree in computer science.

He landed a good job and things were going smoother than he ever believed they could when he unexpectedly became a daddy at age twenty-seven. It was a pure case of two people being irresponsible. The baby's mother meant nothing to him; she was just a girl he had met when he drove up next to her at a red light and asked for her number. They dated occasionally for about eight months. "It was basically a sexual relationship, no real commitment."

Knowing he didn't have real feelings for the mother, Maurice asked her to get an abortion. She refused and clearly resented him for even suggesting it. That moment sealed their fate. From that point, they would always be adversaries in the raising of their child.

Maurice knew that if the baby was going to be born, he wanted to be a good father. Since the baby's mother didn't have much money, he bought two of everything—cribs, car seats, a wardrobe—and took a set to the mother's house. It was there that he found out she had married another man two weeks before the baby was due, and she planned to put the new husband down on the birth certificate as the baby's father.

When the new husband walked in, angry words were exchanged. "I said some things I shouldn't have said to try to hurt her in the way that I was hurt," Maurice said. "She called the police. They arrested me that night and put a restraining order on me. I was not allowed to be at the hospital when my daughter was born."

Maurice immediately went to court to seek custody. A paternity test proved that he was the baby's father, which overruled the mother's insistence that Maurice wasn't the father because he hadn't signed the birth certificate. To Maurice, it seemed his ex-girlfriend's point in marrying the other man was to assert that Maurice didn't have any claim to the child. The baby's mom and her new husband divorced shortly after the baby was born.

Eventually the court awarded Maurice joint custody, with visits every other weekend and on Wednesdays. "I wanted more time than that but her mother wouldn't give it to me," he said. "Basically, everything I've had with my daughter, I've had to get a lawyer and go to court for it."

The situation with the baby's mother grew so aggravating that many times Maurice wondered why he put up with it. He'd seen other men walk away from their children when things didn't work out with the mother. But somehow, he just couldn't see himself causing a child the pain of growing up without a father. His daughter needed him, he was convinced. When she was two, it alarmed him to see welts on her naked bottom. "There's nothing a two-year-old can do to deserve to be beaten like that," he knew. As his little girl got older, teachers sent home reports that she hit and fought other kids at school. He knew there was a connection, and wanted nothing more than to bring the little girl into a home that was loving and violence-free.

But he and the girl's mother continued to battle. He kept trying, unsuccessfully, to draw the judge's attention to the mother's instability. She was evicted three times from apartments in the first years of his daughter's life. Eventually she moved into a women's shelter, which pushed Maurice over the edge. He fumed to Rameck: "I own my own house, my daughter has her own room here. There's no reason my child should be in a shelter."

Finally, the parents agreed informally that Maurice would keep their daughter while the mother got her life together. Maurice now had control of their daughter's life, and was shouldering the full cost of rearing her. But the arrangement had one flaw—his daughter's mother had no intention of returning the $600 a month that the child support enforcement agency was still taking out of his check.

"Take me to court—I'm not giving you anything," she taunted him. Maurice felt helpless. "This went on for months. I didn't want to go back to court. I had been eight or nine times previously. Each time I had to pay a lawyer thousands of dollars and I only got a little piece of what I wanted."

After nine months in the shelter, the girl's mother managed to rent an apartment and got back on her feet, so the parents began sharing custody. Once again, Maurice noticed the ill effects of the mother's influence on their daughter. The girl, now four, again seemed more violent. It also appeared that while visiting her mom, she regularly spent the night with some kids who touched her inappropriately.

Maurice had little faith in the court system, but after two months of praying and fasting, he gave the courts one more try. This time, the judge listened to his recitation of the problems and awarded him residential custody. The judge also told his daughter's mother to take parenting classes.

Maurice estimates that over the years he spent at least $15,000 trying to get full custody of his daughter—and he's definitely not wealthy. "Just imagine if I had been able to put that money in her college plan," he said.

His daughter still has angry outbursts, and he's learned it's a slow process to change a child's habits. If she doesn't get her way, she'll push, shove, and hit. Maurice, who remembers getting beaten as a child just for having the wrong facial expression, believes there are better ways to discipline a child than spanking. He's come up with softer ways to get his point across, such as giving her a time-out, warning her she won't get dessert, or telling her she has to go to bed early without a bedtime story. Because his daughter is very independent, even threatening that "you won't get to wash your own face today" is a good way to persuade her to change her behavior.

"I can't stop the influences she gets from the other side of her family," he said. But over time, he can see the results of giving his daughter a healthy routine, with lots of attention, exercise, and a regular bedtime. During summers and on weekends, they go on adventures to the zoo, parks, the beach, and live shows. Maurice takes pride in giving her experiences that he hopes will bloom into happy memories when his daughter grows up. "When we were children, we probably did that kind of stuff three or four times in our entire lives," he said. "As she grows up, she'll have a better appreciation for things."

AL-TEREEK

One of my first friends to get married was Al-tereek Battle, who wed his college sweetheart not long after he graduated from Rutgers. As I watched Al-tereek exude happiness in being a husband and a dad, I couldn't help but think it was a pretty impressive feat for a guy who didn't even meet his biological father until he was eight.

If you ask Al-tereek, now thirty-two, how he prepared himself to be a father since he didn't have one in the home, he'll answer that he had to teach himself. He observed and followed the lead of the strong men in his life: his older brothers, his coaches, the staff of the local boys' club in his hometown of Passaic, New Jersey.

And what was his best source of inspiration? You won't believe his answer: television.

The TV was the center of the household during Al-tereek's childhood. It was a huge color television that dominated the living room, "the big floor-model joint with the knob that you pull out," he remembers with a laugh. He sat in front of it religiously to watch all the family-oriented shows of the 1970s and 1980s, like *Family Ties, Good Times, Little House on the Prairie,* and *Happy Days.*

His family didn't at all resemble the nuclear versions he saw on TV. For one thing, he was chilling with his mom's boyfriend while watching his favorite sitcoms. His father wasn't in his life at all. As a little boy, when Al-tereek finally got up the nerve to ask his mother why his older siblings didn't look like him, he learned that he had a different father. He went to North Carolina to meet his father a few years later with a child's heart full of hope that they could start a relationship. But nothing happened. To this day they've seen each other only a handful of times.

Al-tereek much preferred the fathers he saw on the screen, so he latched on to those images. "I pulled a lot of positivity from what I saw on TV," he said. "When I was growing up, all the TV shows used to deal with family. I was getting a peek into how life should be. I guess I merged those images into my life. I told my mom when I was little that I was going to get married at age twenty-five, have a son and then a daughter. I knew that was what I wanted."

Talk about the power of visualization. Sure enough, that's almost exactly how his life unfolded. At age twenty-six, he married Tynicka. Two years later, they had a son, Jai, and two years after that a daughter, Bobby Marie.

Al-tereek has shown me it's possible to work through all the baggage of childhood and have a successful marriage, but it's definitely *work*. Although Al-tereek's mom was his biggest inspiration, he also feels that being raised in the household of a strong single mom had its downside: he never learned to compromise. "My mom's rule was the law," he said. "When there's no father, there's no second opinion. So you end up thinking one-sided, and you go out in the world without a complete skill set."

His point is a powerful one, although I think it gets overlooked as the number of births to unmarried moms zooms upward in cities across the United States. As what once was taboo becomes commonplace, I think the trend is more than just a statement on men's unwillingness to be responsible dads. It also reflects that women are realizing that it can be easier to raise a child alone without having to deal with a man's input or influence. Al-tereek said his mom definitely fits into that category. "My mom, she didn't feel that she had to deal with any other person while she raised us. It wasn't necessary. She was able to create her life and have some success with all her children. This was her mission, and she accomplished it."

Single moms certainly deserve respect, but it's undeniable that their kids grow up like Al-tereek and like me, too, with no clue of how to dance the give-and-take of a committed relationship. For example, Al-tereek held firmly to his family's tried-and-true method of paying bills in person at the last minute, but finally he had to admit that Tynicka had a point when she suggested that mailing them in earlier would be easier and less stressful. "If you don't know how to give, how to stand down, how to allow another point of view, you cause a lot of conflict," he said. "I'm still teaching myself to let stuff go, that I don't have to win every time. When I behave like the whole world revolves around me, that's a by-product of having been raised with only one perspective."

To his credit, Al-tereek recognized he had some emotional work to do. Since marrying Tynicka, he not only admitted that her method of paying the bills was smarter, he realized he had to compromise in other areas, too.

Why Al-tereek's own father didn't crave to be with him during his crucial growing-up years, he'll never understand. But he and his dad are reaching out to each other now. Although letting go of wounded feelings is difficult, he doesn't want to deprive his children of a chance to know their grandfather. "The biggest part of being a great father," Al-tereek has concluded, "is being a great man."

Perhaps because of the pain of his childhood, Al-tereek now takes pleasure in creating a warm, safe world for his children. "Every time I come home from work, they make me feel like a king," he said. "As soon as I hit the door, they start screaming from upstairs. They go nuts, yelling 'Daddy, Daddy!' It's like I'm coming through the tunnel in a football game, like I'm the star quarterback. I get charged up just to come home."

"He totally relishes that he's got his own family with its own traditions," said his wife, Tynicka. "He's totally elated. I hear him bragging about it with his friends: 'Yeah, we just cooked up a big Christmas dinner over here.' He really appreciates those things."

Al-tereek has truly embraced the concept of family, and any observer can see that he has found peace and completeness with his marriage and children. It's funny how we all search for fulfillment during our lives, and often it's sitting directly in front of us. We have only to open our eyes.

DARRELL

What if my childhood dreams had come true? What if my dad had given me attention, encouraged me in sports, and been a source of advice and support? My guess is my life would look a lot like that of eighteen-year-old Darrell Terry, Jr.

It's almost uncanny the way his relationship with his father resembles my early fantasies.

His dad, forty-four-year-old Darrell Sr., has been my good friend since I met him in 2000. He is vice president of administration at Beth Israel Medical Center in Newark, where I did my medical residency. I was intrigued to learn then that he was a single man raising his son and daughter.

Darrell fathered the children in his twenties with his live-in girlfriend. The couple broke up in 1992, and the kids lived with their mother for the next few years. But his ex-girlfriend, who also had older children, struggled under the weight of being a single parent. One day she complained to Darrell about it.

"What if I give it a try?" suggested Darrell, then thirty-two. She agreed, and the children—Darrell Jr., then seven, and Gabrielle, six—moved into his apartment.

Darrell realized from the outset that he would need to scale back his bachelor lifestyle because his kids came first. "Socially, I had to slow down and make some sacrifices," he said. "I didn't want to bring different women around them, confusing them." He promised himself that he wouldn't bring any girlfriends around the kids unless the relationship was getting serious. His mom, who lived nearby, watched the kids whenever he had a date.

He poured his attention into his kids and it shows. Darrell Sr. had a weekly ritual of playing basketball with his brothers, so he started taking little Darrell along. As his son got older, Darrell Sr. began to teach him the game, and volunteered as a coach with his son's basketball team. As you would imagine, young Darrell's skills were quite polished by the time he became a teenager, and they eventually earned him the title of captain of South Orange High School's state-ranked basketball team. His father, a busy hospital administrator who often travels, missed only one game during Darrell Jr.'s entire high school career. Darrell Sr. delights in all his son's achievements, although he had a hard time accepting it last year when his little boy ended up outshooting him and blocking his jumpers during their backyard father-son tournaments. At age forty-four, my buddy realized his son had become a better player than he is. But that's how life's supposed to be.

Darrell Sr. is a natural leader with outstanding people skills. And I'm fascinated to see that the son has turned out to be a carbon copy of his father. Darrell Jr. was voted homecoming king in his senior year of high school, and he also volunteered at school as a peer mediator. "I feel I can talk to anybody. I always find the right words to say. I've never had a problem making friends," said young Darrell, who believes he got these traits from his father. "Everyone tells me I sound just like my father. I think I adopted his whole personality. The way he treats people, the way he talks. He treats people with respect."

There's no way that Darrell Jr., now at Penn State studying business management—"Trying to be like Daddy," as he himself puts it with a laugh—can appreciate his blessings the way that I can. This kid doesn't have to pretend that he knows what he's doing; his confidence glows unmistakably. And it's no mystery why he's like this. It's the subtle moments of everyday life with a father who was fully present emotionally that gave Darrell Jr. something to admire and emulate. Having a dad to follow helped Darrell Jr. take surer steps and gave him a sense of direction.

Darrell's daughter is also a high achiever. Gabrielle, who still has the "I miss you so much" letter her father wrote her when she went away to Girl Scout camp in fifth grade, is an A student and a community volunteer. She displays the remarkable confidence that a father's attention helps to sculpt.

In fact, things were going so well for the three of them that Darrell Sr. hesitated before disrupting their household with the news that he was considering marriage. Said Gabrielle, "Before he got married, he was like, 'How do you guys feel about it? It's you guys first.' He always made sure that we knew that. He tells us, 'When I wake up, you guys are the first thing I think about.' "

With his children's blessing, Darrell Sr. married Renee, and they now have a one-year-old, Jordan. Darrell Sr. appreciates that his teen children unselfishly approved the idea of a stepmother. "I really love the young adults they have become," he said. "They're kind, considerate, well mannered, a success in so many ways. They're well-rounded kids. They're good people."

Darrell Sr. once told me that he often feels awkward when people rush to pat him on the back after they hear that he raised his children as a single dad. Although it's meant as a compliment, he doesn't want the kudos. It makes it seem as though what he did was optional, and that attitude is harmful, he believes. "I'm doing exactly what I'm supposed to be doing," he says. "No more, no less."

After I thought about this, I had to agree. We've got to stop treating good fathers as if they should be congratulated or celebrated. Good fathering is something that ought to be expected; you're not supposed to get a bag of treats for doing it. Somehow, many absentee fathers have convinced themselves they're doing a good job just because they pay child support or come up with money when their kids ask for it. In turn, I've seen lots of kids and single moms willingly accept this, and act as if a cash injection is all the fathers are good for. Darrell's noticed the trend, too, and it burns him up.

"It's not just money. That's nothing," he says vehemently. "It amazes me that some fathers miss out on this experience. I can't even imagine what my life would be like had I missed out on all these years with the kids. I have a master's degree, I'm a vice president at a four-hundred-million-dollar hospital, and if you ask me what's the best thing going for me, it's my kids."

Chapter 5

SAMPSON

What I Know Best

IN POOR COMMUNITIES, it wouldn't hurt if we tossed out most of what we think we know about fathering and began again. I learned this lesson powerfully through the example provided by my friend Sabu and his son. I'm sad to admit it, but I'd never seen one of my peers approach the job of being a father quite so unselfishly until I watched Sabu in action as a dad, busting his butt to get to his son when Mekhi's sick, and turning down invitations to go party so they can spend quiet time together.

And now that I've observed him, I get it. Good parents never stop asking themselves the question "What's best for my child?" Or as another friend of mine said, "When I became a dad, I had to realize it's not about me anymore. My child has to come first."

As men, we never discuss our responsibilities as fathers. At the barbershop, we'll talk about everything from cars to videos, from sports to supermodels, but somehow the subject of fatherhood never comes up. That's crazy. Although almost everyone in the barbershop has kids, it's as if we find every other possible topic to talk about except that one.

We're forever judging one another by our cars, our careers, or our hustles. But we never make it a priority to talk about how our children are doing. We don't compare notes on our kids like many mothers do. In no way do we measure our success as men by our performance as dads.

It's not that men don't want to be better parents. But our beer-and-sports culture pushes men in the opposite direction, making us look weak or sissified when we strive to learn more about being a good dad. I'm sure my own father wanted to resolve things with me but he didn't know how. The hardest thing for a father to admit is that he needs help.

Then there's the fact that as a society, we've been conditioned to react immediately when someone criticizes the way we're raising our children. The fact is that so many fathers are explorers without a compass, trying to figure out how to do this job when we didn't have a dad in our own lives. If you have young children, take this quick quiz and see how in tune you are with them:

Do you know where they are at all times? Do you know their friends? Are you involved in your children's school activities? Have you made sure they participate in extracurricular programs? Have you established clear rules in your house? Do you know what kind of music your children are listening to? Do you know what kinds of sites they're accessing on the Internet? Do you know whether the TV shows they watch are age-appropriate?

Here are some suggestions, large and small, for improving fatherhood in our communities:

Model the behavior you want your child to copy. Avoid heated disagreements with your childen's mother. By talking out your differences, you teach your children the importance of compromise and conflict resolution.

Realize that fathering isn't just financial. Don't just spend money on your children, spend time with them. Why pay $60 for a video game when the same money can give your kids an experience they'll always remember? Take them to concerts, to explore careers they're interested in, to hear interesting speakers. Expose them to the world. You'll help instill a love of learning.

Discipline with love. All children need guidance and discipline, but not as a punishment, the National Fatherhood Initiative advises. Remind your children of the consequences of their actions, and provide rewards when they live up to your expectations.

Be readily available. Let your children know that you are there for them. It isn't enough to say it. You have to show it by being accountable. Show up and take interest in their activities. Encourage them to join after-school and extracurricular programs. These are extremely important to their development and success in life.

Create rituals with your child. Strengthen your bond by putting in place some regular activities. These can be large or small; no matter whether you spend Friday nights on the couch with your kids watching videos or once a year take them to the ballpark for the home opener, I can guarantee that they will look forward to these shared moments. Birthdays are especially important. It creates a lifelong memory for a child when Dad reliably takes the time to bring him an ice cream cake on his birthday, to give him a gift-wrapped book, or to take him to play laser tag every year. Rituals like these build trust, by making a child feel as if he's the center of Dad's universe.

Teach through example. Accept that it's *your* job, as a father, to caution your children against drugs and irresponsible sex. Don't leave this task to the streets. But instead of running down the ten rules never to break, use your own real-life examples to paint a picture for your children. You may not even realize it, but there are events in your daily travels that can help them learn important lessons. And if you haven't been a perfect citizen, then let them learn from your bad decisions. Advise your children that there are real-life consequences to selling drugs, from going to jail to being the victim of stick-ups and drive-by shootings.

Talk to your child. This one seems so simple, yet it can be the most difficult to master. Think of the times you've been sitting in the car, bus, or train with your child and there is complete silence. Open up and encourage conversation with your child, especially about the sticky subjects of sex, crime, and drugs. Today's children have been exposed to thousands of hours of violence thanks to television and video games. No wonder they are desensitized to the real-life violence in their neighborhoods. Take time to role-play with your children about how they should act when they face peer pressure to use alcohol or drugs or have sex. Many of our children buckle at this point because they just don't know the right words to say. Help fortify your child by teaching him ways to circumvent that negative energy while preserving his coolness.

Build your child's self-image. A lot of urban kids have never been taught the most basic social skills and they spend a lot of time (as I did) trying to copy other kids' behavior. Teach your child to hold his head up and look people in the eye when talking to them, to stand up for what he believes in, and to never let anyone's harmful words destroy his self-image.

Be your child's hero. Don't depend on actors, musicians, or sports figures to be the role model. At the end of the day, you're the one responsible for guiding your children through life. Teach them the difference between right and wrong. It's up to you.

Show affection. Don't be too macho to show that you care. All kids long for their dad to protect and love them.

Once you master all these skills, then help someone else. Reach out to someone who isn't being an attentive father and let him know that his children need him, and that they should come first. We heartily encourage you to do what we did, and sponsor a roundtable discussion where men can come together to share and discuss their challenges with their children. When we tried this, in October 2006, it was a moving experience for all eleven men in the room. We held the meeting in Sabu's living room. For two hours, we sat in a circle and discussed the things that really matter—the well-being of our children. It felt so therapeutic, it was almost like being in church. Sitting in a circle with men I respect, hearing them share stories of fatherhood, taught me so much about the joys and responsibilities of being a dad. These are honorable men who stayed in their children's lives, and each has become a better man for doing so. When I become a father, I know I'll draw on the insights they shared.

For suggestions on how to sponsor a roundtable discussion on fatherhood in your neighborhood, visit our website at www.threedoctors.com. It's our dream that this topic of discussion become part of men's everyday lives. If only we stopped to ask one another "How's your kid doing?" at the bus stop, the barbershop, the grocery store. Who knows how much we can shake things up just by starting the discussion? It would be wonderful to see fatherhood become part of our everyday conversations.

RAMECK

Chapter 1

RAMECK HUNT

The Beginning

M<small>Y FATHER WASN'T</small> the kind of guy you'd call a player. Bookish and shy, he kept a low profile at his Catholic high school in the early 1970s.

But when the Newark public school girls suddenly discovered him, they realized they had found a good thing. My dad was good-looking, with a sweet style of talking that made you think you were the center of the universe. By the time he left for college in Massachusetts, two cheerleaders from rival high schools were almost brawling for his attention.

Dad obviously had a hard time choosing a winner, since both were pretty. Arlene was sassy and brown-skinned, and had flirtatious dimples. Sharon was the classy caramel-colored one who had endeared herself to his family. They pursued him with a passion they should have been devoting to their schoolwork. Frankly, I think my low-key dad was no match for these two strong-willed, sharp-tongued beauties.

So he did the convenient thing. He lied to both, denying all the rumors and telling each girl she was the only one in his life. He ran a good game until the day he came home from college and bopped into his living room, where he found Arlene and Sharon sitting on the couch waiting for him. They weren't smiling.

They had a joint announcement to make. "We're both pregnant and you know you're the daddy. Now what you gonna do?"

My dad's face fell. Muttering something like "I can't handle this," he ran back outside. It was a fitting preview for how he would handle the duties of fatherhood.

This story of how Dad got ambushed by his two pregnant girlfriends in his own living room has been confirmed to me many times. It's like my own personal legend, proof that I arrived gift-wrapped in scandal.

I know that my mom, Arlene Hunt, had dreams of marrying my father when she was in high school. He was a college boy, and quite a catch. His name was Fred Jones, which he later changed to Alim Bilal after he joined the Nation of Islam. Neither of those names really mattered to his relatives, who have called him "Bobo" since he was a kid because he was bowlegged. My father aspired to be a chemist and won an academic scholarship to Assumption College. Determined to make sure his future would include her, Mom held on tightly to my dad, especially after she started catching glimpses of Sharon hanging out at his house with his mom and siblings.

My mom, who got pregnant at sixteen, insists that I was a planned child. According to her, she and my father tried for two months to conceive a baby as a way to get my mom out of a new high school that she hated. This was during Mom's junior year, at a time when her mother moved the family out of Newark to Plainfield, a working-class suburb that my grandmother had picked about half an hour away. Mom missed her old school, where she and her friends were popular for the parties they threw. To her mind, having a baby was a ticket out of dull Plainfield High. Although she still thought like a kid, Mom was impatient to act like a grown-up.

She continued to run into Sharon at her boyfriend's house, so she questioned my father about her. "I'm not serious about that girl," my dad always told her. But the rumors started to mount when the two girls started taking classes from three to six P.M. every day at Central High School, the area's after-school program for pregnant girls in the early 1970s. Mom heard the whispers: *Your boyfriend's messing around with that girl. She's having his baby, too.*

When confronted, my dad denied the rumor. So my mom, never shy, took it upon herself to call Sharon Jenkins and get some answers.

The truth broke Mom's heart: My dad had fathered Sharon's child as well. Mom's heart would get trampled again in coming months as my dad began a drug addiction that would cut short his college career and cripple him for decades. In time, she'd turn to drugs herself to cut the pain and disappointment she felt.

But for the moment, she was pregnant and coping. She initiated a strange but practical alliance with my dad's other girlfriend. "These babies are going to need to know they're brother and sister," she insisted to Sharon. "I don't want to look up twenty years from now and see them coming in the door saying they're in love with each other. We need to raise them like family."

Sharon agreed that they needed to stick together. And that's how it happened that my father found his two girlfriends lying in wait for him when he came home from college.

I was born on May 1, 1973, at Orange Memorial Hospital. My half sister Quamara arrived eighteen days later.

It ended up working to Sharon's advantage that she was so friendly with my dad's mother. As a result, baby Quamara was always welcomed at my dad's house, where she was lovingly fussed over.

Quamara also ended up getting to enjoy more of my father's attention than I did during our youngest years. After I was born, my dad seemed to declare Sharon the ultimate victor in the girlfriend wars, and the threesome moved into a studio apartment together. But Sharon remembers the arrangement didn't last more than four months. She'll never forget the day it ended, when my sister was about a year old. My father had closed himself off in the bathroom for an unusually long time. "All right, I'll be out," he shouted after she banged on the door.

Finally the door to their tiny box of a bathroom swung open and she could see him sitting on the toilet in an undershirt and boxers, eyes glassy, his face serene. He was slumped back with a hypodermic needle sticking out of his arm. She knew he dabbled in drugs, but she hadn't realized how bad it was until that day. Sharon screamed out of shock. My dad, she thought, had so much going for him. She never thought he'd be the type to throw his life away like that.

She cried. And then she threw him out.

Not long after that, Dad was arrested for armed robbery. He was in prison before my second birthday. He wasn't there when I took my first steps. He didn't hear my first words. My dad missed all those milestones because of his addiction.

Still, my mother regularly brought me to the prison to visit him when I was little. She seemed hell-bent that he fulfill his fatherly duties, although he couldn't do much more than hold me on his lap and talk to me during our short visits. Dad did several more prison stints after that, ranging from eighteen months to two years. I grew up thinking the prison was his home, that my dad lived in a faraway kind of dormitory.

When he wasn't locked up, he was prowling the streets of Newark, searching for a fix or a way to pay for one. Mom always knew how to track him down, and she would call him up with a taunting tone in her voice: "Come over here, let your son spend time with you. He needs to know who you are." During the times when he managed to hold a job, she went after him aggressively for child support. She never got much. It burned Mom up inside that Sharon never had to bother with court-mandated child support. Although Dad didn't support Quamara, either, my dad's mother doted on her, babysitting her frequently and buying her necessities and gifts. She even outfitted my sister's bedroom, buying her an elegant silver-and-white daybed and dresser.

My mom loudly complained to my father's mother about the blatant favoritism she was showing to Quamara, which did nothing to improve the situation. The keepsake baby photo of Quamara and me dressed in matching red velvet outfits and smiling doesn't give a hint of the full-scale feud my mom was engaged in.

I was too little to know all of this. My childhood memories are happy, even though my dad wasn't around.

I didn't question his absence. In my world, daddies were kind of an oddity anyway. It was the rare kid who had one in his life.

In fact, I didn't hunger for my father at all as a child. My mom did a great job of filling that void, so I never realized how important it was to have a father, or what I was missing out on. She kept me dressed nicely, and took me everywhere with her. In the pictures I see, I'm always wearing nice clothes and a bright smile.

My mom had two distinct personalities. She had a doggedly practical side that insisted on personal responsibility, causing her to loud-talk my father constantly about his shortcomings as a parent. This is the side of her that pushed on until she got her high school diploma in 1973 and landed a well-paying job at Bell Laboratories in New Jersey in 1976.

She won't forget the day a scientist there told her, after a conversation with me, that her preschool-age son was "going to be somebody someday." My mom believed the same thing, and she always let me know firmly that she expected the best from me. With her Bell Labs paycheck, we moved into an apartment that she decorated nicely. Even without the benefit of steady child support, Mom made sure I had the toys and clothes I needed. One memorable year, we went to Disney World, where she bought me one of my most prized possessions, a Mickey Mouse phone.

Mom knew how to handle her business, although she often had to cart me along while handling it. We spent a lot of time together, at the Laundromat, running errands and paying bills. Just like any good mom, she made sure I ate all my food. She put a home-cooked dinner on the table every night, and wouldn't let me get up from the table until I had cleaned my plate. Once, I remember, she cooked lima beans, which I despised, and she made me eat every last cold bean, which was pure torture. But that was the kind of household she ran, strict but loving.

Then there was the other side of her, the side that loved to party. She was a young woman, after all, and still looking good. Many nights, our apartment was crammed with people and full of good music. She trained me to go to bed promptly at nine. In the morning, I would wonder about those funny-looking cigarettes sitting in the ashtray wrapped in E-Z Wider paper. I later realized it was marijuana.

She loved to dress up and go out. Mom sometimes even partied with Sharon when they were both young mothers, leaving Quamara and me in the care of my mom's younger siblings while the two of them went out clubbing.

On weekends, when Mom needed a break, she never hesitated to drop me at her mother's house in Plainfield. When we get together as a family and reminisce, as we often do, we all laugh about it. I remember our routine so well. She'd drive up in front of my grandmother's house unannounced and motion for me to get out of the car and walk up the stairs to the front door.

"Ring the bell, baby!" she'd call out to me, her foot ready to hit the gas pedal.

And in a flash she'd drive away, the instant her mother or one of her brothers or sisters opened the door.

My relatives inevitably would groan that Arlene had pulled another fast one, but they never truly minded. I might be the most frequent uninvited guest their house had ever seen, but this was one place I was loved warmly. I never felt abandoned when she dropped me off there. After all, it had been the first house I had ever known.

My grandmother had seven children, and I called her "Ma" just like they did. Most of my relatives consider me her eighth child.

Ma knew I needed stability in my life, and she provided it. I remember a lot of laughter and good times while I was there. My uncles and aunts would pile into the house on weekends, to play card games like Tonk and Spades, and just to spend time together.

Ma ran a child-friendly house, where it was normal to sit in the living room playing family games until way into the night. Monopoly was our game of choice during my early years. We'd put on the top records of the 1970s, and my dance moves often served as the featured entertainment.

My grandmother, who worked the night shift at the post office, expected her kids to be hardworking and self-sufficient. All her children learned to cook, clean, and sew, even the boys.

She wasn't happy with my mother's occasional bouts of irresponsibility, and they often argued about it. My uncle Sheldon remembers one day when he watched from the house, openmouthed, as my mom sped up the snowy street with me in the car. She was driving so fast that the car spun out dangerously. Sheldon didn't want to rat on his sister, so he didn't mention to Ma about the unintentional doughnuts we were doing in the car. But, according to my uncle, I was so alarmed that I ran in the house and tried my best to file a report of the incident. I was just a toddler, so I spun myself around and around in a circle, saying "Mommy, Mommy," until my grandma got the picture.

This was the second most important place in my universe, and it was yet another place in my life where there was no husband in residence until Ma married a man we called Hook. He was a heavy drinker at times, but he was a nice guy and an extremely good cook. After he arrived at Ma's house, our evening meals got a lot more memorable. Unfortunately, a few years after Hook and Ma married, Hook was killed by a city bus one winter morning. I hurried home from school that day, getting off the bus at the same stop where police investigators had spread sand to clean up his blood. Hook's death was tragic. He had really shared the responsibility of running the household and he'd given Ma the companionship she deserved. His presence was a short-lived blessing in our lives.

Before she met Hook, Ma had married and divorced. But I didn't suffer for lack of a male authority figure when I was at her house. If I acted up, all Ma had to say was "Uncle Rasheed's gonna get you." I'd straighten up in a second.

My mom's brother Rasheed served not only as my disciplinarian, but also as one of my biggest childhood inspirations. Although my mother and two of her brothers converted to Islam when they were in high school, my uncle Rasheed took it the most seriously by far. He didn't smoke or drink, and he made a point of staying far away from drugs.

He felt the Muslim faith helped him focus his life, giving him some structure and a reason to resist the negative influence of the streets. He had a bootstraps work ethic that fascinated me. He seemed to know a little bit of everything, from car mechanics to carpentry to photography.

"Where there's no vision, the people perish," he used to say, and it was clear that Uncle Rasheed had a strong vision for his future. He did what others feared to do, launching several successful businesses in Newark and Plainfield without support from anyone. Just watching and listening to my uncle taught me that I could achieve any goal I wanted if I set my mind to it.

Uncle Rasheed's father—my grandfather—had been an alcoholic, and he and Ma divorced when their children were young. Uncle Rasheed understood a boy's need for a male mentor, perhaps because he didn't have one when he was a child. My uncle's strained relationship with his father, Raymond Hunt, had come to an abrupt end one day in an abandoned photo studio.

Rasheed was about nineteen at the time, when his father called him to let him know about a place with photo equipment that had gone out of business. Rasheed, who planned to launch a photography business, arranged to meet his father there. My uncle invited his girlfriend along to see the place and meet his father.

But as Rasheed walked through the seedy building, looking to see if there was anything worth salvaging, his father disappeared with Rasheed's girlfriend into a room and tried to touch her sexually. The alcohol had warped his judgment to the point where he saw his son's teenaged girlfriend as a possible conquest.

Once the girlfriend told my uncle how she'd had to break free from his father's advances, Rasheed shoved his father, ready to fight him. That moment severed any hope of a possible connection with his father.

As a boy, I had the distinct feeling that most fathers were free-floating men who weren't connected to anybody. They didn't have to shoulder responsibility; that was the mom's job. They didn't have to take their kids for haircuts, pick them up from school, or sign them up for sports. Dads lived in far-off places and maybe you might run into them occasionally. That was the scenario at my own house, and at Ma's house, too.

Ma had been quick to divorce Raymond Hunt, the father of her oldest four—Rahman, Rasheed, Venus, and my mom—after it became clear he was an alcoholic who couldn't hold a job. Actually, a lot of his problems were likely related to his mental illness, which he medicated with alcohol.

She then started a live-in relationship with Theodore Green, the father of her three youngest children, Vikki, Sheldon, and Nicole. He wasn't exactly an attentive dad, either. He, too, was an alcoholic, and his children remember times when their father came home so drunk that he knocked the front door off its hinges while fumbling his way inside. He was, as my uncle Sheldon puts it, the kind of father you strive *not* to be like. Although he battled with alcoholism, there were a lot of good things about him, and his children loved him.

To this day, my aunts and uncles tend to shrug off the fact that they grew up without stable fathers. Ma, the most sensible matriarch you could imagine, trained her children not to waste their time worrying about people you can't fix. The Hunt motto, instilled by Ma, is not to wallow in problems but to do something about them.

My aunts and uncles considered me lucky, even spoiled, because at least I occasionally got invited to my father's mom's house. That was way more of a fatherly connection than they had experienced.

My mother always sounded bitter when she talked about my father's family. "Your father's no good. And your grandmother doesn't love you," she would say. I didn't know what to think, but I had to admit some of the questions she flung at me touched on awfully sore spots. "Why don't they invite you to their Sunday dinners?" she'd ask me. "Why didn't they call you for Christmas?"

Just when Mom had me convinced that Dad's family didn't like me, they'd call and invite me over. I felt a confusing sense of dread whenever we were in the car heading to Dad's mother's house. It was something I couldn't explain. I wanted to visit them, despite Mom's complaints that "they don't treat you right over there." But I did feel that I had to be on my best behavior when I was their guest, although other kids on that side of the family were allowed to do whatever they wanted.

Whenever I spent time over there, I felt out of place. I didn't recognize many of the faces, although Quamara seemed to know everyone. Everybody seemed to belong except me. Just the act of inviting me seemed to be a big enough concession. They didn't work too hard to reach out and make me feel welcome once I got there.

I didn't know if I was entitled to feel this way, or if I was letting Mom's rants get to me. But my sister's mother, Sharon, assures me that she observed big differences in the way Quamara and I were treated when we were young.

Sharon remembers one day I was visiting, sitting well behaved on the couch, when Quamara told her grandmother, "I want some ice cream." Even though there wasn't any in the freezer, my father's mom scurried to the corner store to buy some for her precious grandbaby.

When she came back, my grandmother handed Quamara the promised ice cream, but she didn't offer me any. It wasn't surprising to Sharon, who had noticed the unequal treatment before. But this time, she decided she was going to take a stand.

Before Quamara took a bite, Sharon asked, "Does your brother have any ice cream?"

Quamara shook her head no.

"So what are you going to do about that?" Sharon quizzed her.

Quamara looked at the ice cream and slowly, dutifully, handed it to me.

"That's right," Sharon told her. "That's what I want you to do every time you're over here and you have something and he has nothing. That's your brother. You always have to share with him."

My father's sister, Lora, who was friends with my mom, says she also protested that it wasn't right that my grandmother seemed to have lingering questions of whether I truly belonged in the family.

Later, as the years rolled on and I became an adult, my father's mother and I became much closer. As I came to know her better, I respected how much she had sacrificed to provide education and advantages for her children. I recognize now that she must have had high hopes for Dad's future, and it had to have been a crushing disappointment when he fell so short of his goal. It wasn't in her plan to see her smart, talented son go to prison when he should have been in college. And she certainly hadn't envisioned him fathering two babies at the same time.

When Dad wasn't in prison, I usually visited him at his mother's house. This happened maybe a couple times a year, from the time I was a baby until I was a preteen.

My memories of this early period are fuzzy, probably because I saw so little of him. But I remember that I thought my father was the nicest man in the world. To me, he was a loving, mild-mannered man who was good-looking and muscular.

Every time I saw him, my heart would leap. Happily for me, my dad seemed as excited to see me as I was to see him.

I remember my father always being the life of the party. He acted like one of the kids and would play with us when the other adults were in another room, doing their own thing. The younger set loved playing music, and we could always talk my father into getting up and trying the latest dance moves. We'd howl with laughter as he tried to dance like us. He didn't care. He was just having fun and he enjoyed entertaining us.

I don't remember ever being the center of his attention. Anything we did, it was with a group. Still, I always felt happy and supremely satisfied just being around him. If Dad was in the house, I felt welcomed and warm.

My dad often surprised the kids in the house with gifts. I always appreciated anything he gave me, even if it was small. The present I remember best was a bright red electric keyboard that he gave me for Christmas when I was around age eight. It came with a strap so I could wear it like a guitar and really get down like Prince or some other superstar.

As a kid, I was always entertaining, and now I could strut around in front of my audience and perform a real concert with live music. It had a ready-made bass line, so all I had to do was add some key strokes to make a song that sounded halfway decent.

I practiced on my keyboard for hours, trying to get my act right. Such a wonderful musical instrument had to be really expensive, I remember thinking, which made me love my dad even more. I thought it was one of the best gifts I had ever received.

I never blamed Dad for not being a regular presence in my life. I figured if he couldn't visit, there was a good reason. I didn't spend any time wishing he could be with me. Back then, I was just a happy little kid who was delighted to bask in my dad's attention. The funny thing was, in another compartment of my life that I kept completely separate, I already was engaged in an active quest to teach myself to become a man.

In my single-mom-headed household, I could already tell there were things I needed to learn for myself. I knew boys behaved a certain way, with a certain roughness. I was always on the lookout, searching for clues about how to act. But I didn't connect the dots, back then, during the fleeting time I spent with my father. Maybe because I couldn't get any time alone with him, maybe because he wasn't around too much, I didn't rely on Dad to decipher the mysteries of becoming a man. Nor did he take those opportunities to offer his son any tips on becoming one.

Instead, as a boy, I tried to keep my antennae up at all times, to pick up on anything that might be appropriately manly. "Hey, that must be something we're supposed to do," I'd say to myself whenever something that seemed loaded with testosterone popped up on my radar screen. And that's what drew me, when I was about eight years old, to sign up for the Pop Warner youth football program in my Plainfield neighborhood.

I was no fan of football. I had tossed a ball around casually with my friends, and my mother adored the Dallas Cowboys, so I knew how to drop some names of football stars, but I didn't know any more than that. I didn't know the intricacies of the game, I couldn't tell a defensive end from a running back. But playing Pop Warner definitely seemed like the thing to do. In my neighborhood, all my friends couldn't wait for the season to start.

Inside my head, a loud debate was roaring.

It was one of many times that I acted in the role of my own father, since I didn't have one in the flesh to train me and cheer me on.

"Boy, you better go up there and sign up for Pop Warner," I told myself sternly and silently.

"I'm scared, I don't know how to play," my heart answered.

"Be a man, you've got to give it a shot," I told myself. "Now march your butt up there and sign up."

Answering dutifully to the fatherly voice I'd manufactured, I prepared to report to Cedarbrook Park that summer for the first football practice.

First I told Mom that I needed some equipment. She took me to the sporting goods store to pick it out. I didn't even know what I needed, so the clerk helped me select everything. I felt really excited when I walked out of the store with a bag full of shoulder pads, knee pads, cleats, helmet, and a uniform. It felt great, like a new adventure in my life.

I hurried home to try everything on. I was feeling like a real man then. I tried the pants first, fitting the knee pads into the sleeves in the pants. Then I put on the shirt and helmet. I snapped the chin strap and looked at myself in the mirror. Boy, I was ready to go. I was more enthusiastic to play than I ever thought I would be.

I took another look in the mirror and realized something looked funny. I had forgotten to put on the shoulder pads. Grabbing them, I was tempted to just hang them over my shoulder, but I hadn't ever seen anyone wearing them outside their uniform before. So I took off my jersey and put the shoulder pads over my head. I tightly tied the laces across my chest and adjusted the pads evenly. Then I tried to put the jersey on over the pads but it wouldn't fit. I couldn't ease it over the shoulder pads.

I tried again and again, but I just couldn't get it. I didn't know what to do. I got so frustrated that I took the jersey off and threw it in the corner. If there ever was a time I wished I had a dad or brother around, it was then. What was I going to do? The first practice was the next day, and I didn't even know how to suit up right.

The next day, I dreaded waking up. I was ready to quit before I even started. But my mother would have killed me if I didn't go to that first practice after she spent all that money on the uniform.

When I got to Cedarbrook Park, I saw a bunch of kids with their parents or older brothers standing around to cheer them on. I was there alone.

The coach came over to me, asked what my name was, and checked his list. He asked what position I wanted to play and I couldn't come up with an answer. After he realized I had no clue, he put "linebacker" next to my name.

That made me more uncomfortable because now I was about to start playing a position that I didn't even understand. Why couldn't he have put me down as a running back or quarterback? I knew what those guys did. I was upset at myself for not saying one of those two positions, but the truth was, I wasn't sure if I'd have been good at either one, and that's why I didn't say anything.

Then the moment of truth came. The coach yelled out, "Suit up!" While all the other kids got excited by what the coach said, and their parents and brothers smiled from the sidelines, my knees buckled. I had no idea what to do. I didn't know how to put my jersey on over my shoulder pads.

What to do? I was frantic. I feared that if I asked anyone for help, I'd be the laughingstock of Pop Warner football. Pulling the coach aside wasn't an option, I thought, because he'd realize in an instant that I didn't know jack about the game. Finally the scared little boy inside me won out. I gave up, gathered up my stuff, and turned around. Hoping nobody saw me leave, I headed home. I felt dejected.

I blamed myself.

I thought it was my fault that I couldn't put on the football pads. It didn't occur to me that I didn't have anybody in my life to teach me to do it.

It was my fault. I had to be inadequate.

I fell into a habit of thinking it was my own fault whenever I couldn't master something.

That's because I've always been pretty independent. My family still laughs at the memory of how I nonchalantly boarded a public bus as a five-year-old and rode to downtown Plainfield alone. When I finished checking out the sights, I found the right bus to take me home and climbed on board. I arrived home at Ma's safely, to the surprise of my panicked family.

As I got older, Mom and I moved around a lot, bouncing between Ma's house and various apartments that weren't in the best of neighborhoods. I was always walking into a new social setting, every year or so. One thing I learned quickly growing up in the 'hood is that you had to be tough.

Being a good student, I knew that I had a nerdy side. The older I got, the harder I worked to conceal it, in order to be perceived as tough. This became a tall order once I reached fifth grade and was selected for my school's Gifted & Talented program. Now I couldn't hide my good grades any longer. With the other gifted students, I had to publicly rise and leave at the end of third period to go to special classes. This made it all the more important for me to work hard at being considered cool.

Since turning to Dad for advice wasn't possible, I did what lots of my peers did. I turned to the streets. In my search to construct a manly personality for myself, the streets became my best classroom. I started imitating whoever it was in my neighborhood that seemed the biggest and baddest at the time.

First I settled on a guy I admired named Buddy, who was the best gymnast I'd ever seen. Of course, I'm talking about gymnastics ghetto-style, where you find some dirty old mattresses and teach yourself to flip on them. Buddy was so good, he could somersault and do back flips on any surface, whether grass or concrete. I thought Buddy was so amazing that he probably could qualify for the Olympics, although this being the 'hood, there was no way that would happen.

Because of his gymnastic ability and his good looks, Buddy pulled all the girls. But Buddy wasn't soft. He could fight, so nobody messed with him. So I convinced myself that I should act like Buddy.

But the problem was, I couldn't flip. I tried and failed miserably. Too embarrassed to ask him how to learn, I decided to switch and imitate his brother, Andre.

'Dre was a good athlete but the quiet type. He didn't start any trouble but he knew how to kick butt if somebody messed with him. Ladies liked him, I noticed, because he was mysterious.

So I devoted a few weeks to imitating him until I realized I just couldn't pull it off. I talked entirely too much to be the strong, silent type.

This went on and on. It was frustrating. I kept trying to find the right role model to copy, but none of them fit.

It certainly helped to have a father or older brothers, I noticed. My friend

Sean also was in the Gifted & Talented program, but he was no geek. I considered him the epitome of cool. But then again, he had the benefit of having older brothers who helped him polish his game.

Sean taught me a lot. You could say he was the kind of tutor who believed in "experiential" learning. He knew I hadn't had much experience with girls, so one day when we were preteens he volunteered to let me watch him in a sexual encounter with his girlfriend. When he invited me on the adventure, he had a "Pay attention, sonny boy" patronizing attitude, but it didn't matter to me. It sounds kind of weird but little kids are curious and will do almost anything to satisfy their curiosity. So I went with him to his girlfriend's house at a time when her parents weren't home. The "lesson" took place in the basement. Sean had a well-thought-out plan: If for some reason her parents came home unexpectedly, he and his girl would stop the "lesson" and act as if we were watching television or playing Ping-Pong.

But we weren't interrupted. From my front-row seat, I got my first peek at sexuality, a much-publicized and discussed phenomenon among my peers. I'd seen music videos with men and women acting suggestively but I hadn't ever seen sex in action. Now I had an idea what the fuss was all about.

Sometimes I let friends drag me into crazy and even dangerous things. Once when I was about sixteen, I was hanging with some older guys from Plainfield on the day before Thanksgiving. I wasn't a heavy drinker, but on this day I went in with them to buy some forty-ounces. Then we headed to our hangout spot, on the steps in back of a nearby school, where we passed the beers around and got a little tipsy.

There were about six of us laughing and talking when a crackhead from the neighborhood wandered up. "Can I cop a rock?" he asked, trying to see if any of us could sell him some crack. One of the guys I didn't know so well jumped up, ready to make a deal. The two of them walked away, made their transaction, and then the crackhead disappeared.

Minutes later, we looked across the schoolyard and saw flames rising from the man's crack pipe, which threw the guy who'd sold him the rock into an instant rage. "I told him not to smoke that up here near the school," he said. "I'm gonna go kick his ass." The rest of us prepared to rumble, too. I have to admit, our logic was a little hazy: although we thought crack smoking near the school was unacceptable, we didn't see anything wrong with drinking forty-ounces right next to it ourselves. But we thought we were tough, and we were used to protecting our turf. It was common for us to get in scuffles with rival crews. Beating up this sorry crack addict was going to be easy. So we all ran over to him.

"I'm sorry, I'm about to leave," he said hurriedly when we confronted him. But hungry for one last hit, he knelt down, flicked his lighter, and lit the crack one more time. For us, that was the last straw.

One of my friends punched him in the head. The pipe flew and broke into pieces, and the crackhead sagged to the ground. "Wow, you dropped him," we said admiringly.

Next, it seemed that everyone else wanted to get that same thrill of knocking him down like in a boxing match. For at least five minutes, we smacked him around until he fell to the ground, always lifting him up to take another blow. He looked like a human punching bag.

Then I remembered something. In my trench coat pocket was a knife I had just bought at my uncle Rasheed's shop. In an effort to impress my friends, I pulled it out. "Look what I got," I told my friends, and flicked the knife so that the switchblade popped out.

Suddenly all eyes were on me. And I found myself in a position I had no desire to be in. My mind raced. "What am I gonna do?" I asked myself. "I don't want to stab this guy. But if I just close the knife up, they're gonna call me a punk."

I figured I had to do something, just to keep my reputation intact. I wanted them to know I was cool and tough. So I stepped forward and poked the crackhead gently in the thigh. It barely broke the skin. As I retracted the blade I became nauseated; I was sickened by what I had just done.

Leaving the guy moaning on the ground, we walked away from the scene.

I headed to the store with my friends so they could buy cigarettes. Then I stupidly went back with them to the same old hangout near the school so they could have a smoke. The police walked up to us. "A guy got beat up back here. Do you know who did it?" Although we denied knowing anything, they searched us. And they found the knife in my pocket. My heart sank.

I ended up in jail on a charge of attempted murder because we had beaten him up so badly. Luckily for me, the case was thrown out after the victim failed to show up in court. It was then that I realized that being a tough guy wasn't me. It just didn't feel right. Finally, I just let it go.

I figured out that I needed to just be me. The problem was, I had been such a shape-shifter in the past that I didn't know who "me" was.

It wasn't until I went to high school and hooked up with George and Sam that I found the perfect fit. They were fun-loving and adventurous but they also knew how to knuckle down, study hard, and get good grades. With them, I could strike the right balance. I could be smart and cool at the same time.

But before that, I was always on a search to find the right personality.

I often wondered why many of my friends were better than I was in sports. The answer was obvious: I rarely spent any time practicing, so why would I be good at sports?

Somehow I couldn't grasp the fact that I needed to practice my jump shot over and over in order to improve my game. I could have really used someone in my life to remind me to go outside and do the shooting and running drills that make people better athletes. My dad could have handled the job easily if he had been around. Dad had been a pretty good athlete when he was young. He played high school basketball, and when he got to Assumption College, he made the varsity team. But it really wasn't a testament to his skills. Dad shared a room with a black student who was there on a basketball scholarship, and after hanging out with him, Dad decided to try out for the team. He showed up at the tryouts, ready to compete for a slot. But the coach just handed him a jersey and told him to suit up. It was the 1970s and he was black, so naturally it was assumed he had to be good at basketball. He remembers that he had to correct his professors often, letting them know that it was actually an academic scholarship, not a basketball one, that got him there.

By the time I got to high school, I was a pretty good basketball player, but I didn't stand a chance of catching up to the sports skills of guys my age who'd been practicing and playing competitively for years. So I developed a motto: "I don't play sports, I play girls."

There was some false bravado behind that slogan, though, because I really didn't know how to talk to women. After all, I couldn't stand next to a guy and take notes when he was getting his mack on. Nobody told me the secrets. It seemed to me, once again, that not having a father in my life had handicapped me. Fathers, I believe, help instill a confidence in you. But I didn't have that. I worried endlessly about finding the right thing to say. I was afraid of approaching girls because I didn't know how to break the ice. If I looked at a girl and she didn't smile, I would think, "She's not interested," and I'd back away. I didn't have anybody to explain the "She's playing hard to get" ploy to me, and as a result, I gave up too easily.

The only thing that saved me, and helped me carve my playboy image in high school, was that I didn't have to pursue anybody. Girls openly flirted with me and told me they found me attractive.

The only downside to this was that I rarely got the girls I wanted— instead, I had to take the ones who wanted me. When we were in high school and college, Sam had the confidence I lacked. Sam was never afraid to go up to a girl and he could always think of something to say. He's always done that, and he usually was pretty successful.

I, on the other hand, seemed to just exude nervousness when I approached a girl. I remember going to a party when I was about fifteen, where I met a girl who was so pretty I would have done absolutely anything for her to be my girlfriend. I guess she could see this in my lovelorn puppy-dog eyes, because she led me to her cousin's bedroom and we started making out.

We talked on the phone for about a week after that, but then she lost interest. I'm sure she could see how infatuated I was with her, and that she was in control of the relationship. She knew exactly how far she wanted it to go, and she hit the brakes long before I wanted it to end. I thought about her for months afterward. Every time the phone rang, I wished it was her. I ran into her a few years later, and she was dating one of the neighborhood hustlers. I spoke to her, but I don't think she remembered me. I didn't even try to refresh her memory or get her number. I didn't think I had a chance against a guy who had a wad of money in a rubber band.

After a few ego-battering episodes like that, I realized it made more sense to let the girls chase me than to go chasing after them.

The person you grow into, I've realized, depends largely on what you've been exposed to as a child. One of my cousins, for example, loved going fishing with his father. I, on the other hand, couldn't see what the big deal was all about. What was so exciting about fishing? You just sit there for hours, with your line in the water, even if nothing happens? I didn't get it.

But now I think I'd probably enjoy fishing today if my father had taken the time with me that my cousin's father did. If my father had taken me out on the lake and explained to me, "Son, this is peaceful. I'm going to teach you patience," maybe I'd be a more patient person today as well as a competent fisherman.

But those kinds of lessons aren't a priority in the many homes where kids are growing up fatherless. When you learn what the streets have to teach you, it makes for a haphazard lesson plan. It makes me think of the first time I drank beer, when I was sixteen. I thought it tasted awful. But I knew that I was supposed to like it, because all the guys did. Now I've grown to like the taste of it. The streets made sure I learned that lesson well.

I WAS DEEP INTO the job of borrowing people's personalities, busily designing my way to a manly reputation, when my father arrived back on the scene.

I was about twelve when Dad became a more consistent presence in my life. He had just completed a two-year prison sentence and moved in with his girlfriend, a woman named Beverly. Not long after that, they had a child, my half sister Daaimah.

This is where my real memories of my father begin. I could finally start to carve out a real relationship with him.

At first it was hard even mouthing the word "Dad." I just hadn't had much occasion to say it during the earlier years of my life. It sounded so unfamiliar. My mouth wasn't used to saying the word. As I got older and spent more time with him, though, it rolled off my tongue effortlessly.

I know that Dad still struggled against his drug problem for many more years after he was last released from prison. But he also tried valiantly to be more of a father to me. And I appreciated that.

My father and I had a low-key, low-pressure relationship. He never tried to come on strong, like a big-time disciplinarian. I think he realized that it was a little inappropriate to come in and out of my life and then announce, "I'm your father, so do what I say." And that was fine by me. It would have turned me off for him to be a heavy-handed father.

Instead, he fit more into the mold of a dad who was as much a friend as a father, similar to George's surrogate father, Shahid. He gave great advice, and that's exactly what I wanted. I craved learning about him so much that I must have asked a thousand questions an hour.

I wanted Dad to tell me about himself. He was really a stranger and I didn't know too much about him. I wanted him to reminisce with me, to reveal what his childhood had been like. I wanted him to pass down things to me. I wanted to know the secrets of manhood.

Hungry for that father-to-son wisdom, I would hit my father with questions as soon as I saw him. Dad seemed caught off guard by my constant probing. "Tell me about when you were my age," I would beg him. "What was it like? What did you wear? What did you do for fun?"

There was so much I needed to know. I felt ignorant. I was getting old enough to realize that my dad didn't do the things that traditional fathers were supposed to do. He didn't tuck me in at night, he didn't help choose my school or check my homework. He didn't know my friends, he didn't pay for my school supplies, my food, or my shelter. My upkeep had been almost completely provided by my mom and her family.

I didn't know what a dad was supposed to supply. But whatever it was, I knew I wasn't getting it and I wanted it.

Yet I respected my father. Once he came back into my life, he always kept his word. Dad never made promises he couldn't keep. Mind you, he didn't make many promises, so he didn't have as many to keep.

I didn't ask him for a whole lot. I never asked him to buy me a car because I knew he couldn't. But the little things, I knew he could manage.

One thing I loved about Dad was his soft-spoken but thought-provoking way of talking.

When Dad found out that I had gotten in trouble for the incident with the crackhead, he had a serious talk with me.

"You didn't stop to think, did you?" he asked me. "You've got to think about the decisions you make. You see the consequences now, don't you? You could go to jail. You're doing so well in school, you want to go to college, why destroy it now?"

Dad sounded more like a counselor than an angry father. He helped me see how the split-second decisions I make can be detrimental. He was almost like a psychologist. He didn't give me the answers. Rather, he wanted me to see the answers for myself.

"I've been in these kinds of situations," he added. "You don't want to end up like me."

I really paid attention to what he was saying. I knew it was coming from somebody who knew what life behind bars was like.

Yet our conversations always seemed short-lived. Since he wasn't a full-time father, he couldn't be there to advise me through my everyday problems. I had to keep stumbling through on my own.

I came remarkably close to getting a live-in father figure at one point, though. So close, in fact, that I allowed myself to hope things were getting ready to change. Bobby was a boyfriend of Mom's who stole my heart when I was about ten years old. If I could have had a magic wand that let me make a decision that would affect my mother's life forever, that would have been the moment I'd have waved it. I'd have made her marry him.

Bobby was a great guy. He worked with Mom at Bell Laboratories. Thin and tall, he was a handsome man who wore an Afro. They started dating when Mom and I were living in an apartment in suburban Hillside, in a building that resembled Brooklyn's brownstones. Soon Bobby moved in with us and became like my live-in father, something I'd never had.

When he came home from work, he always said yes when I asked him to play backgammon or video games. I could easily talk him into playing Uno with me or a game of Sorry. We would spend hours engrossed in games in the living room, occasionally jumping up to put one of Bobby's favorite albums on the stereo. To this day, if I hear "Off the Wall" by Michael Jackson or Donna Summer's suggestive "Hot Stuff," I think of those game sessions. If Bobby wasn't in the mood to play with me, he never showed it. He never skimped on attention, and over time we became a real pair. I could tell the feeling was mutual: I liked playing around with him, and he liked spending time with me. Sometimes it was lonely being an only child, but having Bobby around filled that void and it felt great.

One added benefit was that my no-nonsense Mom seemed to take more of an interest in playtime once Bobby arrived. If she came home and found us playing backgammon, she might take a few minutes and play the winner. Thanks to Bobby's presence, Mom softened up a little, taking time for more fun and games, I couldn't help but notice. Soon, the three of us started to spend time doing more of the things that families did together.

Bobby was good to me, and more important, he was good to my mother. By the ripe age of ten, I had realized that Mom's choices of men didn't seem to be helping her with the things she was going through. I was in fifth grade, and already I felt like her protector. Bobby wasn't into drugs, and he seemed to be a healthy influence on Mom.

He wasn't the type to party hard, and was more of a homebody. In my eyes, he was a regular stand-up guy, even a little corny. Bobby never attempted to discipline me; he left that responsibility to my mom, who was up to the task. And I never turned on him with the "You're not my daddy" line that a lot of kids aim at their parents' live-in partners. I appreciated everything he did for us, and I wouldn't have dreamed of being disrespectful.

I could feel the difference in our lives financially after Bobby began handing his paycheck dutifully over to Mom. We were able to do more and have more. Mom even got to pursue one of her dreams, training for a career working at the airport, while Bobby took care of us. Suddenly I could see the difference that a reliable man makes in a household. I never knew how I wanted and missed and cherished this kind of a connection until Bobby showed up.

Then Mom started dating a new guy while she was still with Bobby. It was someone from her past, a guy she remembered from her years as a teenager hanging out at Twin City Roller Rink in Elizabeth, New Jersey. Back then, my mom had thought he was so cool. He had been one of the smoothest dudes at the rink and was well known throughout his neighborhood. When she bumped into him thirteen years later, he had recently been released from prison. Mom felt flattered to be hotly pursued by a guy she once had a huge crush on. I think he was exhilarating to my mom, a change from the *Leave It to Beaver* lifestyle she had found with Bobby.

I remember walking up the stairs to my grandmother's house the day that Mom broke the news to me that she intended to break up with Bobby. "No!" I said, banging my fists into her. "Why are you doing this? You're making a big mistake."

Then I tried to talk sense into her. "You can make it work, Mom," I begged. "You need to get back with him." But she wouldn't listen.

Then something happened that I'd never done before. Tears started rolling down my cheeks. I had never cried for any of my mother's boyfriends until that moment.

I had let myself believe that Mom and Bobby would live happily ever after, but now I had to face the fact that she meant what she was saying. It was over. I was crushed. Part of my reaction was selfish—I really liked those after-school game sessions—but I knew that Bobby provided us with a lifestyle we hadn't known before. For the first time, we were doing well. Mom wasn't going out on the town; instead, we were going out for family dinners. Bobby had been the first man Mom ever brought home who I felt was the right guy for her. There was no way she could justify her decision to me. All I knew was that we finally had a happy family and she was messing it up.

But Mom had already made up her mind. Bobby wasn't the kind of man she wanted. He acted weak, he didn't know how to take charge, manage money, or make decisions. The only real relationship in the apartment, she said, was between him and me. "It was more of a twosome than a threesome," is how my Mom describes it.

That day, I felt like I had lost my best friend. It was a pain like I can only imagine a son feels when his parents divorce. I already had missed out on knowing what it was like to live with my father in the same house. Now here she was snatching away the closest thing I had known.

Mine wasn't the only heart that was breaking. Bobby loved my mom and couldn't understand why she was acting so distant. But he finally got the message that their relationship wasn't salvageable after Mom became pregnant with her new boyfriend's child.

Bobby moved out of the apartment. And I never saw him again.

In what seemed like a flash, I had to adjust from perhaps the most blissfully childlike period I'd ever known to a situation that demanded I become man of the house. I didn't resent it at first, though. Mom really relied on me once the Bobby era ended, because around the same time the baby was born, the new man in her life was arrested and returned to prison.

My sister Mecca arrived in chilly January, when I was in sixth grade. Mom and I had already given up the Hillside apartment and moved back into the safety net of Ma's house for a while. My mother landed a steady job at the post office, and as soon as she saved some money, she moved us into an apartment in Plainfield, a few blocks from Ma's.

Now we had a family of three, and I was given the job of father. I took that responsibility to heart, even though I was only twelve.

In the mornings, I'd give Mecca a bath in the beige baby tub. And then I'd comb her hair. That was the most challenging part. I remember trying to arrange and part her hair, putting it in two or three pigtails, and snapping the ends closed with plastic barrettes. I was proud of myself for doing her hair. The only problem was braids. I could never figure out how to braid, so I settled for twists. After my hair-care sessions, Mecca always looked good when she went off to day care. Then I'd get myself together and head to junior high.

After a while, though, it started getting tough being the patriarch. Mom was working a midnight shift at the post office, so I pretty much served as Mecca's primary caregiver after school while my mother slept. As a result, I wasn't able to go out and roughhouse with my friends because I had to babysit. I complained to Mom that it wasn't fair. "I'm a kid, Mom, I want to do kid things," I'd protest. "I'm only twelve, I want to go outside and play."

"Who's going to watch your sister?" she'd throw back at me.

So I got resourceful. I would just take my baby sister out with me. I found some girls in my apartment complex who would sit on their porch with Mecca and give her a bottle or fix her hair while my friends and I ran back and forth nearby.

But that solution didn't last long. There was only so much a twelve-year-old could do with a toddler in tow. I was miserable. And to top it off, I also had to watch my grandfather Raymond Hunt. He had been living on the streets when Mom found him at Newark's Pennsylvania Station and decided to take him in and clean him up. It was a well-intentioned gesture. He was a war veteran and an alcoholic and was suffering from mental illness. But my grandfather didn't talk to us, he only mumbled to himself, talking to the voices he heard in his head. He needed to be in a mental hospital. Instead he was parked inside my bedroom. I used to be proud to let my friends hang out in my room, which was decked out with *Star Wars* curtains and cool bunk beds, but now I was ashamed to invite them over. My grandfather often soiled his pants, so my bedroom stank. To make matters worse, Mom asked me to make sure he took baths, which was not the easiest mission. Sometimes I resented all the responsibility I had to shoulder, and then I instantly struggled with guilt over those feelings.

Finally Mom realized we couldn't take care of him anymore, and she took him to the veterans' hospital and dropped him off. The hospital discharged him a few days later, and my family never saw him again.

But I was still in charge of Mecca. My grandmother was helpful, though. Sometimes I could take my sister over to her house and my relatives would watch Mecca so I could have a little time for myself. It was a hard situation for a preteen, but I didn't feel entitled to complain. What else was I supposed to do? My mother had to work, so she couldn't be there for my sister. So I just tried to make the most of it.

This topsy-turvy period was the tipping point for my mother, I think. It added more hurdles to her already complicated life. With neither my father nor my sister's father to support her and her children, our lights started getting cut off periodically and there wasn't much food in the refrigerator. When I was younger, Mom always kept me looking sharp, with fresh haircuts and new clothes. But now she let me know, at age twelve, that I needed to get a job and buy my own school clothes.

Mom's behavior was changing. I could hear whispers in my family that my mother was doing some unhealthy things, but Mom always protected me from seeing any evidence of drug addiction. All I knew was that she told me she had to find a way "to numb the pain."

But despite whatever Mom was doing secretly, she kept a firm grip on her plans for my education. All my life, my mother had made it clear that she had high expectations for me academically. I noticed she was much stricter about good grades than my grandmother was. For Ma, a B or C would have been acceptable, but my mother knew I was capable of much better. It disappointed her when I brought home anything lower than an A. It was my mom who taught me to excel in school, because she didn't accept anything less. Mom made it so clear that I would be going to college that I grew up thinking I had no other choice. College was just a given. Even though a lot of my Plainfield friends hadn't given much thought to college, I knew I was different.

And that's how it happened that when the time came for me to go to high school, my mother decided without consulting me to send me to University High School in Newark. University was a magnet high school, perfect for students who were college-bound. At first I was furious at her. The members of my junior high "posse" had been dying to start at Plainfield High. We were going to run the place. But the wheels were already in motion and I was set to start at University High in September 1987. I took the news hard after realizing there was nothing I could do. I would have to move back to Newark and live with my uncle Rahman so I could be close to my new school. I hated the idea. That was the last time I ever lived with my mom.

But I recognized that getting away from all the instability in our apartment was a reprieve. Things were shifting in our household, and not for the better. So I decided to look at this as an opportunity. I vowed to visit my sister regularly. Looking back, a part of me regrets ever leaving her alone with my mother.

As time went on, I didn't see Mecca as much as I should have. Then I started to hear that she was getting into trouble at school for bad behavior, and her schoolwork was suffering. When I took a closer look, I realized that she was going through a lot at home. Mom didn't have a reliable babysitter anymore, and as a result, she had taken to bringing Mecca along to some places a little girl had no business being. Mom's addiction had taken over, and she was no longer being discreet about the company she kept.

By the time I realized how bad things were with my sister, I was already on my way to Seton Hall. I wanted her to start doing better in school and to reverse the bad habits I could see she had picked up, but I didn't know how to motivate her.

So I decided to expose her to something different. I wanted her to see what education could do for her. Even though I was immersed in my college workload, I often brought Mecca to campus on weekends. She was eight or nine by then.

Although I was now taking tough classes like organic chemistry and getting A's in them, I still had never mastered the art of hair-braiding. Luckily I had a number of female friends who volunteered to do Mecca's hair for me. I also confided in them about Mecca's behavior, and they offered to teach her how to be a lady, something I knew I couldn't do.

It excited Mecca to come to Seton Hall and hang out with me and her newfound college girlfriends. I urged her to do well in school, promising that if she brought home a good report card I would buy her a new pair of sneakers or something else she wanted. I got on my soapbox often, telling her how important education was, the way that Mom had lectured me.

I even talked to her about sex. I knew somebody had to do it. I didn't even want Mecca to have boyfriends, let alone sex, so I tried my best to scare her away from sex with my fatherly talks. "Sex is something for grown-ups," I told her. "You've got to respect your body and never let any boy disrespect it."

And the surest way to do that, I told her, was not to have sex. "Your body is your temple. It's a prize and you can never give a prize like that away so easily." A girl had told me that line once, when I was trying to get into *her* temple, and I thought it was effective, so I passed it on to Mecca.

But I did tell Mecca that if she ever did have sex, she better protect herself. I worried about her constantly once she became interested in boys. But I couldn't control everything.

Mecca lived with my mom until she was fifteen, and they fought frequently. With all that was going on in my mother's life, she wasn't able to be the mother to Mecca that she was to me. Finally, Mom gave her permission to move in with her cousin in Philadelphia. Within a few weeks, I felt as though all my hard work had come undone. Although her cousin tried her best to watch over my little sister, Mecca decided to have sex with a man in his early twenties at her cousin's house when no one was home. She got pregnant after that one encounter and returned home. The cycle of fatherlessness continued in our family. Like our mother, Mecca had created a baby, Inasha, with a man who wouldn't be a real presence in his child's life.

Now in her twenties, Mecca has grown into a take-charge, street-smart mom shaped in the ever-recognizable mold of our mother. But there's no doubt that Mecca listened to the messages I tried hard to instill in her. Sometimes when you plant a seed, it takes a little while before it starts to grow. She's a responsible young mom who has stayed away from drugs, with her own apartment in the Newark area, a car, and two jobs.

I'm touched to see that the time I put in, as a worried older brother, has paid off. "Rameck was the only father figure I ever had," says Mecca, who'll promptly correct anybody who suggests she grew up without a father. "I'm accustomed to having a father. Rameck is my father. That's who I call when I need someone."

Helping to raise my sister taught me that parenting isn't easy. No matter what you tell kids and how much love you give them, they still will make mistakes. But I also learned that no matter how many mistakes they make, as long as you keep loving them and telling them the right thing, they will find their way back to the right path.

My experience with Mecca changed me. I started to ponder the power of fathers. Although I'd been raised in an environment where fathers weren't plentiful, I was getting old enough to realize the necessary role that fathers play in a child's life.

Where was the kind of dad that you saw every day when you came home from school? Why was he missing from my world?

A dad that you saw every day, I began to realize, could help you a lot more than one you saw only every once in a while.

An everyday dad can keep a child from seeking the answers to life's questions in the streets. An everyday dad can remind a kid, over and over again if necessary, about the importance of practicing sports. He can show a son how to treat women with respect, so a boy won't have to copy what he sees in movies and music videos. Or show a daughter that she's loved, so she won't feel the need to fall into bed with every boy who tells her she's cute.

How did it happen, I wondered, that people stopped expecting men to be full-time, devoted dads? It's not unusual to hear single mothers say, "I don't need a man, I can do bad by myself." And it's not unusual to see men who fill their days with the pursuit of women, drugs, or liquor—men who concern themselves with everything but the job of taking care of their children.

I needed to look no further than my own father to see how an extraordinary man could get sidetracked by the unhealthy messages in our community.

My dad, I knew, could have had it all. A great career, a good middle-class life. And it was obvious from his generosity and attentiveness that he would have been a devoted dad to Quamara, Daaimah, and me if drugs hadn't stolen him from us. I could truly empathize with him. Heck, I'd almost gone down a similar road. In high school, my friends and I frequently got ourselves into trouble. I was just fortunate that I got steered back onto the right path.

Sometimes I remembered how my uncle Sheldon used to tease me: "Your father's not your real daddy." That stuck with me for years. It wasn't until I started being around my father more that I realized how alike we really were. I'm a doctor by training and believe in science, but if there ever was a doubt about genetics, being around my father wiped away any doubts I may have had.

I may not have inherited his looks, but I certainly inherited some of his personality traits. He had been a top student, like me. And he had tried his best as a youth to shun that brainy reputation, just as I did. The very reason Dad developed his drug habit was his desire to be part of the in crowd. I could relate to that. When I had whipped out that knife on that crack addict, I was trying to be cool, to gain respect—just like my father had.

I realize now that my father's open, loving approach balances out the more practical influence of my mother's side of the family. My mother's insistence on good grades and Ma's sturdy, tough love gave me the perseverance to achieve my goals. The Hunts firmly believe that everyone has to swim on their own, and that there's no sense in enabling anyone's bad habits. They gave me determination, which translated into my ability to push past my father's obstacles and achieve more than he did.

On the other hand, I've learned the power of pure, forgiving love from my father. I've seen his family extend a well-intentioned helping hand over and over, even when people take advantage of it.

The very reason I've shown the endless capacity to forgive and encourage my father is, I'm sure, because he showed such warmth and unconditional love every time he laid eyes on me.

My father's influence gave me the compassion to keep loving him, despite his relapses. And there were many.

Dad went to drug rehabilitation programs many times. Every time he got out, he found a good job quickly. I think it was because my father was such a genuinely nice man that he always bounced back. People were always rooting for him to kick his habit, so they bent over backward to help him.

Dad would work for a while, earning good money, but then he'd mess up and get fired. It was a never-ending cycle of disappointment.

Every time he would get out of rehab, though, I would cheer him on. "Dad, you can do it this time," I told him.

"I'm going to try, son," he would say. I don't know if he believed it himself.

But I believed in him. I tried to be positive and upbeat, because I always wanted to convince him that this was going to be the last time.

Sometimes when I encouraged him to get off drugs, he told me he felt defeated. It was then that he suggested that perhaps his sole purpose on this earth was to serve as an example to me.

"I don't know the reason God is taking me through this, but I have to believe that a part of that reason is for me to show you what not to do," he would say. "Maybe that's my role on earth—to show you what not to do."

I couldn't accept that. "That's a cop-out, Dad," I would tell him. "You're so smart. You've got so much going for you, you've just got to turn your life around."

I knew the dangers of his addiction and I was scared for him. "You could die, Dad. You've got to stop."

"I know," he would reply unconvincingly. "I'm trying."

I never gave up. Throughout high school and college, I kept cheering him on.

Fate's a funny thing. More than once during my childhood, it put me in the position where I had to serve in a caretaking role to the men who rightly should have been fathering me.

But the bond between my father and me isn't fragile. It has survived a million disappointments. I never stopped hoping that my father would one day have the life that he deserved.

Chapter 2

ALIM BILAL

The Beginning

I REMEMBER WHEN RAMECK first told me he wanted to be a doctor. He was in high school.

I told him to go for it. I never let on that his words had sent icy shivers down my spine.

I knew medical school wasn't free. And it's a sorry moment when a father realizes he can't help his child. Back then, I was a drug-abusing ex-felon who had no idea where to find the money to help Rameck's dream come true. That hurt me so bad. I felt like less than a man. As Rameck's father, I felt a responsibility to pave the way for my son, my smart, bold man-child who had kept his grades up, his nose clean, and had managed to avoid the traps that ensnared me. But since I was bouncing in and out of rehab programs at the time, I knew there was nothing I could do. I felt worthless.

During Rameck's high school years, I managed to keep a job—but just barely. I worked as a supervisor with the Newark water department, supervising crews at excavation sites. It was a steady job, but it just didn't feel right. Going to that job every day reminded me that I had blown every chance I had ever gotten to achieve the dreams of my own youth. I had lost a college scholarship, and nothing had ever come of my desire to become a world-class chemist. So I kept using drugs to make myself feel good. I had a government job with good benefits that paid the bill for me to go through drug rehab several times. But I always relapsed.

By the time Rameck expressed his desire to be a doctor, I was in my forties and the father of three children. Heroin had been a part of my life since my fateful first year in college, when it seemed like I gambled away my whole future in one fell swoop by acting recklessly during my Christmas visit home. I went looking for my old friends from high school and found them in an apartment getting high on heroin. When they told me to give it a try, I didn't have the backbone to say no. I promptly got hooked, and college became unimportant. Two years later, I was headed to prison for armed robbery.

During my freshman year, I also dated two different girls, both cheerleaders from different high schools. That's how Rameck and his half sister, Quamara, came to be born just a few weeks apart.

In the annals of fatherhood, it wasn't the greatest of starts: I had two children by two different teen mothers and I was on my way to prison before I had even turned twenty-one.

Disappointed isn't the word to describe how my family felt, as they watched my life swiftly unravel after high school. Shocked is more like it.

My siblings thought I was a genius when we were kids. They boasted that I could take any electronic item apart and put it back together again. I loved looking inside radios and telephones to see how they worked.

I'm the second oldest of six kids. We didn't have much, we lived in the projects, but my family was certain that someday I was going to be rich and important. I loved math and science, and my family just knew that I would grow up to be a famous scientist. They had me thoroughly convinced. I went through my childhood believing in the destiny that my family envisioned for me.

My parents, Fred and Winnie Jones, met and married in North Carolina. Neither one had a high school diploma when they decided to move north in 1961 with their children in search of better opportunities. I was eight at the time.

Newark, they decided, was the place they would settle. We got a brand-new apartment on Prince Street. It was in the projects, but it was nice. Five bedrooms, everything new, and we were one of the first families to move in. I remember a time when our apartment complex was a closely knit community where everyone looked out for one another. But over time, drugs and alcohol crept in to pull our little community apart. Our family wasn't spared.

My mom was strict, with high expectations. She wanted the best for us, and was determined that we wouldn't go to public school in Newark. A resourceful woman, she found a job in a church rectory, cooking and cleaning for the priests. It helped her get a tuition discount so her six children could go to Catholic school.

Mom believed sincerely in the power of education. She herself only went to the eighth grade when she was in North Carolina, but after we moved to Newark, she went back to school. She earned her high school diploma, and then enrolled in college. She became a registered nurse.

My father got a job in Hackensack as a printer, and he worked there for decades, until he retired. He went to work every day and didn't do much more than that, as far as I'm concerned. He was a quiet, withdrawn man. He loved us, we know that. But his emotional absence helped me form some opinions, early on, about what kind of father I would become. My father suffered from alcoholism. He wasn't able to break free and teach me some things that would have helped me negotiate life. I made myself a promise as a child that I would never be that type of father.

My dad was named for his father, Fred Jones, who lived in North Carolina and, from what I could see, shared the same type of loner behavior. He lived by himself and didn't say much.

I had the same name. But I didn't want to be like them. Somehow I knew, at an early age, that children shouldn't receive the silent treatment from their father. I wanted my dad to be more than just a provider. A good father, I believed, has got to be someone who listens, someone who communicates, and above all, is a great teacher.

My parents were a good-looking, well-dressed pair when they were young. Yet everything wasn't pretty behind the scenes. My father's alcoholism made him abusive. Once when I was a teenager, my mother took him to court for domestic violence, and the lawyers actually put me on the stand to testify against him. Later my parents reconciled and stayed together for several more years. My father was, after all, a good provider—better than most.

Our mom knew the dangers that lurked in our low-income neighborhood and she tried her hardest to insulate us from them. She had us baptized Catholic and made our church and school the center of our world. She strictly enforced her rules and curfews, and made sure we concentrated on our schoolwork. Everyone in our neighborhood complimented Winnie Jones on how well behaved her children were. She took pride in thinking she had the perfect kids.

But she couldn't insulate us completely. One day when I was in elementary school, two boys attacked me on the way to school. They stole my lunch money and knifed me in my side. Doctors had to remove my spleen as a result of the stab wounds. That day changed me. I knew I had to toughen up or else I would get run over.

Although I still kept my grades high, I started rebelling in my own way. Around my junior or senior year of high school, the Black Panthers came to Newark. And with them came the black Muslim movement. I loved listening to all the black awareness rhetoric. It sounded so revolutionary to me.

Members of the local mosque would drive into our neighborhood in vans and pick up anyone who wanted to go to their Masjid temple. I always climbed on board for the ride. Coming from such a demeaning and depressing area, we were some angry kids in those vans.

I soaked up all the knowledge I could at those meetings at the mosque. In my senior year of high school, I started following the teachings of Elijah Muhammad. I remember coming home and convincing the rest of my siblings to join the Nation of Islam. They weren't happy when I told them to stop eating pork, but over the coming years, I would recruit all five of my siblings to Islam. We all wore the required Muslim garb. My brothers and I wore the clean-shaven look, with suits and bow ties, and my sisters covered their hair and bodies with long scarves and tunics.

Soon, I changed my name legally from Fred Jones to Alim Bilal.

Alim means the learned one. I wanted to be known as a deep thinker, a learned person.

Yet my experience with Islam, I reflect now, was little more than a fad. At the same time I was converting to the faith during high school, I was also doing something that was completely out of keeping with its philosophy.

I started experimenting with drugs. My little sister, Resa, who is three years younger, knew it and would cover for me. When I'd walk out of our bathroom, she would go in after me and pick up the coke spoons and other drug residue I'd left behind. She was fifteen or sixteen at the time.

Still, I kept a high grade-point average at Essex Catholic High School. My mother and my parish priest bragged about my accomplishments when I earned an academic scholarship to Assumption College in Worcester, Massachusetts.

I knew as I packed my bags for college in 1971 that I was taking their hopes and expectations with me. I had a lot to accomplish.

But being plunked onto an all-white Catholic campus in the middle of New England was hard for me. Although I performed well academically, earning a 3.5 grade-point average in the first semester, I flopped around socially like the poor kid from Newark that I was. I missed the comfort of my family, and I didn't have Mom's rigid rules. I didn't fit in at Assumption.

Maybe that's why the need to fit in became so all-important when I went home for winter break during freshman year and found my friends shooting heroin. When they asked me if I wanted to take part, I should have had the guts to leave. But I tried it. In that instant, I burned up every opportunity my mother had sacrificed to create.

Mom had done everything she could to keep the streets out of our life while we were kids. But she couldn't protect us forever. One by one, all of my siblings turned to drugs and risky behaviors after they reached adulthood. It was as if our strict upbringing created within us a monstrous urge to try everything we had missed out on. My mom suffered with each of us, through our addictions, health problems, broken families, and incarcerations. She never stopped trying to bring us back from the edge.

When my little sister graduated from high school, Resa became one of my favorite drug buddies. She always said there was no better person to get high with than me, because she didn't have to fear that I was going to turn on her and hurt her. We trusted each other. We drove to Harlem regularly. One of our suppliers there was called "The Claw" because he had an over-sized, grotesque mitt of a hand. Having used up all the veins in his arms and legs during years of drug use, he had started shooting drugs directly into his hand. But his hand had grown hard and engorged because he let it get infected. He eventually had to have it amputated.

On the way back from Harlem, we'd stop at a gas station, eager to get some privacy so we could cook up the raw heroin we had bought. We couldn't go into the bathroom together since it would look suspicious, so I'd go in first and shoot up. Then my sister would take her turn.

Just as Resa thought I was the safest drug partner for her, she was a good sidekick for me, too, because my sister had an uncanny knack for finding just the right spot for the syringe. Her practiced fingers could always locate a vein, so that I could feel that euphoric rush I sought. And when you've been a longtime user, believe me, good veins are hard to find.

My appetite for heroin flared out of control as soon as I tried it. It wasn't deliberate. I truly wanted that rosy future that had been promised to me. I had expected to finish college and start my glorious career. I thought I was so smart that no substance could overpower me. And that's where I went wrong.

Very quickly, I found out that addiction has nothing to do with intelligence, nothing to do with one's morals or spirit. It's pure evil and it has the power to overwhelm everything a person has inside, I don't care who you are. I found out, as I started craving the drug at all hours, that I wasn't special. I let my addiction tear through my life and get between me and my goals. I couldn't even keep the promise I had made to myself about being a good father. I dropped out of college, committed a robbery, and was on my way to prison when my children were born.

Yet I remember feeling a profound sense of love for my newborn son and daughter. It was the only positive thing cutting through the mess I had made of my life. I felt that God had honored me with one of my life's wishes.

Their mothers brought the babies to visit me occasionally while I was incarcerated. I was always overjoyed to see them. I remember walking into the visiting room to see Rameck sitting there, dressed neatly, cuddling with his mom. Just seeing the two of them ignited conflicting feelings in me.

I was happy and proud to see my son, but I wasn't proud of the complicated ball of emotions that entwined yet separated me and his mother, Arlene. She had gotten pregnant in high school and had hoped that the three of us could live happily ever after. Her hopes had been dashed almost immediately when it became obvious that I not only had another girlfriend but was on my way to prison.

I knew how badly I had damaged Arlene emotionally. All those feelings came pouring out when I saw my little son cradled in her arms. I know I seemed detached to her; that was just my way of handling the situation. For the duration of our visits, I would hold Rameck's hand and help him toddle around the waiting room, or I would put him on my lap and feed him. That was the extent of my fathering, due to the circumstances. As he grew older, it became clear that Rameck hungered for more.

He loved being around me and craved my attention. During the periods that I spent "on the street," when I wasn't in prison, he would nearly glue himself to me when we were together.

The boy had a lot of questions. A lot of times I scolded Rameck for talking too much and begged him to just be quiet for a minute so I could hear myself think. I regret that so much now. That was the kind of thing I had resented most about my own father. How could I have gone back on my own vow to be the kind of father who listens when his child has something to say?

Once, when he was about eleven or twelve, we were in my car going to cash my paycheck from a job I had found working on computers. Rameck pelted me with questions: "Why does Mommy say you're not doing what you're supposed to do? Why don't you ever give me any money? Why don't you ever come and pick me up?"

Choosing my words carefully, I gently let him know that my everyday life was a struggle. I told him I was doing my best. At the time, my "best" meant that I occasionally picked him up and spent money on him, and that child support was being deducted regularly from my paycheck.

What he really wanted to know—but didn't ask—was why I didn't give him my full attention. What I left unspoken was the fact that drugs had stolen my focus and were still unraveling my life. Although my children's safety and well-being were important to me, I'm ashamed to say that drugs were even more important.

Several times, the police came knocking at my door to arrest me because Arlene had reported me for nonpayment of child support. I had only myself to blame when that happened. I never got mad at her, and I certainly tried to let Rameck know that he shouldn't feel guilty about it. It was my own fault because I wasn't living up to my responsibility.

I hated the fact that my kids had to take a backseat to my addiction, starting from the minute I woke up every morning. I got out of bed planning what I would do to score some drugs. I had wanted to give my children so much, but I didn't have anything to give.

Because I wanted my kids to have nice things, I hustled even harder at Christmas and birthdays to ensure they had lavish gifts. Once, I surprised Rameck with a bright red electric keyboard that he was crazy about.

I remember quite clearly the day I got it for him. I stole it from a Sears store. There had been dozens of them, stacked in a huge pyramid right by the store entrance. I took one for Rameck and disappeared nonchalantly through the door and into the parking lot.

I loved that feeling of walking in the door at Christmastime and having my son leap for joy because Daddy had brought something special just for him.

By the time Rameck reached high school, I had become a daddy a third time. I was in a relationship with a woman named Beverly, whom I had met not long after I got released from prison in 1979. Once I left the halfway house, I moved in with her. I was working nights and Beverly was working days as a cashier when our daughter, Daaimah, was born. It was my first chance to be a full-time dad.

In the daytime, I would babysit Daaimah. But I also had a habit to support, and since she was there, Daaimah had to go along for the ride.

I would wake up in the morning, then wake up the baby. I'd feed her, dress her, and braid her hair neatly. Then we'd get in the car and find a place to go "shopping" because I needed money for drugs. The two of us would go into a Sears store or a supermarket, and I would put her in a shopping cart. Cute Daaimah served as my diversion. I'd push her down the meat aisle in the grocery cart and pretend to fuss over her while stuffing steaks into my jacket.

I must have had my routine down pat because I never got caught. I felt invisible, untouchable even, when I was rolling the cart through those stores, taking what I wanted. It took years for me to wake up to the fact that our father-daughter outings were warping the precious little girl I had turned into my accomplice. It got to the point where she would say, "Dad, Dad," tug me on the shoulder in the store, and point to something she wanted. Later, when we got to the car, she would be delighted to see I had gotten it for her.

Our partnership ended abruptly one day when Daaimah was shopping with her mother. After they checked out and were loading the car, Daaimah merrily plucked a bunch of stolen dolls out of the hood of her jacket where she had stashed them. Her mother gave her an earful that day. She told her that Daddy shouldn't be doing those things, that he's going to go to jail if he doesn't stop.

I didn't hear about this conversation until later, when I was out doing my thing, shopping for free with my sweet daughter. Right in the middle of the store, Daaimah cried out, "Daddy, take those steaks out of your shirt! I don't want you to go to jail!"

Even as I shushed her, I felt ashamed.

It would be one of many times my children tried to steer me straight, to save their own father. Rameck didn't beat around the bush once he was old enough to see what kind of life I was living. I can't count the number of times he encouraged me to give up the drugs. If anyone had been listening in on our conversations back then, they might have thought Rameck sounded more like the parent than I did. "Dad, you can beat this," he would tell me. "You're a strong, smart man and I know you can do it."

Rameck was my constant cheerleader, but there came a point during his teen years when his behavior began to mirror mine in some alarming ways. I could see some parts of my restless, radical personality starting to pop out in him as he began hanging with some thug friends and acting with violence and anger. It all culminated with Rameck's getting arrested on an attempted murder charge for his role in an attack on a crackhead.

I ached for Rameck not to disappear down the wrong path like I did. "You don't want to be like me," I told him.

Rameck and I had a memorable heart-to-heart talk after his arrest. I tried not to preach at him. But I did want him to realize that he had the opportunity to switch direction before his life became the horror movie that mine already was. Rameck knew I had wasted years of my life in prison, critical years that kept me from being in his life. I had even missed my own sister Jackie's funeral because I was locked up.

It meant a lot for me to offer myself and my own experiences to wake him up and make him realize there were painful consequences for his spur-of-the-moment actions.

Rameck, my smart young son, grasped what I was telling him. He made the choice to stick with George and Sam and go to college. As I watched him grow and achieve, I felt helplessly grateful.

Serving as an example to him felt purifying to me. It gave me a sense of purpose, it comforted me. It gave me something I could feel good about, whenever I started hating myself for falling so short of my goals.

Offering advice, I knew, was the one thing I *could* do. Even when I was hustling in the streets, I stayed in touch and always had fatherly advice to offer if they needed it.

Since we lived in separate homes, I always encouraged Rameck to reach out for me. I wanted him to know who his father was, inside. "My actions don't define who I am," I would tell Rameck, hoping he could understand.

My kids knew how to find me if they needed me. I made sure they knew my phone number at all times. As they got older, Rameck and Quamara called me often to share their problems and worries. It was clear—they forgave me for my flaws. I'm still amazed by the depths of their love and acceptance.

But I'll never forget one day with Daaimah, when she was in fourth or fifth grade and she asked me to drop her off in front of her school instead of walking her in. I probably was high and didn't realize how scruffy I looked. "Dad, don't walk me to the door. You embarrass me," she said. Her words stung me out of my stupor. I realized that even though she loved me mightily, she was ashamed to be seen with me.

I couldn't deny it any longer. Even though my children loved and accepted me the way I was, I wasn't the man that God had destined me to be.

I had lost a lot of good jobs by then because of my addiction. I once crashed a work truck and got fired because I was high. Every time I went to jail, or to rehab, I promised myself I was going to get out and do the right thing. "I'm not going back into the life," I vowed countless times. But whenever I returned to the streets of Newark, I found out that the city hadn't changed, and neither had I.

For eight years, I managed to hold a job with the Newark water department, although I have no idea how. Every time the bosses threatened to fire me, they didn't follow through. I felt really bad, because I had gotten the job through family contacts and I was abusing that familiarity. But I never stopped getting high. The fact that my supervisors never fired me ended up enabling me and keeping me from changing.

The day that the water department finally got fed up and fired me, that was my rock-bottom moment. I lost my apartment shortly after that, since I couldn't afford to pay the rent.

I had been back and forth to so many rehab programs that my medical insurance company said it would only pay for a two-week program. I knew that wasn't enough.

I prayed. "God, why have you taken everything away from me?" I questioned. "You took my job, my house, and I can't get the help I need to kick this habit."

A flood of fear came pouring out of me. I was petrified of failing again. My faith in myself was long gone by that point.

Then I put my trust in God. I signed up for the two-week program.

As I boarded the train to leave for rehab, I made a solemn promise to myself. I vowed to make my children proud of me.

When the two weeks were up, God came through. I found an out-of-state Christian rehab clinic that let me continue my detoxification for free.

While I was there, I thought about how I owed it to my three children to make a change.

In those quiet hours I spent alone, I could hear Rameck's voice encouraging me. "Do it for your kids if not for yourself. Your kids need you," he used to tell me. One day I found a piece of paper and composed a heartfelt poem for Rameck, who was by then in medical school making his dream of becoming a doctor a reality.

It read, in part:

See son, I was there for you from the first day you were born,
But life has snags, so because of fate, your parents' love would be torn.
And even though in your little life, you would pray we could be one,
I wasn't there to help you grow, for that I'm sorry, son.
Sometimes I wasn't there to push you along the way. Only you could run.
Please find it in your heart to forgive me, truly I'm sorry, son.
So when you jump your next hurdle, and that dream of a doctor
  you become,
Just remember I always knew you would do it, I always knew you were
  the one.
So don't forget the mistakes I made, use them when problems come,
And don't forget the words I said. Don't forget, "I'm sorry, son."

I signed it, and mailed it to him. Years later, I was surprised and touched to find out that Rameck had framed my poem and put it in a place of honor over his mantel.

When I completed rehab, I came home newly determined to live up to my children's expectations. It was 1997. I was forty-three years old and finally ready to put my mistakes behind me.

I lived with my mom until I got on my feet.

It wasn't long before I stumbled into a good job. I was at church when a friend asked me if I wanted to work at a local rehab center where she had connections. "Alim, don't you want to be a counselor? You'd be good at it," she said. "I can get you on if you can pass the drug test." I had been clean for months, so I passed the urine test with flying colors. I went through the interview process and got the job.

Immediately I loved the work. It was the perfect fit: working as a rehab counselor, trying to inspire addicts to make a change like I did. I myself had gotten caught up in the social factors that brought clients through the door. I fully understood how your environment can twist you and rob you of good judgment. I was intimately aware of how hard it is to change when you're surrounded by folks doing the wrong thing.

Landing the job motivated me to go back to school, where I quickly earned my associate's degree and became a certified drug and alcohol counselor. Finally, I had found my calling.

When you work with drug addicts, it's impossible to ignore the lasting impact of fatherlessness. I know of young men who were actually taught the drug trade by their fathers, and I think that's unforgivable. I have a young relative whose father told him the way to get the things he wants is to sell drugs. Of course, every child looks up to his father and wants to do what his dad tells him. Now that young man's in the federal penitentiary serving a twenty-year sentence. I think it's a tragedy when a father fails to teach a child right from wrong. That kind of story hurts my heart, but it's a reality.

These guys I've counseled in drug rehab groups are so angry at their own fathers. It's almost always the same story: Their fathers weren't in their lives; they had no male role models; they feel like they were left to fend for themselves.

I'm a living example. My father lived with us, but he never talked to us. He didn't explain things; he never guided us. He was a provider and that was it. He used alcohol as his crutch. I used drugs. Fortunately, my sister Resa and I were able to clean up our lives and move in a new direction. Resa conquered her habit years before I did. Once she made up her mind, she checked herself into a rehab facility and has never looked back. Today, she's a spiritual person filled with peace. A project manager for a major company, she owns her own home in the country, an hour from the madness of our Newark hometown.

Drug and alcohol abuse serves a purpose, I now know. It makes you feel whole, accepted, important. It hides your pain. It covers up the stuff you're not proud of. You can't get better until you start living your life with purpose.

After nearly throwing my whole adulthood away on drugs, I'm happy to say that I've finally figured out what gives life its purpose. It occurred to me on the day that Rameck strode across the stage in his cap and gown to get his medical degree from the University of Medicine & Dentistry of New Jersey. I felt like I had suddenly found my direction after decades of being lost.

I know it was his big moment. But it was mine, too.

Sitting there inside the PNC Bank Arts Center, a huge outdoor arena, I watched the graduates parade in. All I could think was "Wow." The moment felt so auspicious, so full of success. It was a gorgeously clear, sunny morning.

As I sat in that seat watching my son achieve his dream, I saw Rameck accomplishing what I hadn't been able to do. In college, my dream had been to be a chemist, but I ended up letting the chemicals control me. As I admired my son looking regal in his cap and gown, I realized that my dream hadn't been lost—it had only been deferred a generation.

At that moment, there was no drug, no high that could equal my pride in that realization. Although I couldn't undo my own mistakes, I could take pride in the fact that I had helped my child to hurdle over the obstacles that had tripped me up.

Big and little epiphanies started washing over me as I surveyed the scene.

I remember savoring the moment with Rameck's maternal grandmother, who was in a wheelchair and battling liver disease. I was so grateful for her.

She had been the one to shoulder the hardest part of raising Rameck. Both his mother and I had been dealing with our own problems and pain, so she stepped in without a fuss and provided a healthy life for him. She was such a wise, patient woman. Whenever her daughter bad-mouthed me in front of Rameck, she always quietly told Rameck to go figure things out for himself and not to let his mother's bitterness dictate his opinion of me.

She seemed to see the bigger picture of life, and didn't go barreling after instant gratification the way Arlene and I had done. Even in my worst years, she didn't judge me harshly the way the rest of the world seemed to do. Her words, but even more so her example, had long pushed me to be a better father.

On that glorious graduation day, she was in failing health and would only live a month more. But she had survived long enough to see Rameck become a doctor. Her joy was boundless.

I was beginning to understand the supreme contentment she had found in being a steadying influence for a child. It wasn't something that I found easy to grasp during my wilder years. I wished to God I hadn't had to go to hell and back to learn it.

When the ceremony was over, there was the usual rush of people. It took a while for Rameck to find us. He, Sam, and George had to take a few minutes and pose for photographs. The local newspaper was getting ready to do a front-page story about the three of them. It was the beginning of their fame.

I stood back quietly, letting the unforgettable scene unfold. I didn't rush to get to Rameck. I just waited my turn, watching him all the while. Finally our eyes met, and we came together and hugged warmly. I was full by then. He knew it.

It's funny how on milestone days like that, proud parents can't help but think back to when their children were small. As I stood there, I flashed back to the day when Rameck first announced that he wanted to be a doctor.

It had sounded like such an impossible dream at the time. Yet here was Rameck, standing at my side in full doctoral regalia, his cap and gown.

I said to myself, almost out loud, "Parents have to believe in their children."

No matter what their dreams sound like, no matter how outlandish, you have to support your kids, I've realized. Never tell a child they can't aspire to be an astronaut or even the president. What right do we have to tamp down on their dreams? That seems to me to be part of the problem. Parents who had their dreams dashed end up doing the same thing to their kids.

As much as I tried to be there for my children, I must admit that my drug dependence was the ultimate act of selfishness. I should have put my children first. When I finally, truly put my children first and kicked my drug habit, I found that the pieces of my life fell into place.

Now, with my son as my hero, I have found my own place in the work world. I didn't stop with getting my community college degree. I went on to earn a bachelor's in psychology from Montclair State University, and am now working on my master's. I'm studying to become a licensed professional counselor. I'm proud of the man I have become.

I was searching for relief, escape, and pleasure when I stooped to taking drugs. I now know that a much greater joy and pleasure comes from seeing your kids soar over their obstacles. A father's support can go a long way toward pushing kids to ignore the temptations of the streets and to go for their dreams. I now know that you've got to believe in your kids and be there for them no matter the outcome.

Too many fathers today end up denying a future to their next generation, because they don't believe they have anything to contribute to a child's life. They simply give up. They've let the world eat them up and spit them out. Anytime a man allows himself to get caught up in that cycle of drugs and jail, it's obvious that he's given up. He believes there's no other way to survive. He thinks he has no power and no choices.

But these fathers do have power. They have the power to undo generations of hurt by simply stepping into their children's lives and providing the attention and support that their kids need to succeed.

It's tough to teach yourself the ropes of fatherhood when you didn't have a good role model. As someone who testified against his father in a domestic violence trial, I can certainly admit that. My mother so feared for our family's safety when I was a teenager that she took action one day, secretly moving her children to a new apartment while my father was at work. Although my parents never divorced, they remained separated from that point on.

But I believe it's not healthy to dwell on all the things your father didn't do for you. Even if an absentee father dragged your self-esteem down, the glow of watching your child achieve is a wonderful cure for that problem.

I figured it out late, but I'm grateful that I figured it out at all. Some fathers never do.

Chapter 3

RAMECK

Arrested Development

I T'S JUST NATURAL TO yearn to spend time with your dad. I'm sure that's why some of my happiest memories are from those summers when Dad would put me and my sisters in the car and take us to amusement parks and the beach.

Dad made it a Memorial Day ritual to take us to Great Adventure, an amusement park about forty-five minutes south of Newark down the New Jersey Turnpike. To Quamara, Daaimah, and me, it seemed that the drive there was just as much fun as going on all the rides. We'd snack all the way, from a cooler full of fried chicken and drinks. We would have such a good time, singing campfire songs in the car and playing games. Or my father would push a CD into his player, and surprise us by blasting the newest Tupac song while we drove. Anything to entertain us.

You're probably picturing this scene with a carload of kids laughing and talking, right? But guess again.

My siblings and I were all grown-ups, singing at the top of our lungs, stuffed into the car with Dad at the wheel. You would have laughed to have seen us in this arrested stage of development.

I was a grown man in medical school by then, wrestling with a demanding class load, but my dad's triumphant return had me feeling like a little kid. The three of us were getting our first chance at having a real daddy. All of us seemed caught in a time warp, even Dad, who organized the corniest of outings for his three children once he got clean. He seemed to be trying to make up for lost time.

My joy stemmed from more than just our trip to the amusement park. I knew that my lifelong roller-coaster ride had finally come to an end.

I can't explain why I knew in my gut, when my dad disappeared for a year into those back-to-back rehab programs, that he would win his battle this time. I could just feel it. There would be no more relapses.

As time went on, I felt even surer. Although we were allowed only the barest of communication with him—only phone calls on Sunday, or handwritten letters back and forth—I could sense a difference. He sounded less shaky, more determined in his letters. Then his "I'm Sorry, Son" poem showed up in my mailbox. Its beauty and eloquence gave me hope like I'd never allowed myself to feel before.

When Dad came home, he had a new take-care-of-business spirit. First, he tackled the task of cleaning up the mess he had made of his life. He got a job and found himself an apartment. He paid his tickets and got his driver's license restored.

And then he enrolled in school. While working full-time, he juggled a full college load and earned two degrees. I marveled at how he did it all. Dad shared with me that he had written out a one-year plan, a three-year-plan, and a five-year plan for success. Suddenly, he had a point to prove, mostly to himself. He really wanted for himself many of the things he saw me achieving. An unquenchable desire to learn and live as much he could had leaped into his soul.

He felt that he had wasted too many years, and that realization seemed to give him superhuman strength. He even began putting away money to build a retirement home on some North Carolina property owned by our family. Dad put himself on a strict budget so he could stockpile funds for the future. The new possibilities of his life excited him.

Suddenly we had a go-to guy. Dad made it clear to my sisters and me that he wanted us to call on him if we needed financial help. I was doing okay, but he did assist my sisters occasionally if they couldn't pay their rent or make a car insurance payment. This was the father none of us had ever seen.

Often, my phone would ring at night and Dad would be on the other end. "I just called to say good night. I love you," he'd say. We'd talk about our day, and then he'd hang up with an "Okay, I'm on to the next kid." My sister Quamara said it made her feel like a princess when she got those nightly phone calls.

Daaimah, Quamara, and I found ourselves having to adjust to this new family arrangement. Having been raised separately, we had grown quite used to saying "my father" when we talked about Dad in our daily lives. But here we were, sharing a dad for the first time, and realizing that it didn't sound quite right to say "my father" when we were talking about him to one another. Eventually we got used to the fact that siblings call their father "Dad" when speaking to one another. We just had to train our mouths to use the term.

On Sundays, we'd gather at Dad's mother's house in the afternoon. It didn't matter what I was going through at school, nothing could keep me from those Sunday dinners. I kept a board game, Taboo, in the trunk of my car, just so we could divide the guests up after dinner and play. Often Dad, Daaimah, Quamara, and I would end up on the same team. I loved hearing my father's loud laugh and seeing the delight he took in pulling the once-tattered corners of his family together.

Dad's new lease on life came with a side benefit. I got to carve out a better relationship with my relatives on his side. I hadn't seen much of Quamara during my teen years, but with Dad linking us, we became really close in our twenties. I went to her college parties, and she came to mine. George and Sam adopted her as their "little sister" too, although she was our age. In fact, when Quamara's car broke down, George gave her his old car. He didn't charge her a cent. His only request was that she transfer the title and registration to her name before she took it from him. My family was so grateful we couldn't stop thanking him, but he was like, "Man, don't thank me. Quamara's family. That's just how we do it."

My father's mom and I came to know each other better, too, and together we stamped out the early uneasiness we'd felt toward each other. A big turning point came during my early years at Seton Hall when she opened her home to me. I had been in a quandary over where to stay during winter break. Carla Dickson, who ran our Pre-Medical/Pre-Dental Plus Program aimed at retaining minorities, strongly believed that her flock of at-risk urban students should stay on campus year-round. "I don't want you going home and hanging out with your boys. You might get into trouble and not come back," she told us.

Carla searched hard for an on-campus job that would allow me to live in the dorms during the break, but she couldn't find anything. I had no choice: I needed to get my stuff and go. But where? I felt too old to bunk at Ma's house anymore because it was crowded. I knew I'd have to share a bed with either my uncles or my cousins. I had gotten used to college life where I had my own space. I really had to find an alternative.

Then my dad's mother made an offer. "Why don't you stay over here for the winter break?" she asked. Her invitation felt so good. I stayed in her attic room, grateful to be sleeping in my own bed. She treated me like royalty during those few wintry weeks. It was like paradise to feast on her cooking every day. I can tell you with confidence that my grandmother makes the best Sunday dinners in America. My friends and relatives tease me about how much I gloat over how well my Nana prepares a meal. They think I'm playing, but this is the honest-to-God truth. No one can do it better.

There weren't many people in the house, so it really did seem like a serene haven. I could come and go as I pleased. I felt comfortable. Whenever I came in, there would be a home-cooked meal prepared for me, and all I had to do was warm it up in the microwave. I usually arrived late at night. I had a girlfriend at the time and we tried to spend as much time together as we could during the winter break. I tried not to abuse the freedom my grandmother gave me, making a point to come in at a respectable hour. The only night I remember coming in very late was when I had a huge fight with my girlfriend and I went over to her dorm at Rutgers University in Piscataway around midnight. I didn't get back until a few hours later. Even then it wasn't a problem, at least not with Nana. My girlfriend was a different story.

It felt blissful to not have to worry about Nana's attention as I had been doing since childhood. We had come a long way since those early days when it seemed that she favored the other grandchildren over me. I remember always trying to rationalize the reason why. Often I would tell myself that "the other kids spend way more time over there than I do, so it makes sense that Nana would be more attached to them."

Our relationship had improved a bit since then, starting when she made an effort to take me and all her grandchildren to her family reunions down south. I was a preteen, and still struggled with feeling out of place on those trips. Relatives didn't recognize me because it seemed I'd shown up out of nowhere. "Oh, this is Bobo's son," she'd hasten to tell them. But I still felt disconnected, like an unofficial member of her family rather than a true relative.

Just when I had given up hope that a real relationship could ever emerge, she took me in.

If there was any ice left between the two of us, it definitely melted away while I stayed in her attic room, far from the negative influences of my old neighborhood. I'll always appreciate that she reached into my life and rescued me when I needed a safe place to keep me from running wild during that first college break.

Would fate have led me to hook up with my old friends and drop out of school if I hadn't stayed there? I don't know.

But I do know this: The haven she provided for me is exactly what my father so desperately needed at age eighteen—but didn't have. The choices he made during winter break in his freshman year caused his downfall. Just home from his first semester at Assumption College, Dad went looking for his neighborhood buddies and found them shooting heroin. The fact that he didn't say no when they invited him to try the drug would haunt him forever.

When I think about how our lives paralleled until that critical point, I feel unbelievably humbled.

He took one road, and eighteen years later at that same fork, I took the other. The choice he made caused me to aim for stability. And my choice helped give him the inspiration needed later to resurrect his life.

We're inextricably linked, for better and for worse, I've learned. In fact, researching this book has taught me much I didn't know about the similarities between my father and me.

Just like him, I allowed my friends to persuade me to do things I felt uneasy about.

I also found that I respond to women in a way that's very similar to my father. We don't tend to be the pursuers. Rather, we both have a history of sliding into relationships with women who sought us out. Women who loved us with everything they had.

It has amazed me to learn that my father had a love for math and science as a boy just like I did. It's a little embarrassing to admit it, but I'm so excited to finally discover that I'm just like Dad.

Yet I've had advantages that my father didn't have. And George and Sam can say the same, now that we've learned more than we ever knew about our fathers' lives. For instance, both my father and George's father went to college. Yet they didn't graduate. Both struggled with the tremendous adjustment of fitting in. What some might dismiss as a failure, I can admire.

In fact, I think their attempts were heroic. Both were bowled over by the pressures of college and the unfamiliarity of their new environment. You've got to give them credit for being pioneers and having the guts to attempt something they hadn't seen modeled in their own families. Their college attempts shouldn't be viewed as failures but as successes, given the era.

We, on the other hand, had the support of a Carla Dickson, which is kind of like having a prizefighter in your corner. She helped George, Sam, and me tough it out, and taught us to envision ourselves as doctors. From helping us piece together a financial strategy to pay for college to monitoring our grades, she did it all. My father didn't have that kind of support. When he set foot on Assumption College's campus in the 1970s, I know he felt utterly alone. He and George's dad can be compared to the first wave of an army battalion that sweeps in and paves the way for the troops to come. It had to be extraordinarily hard for them. After all, we found it difficult twenty years later. Just knowing that he tried to break through, to make it to college, makes me appreciate my blessings and respect him more.

I know many people who are so disappointed in the men who fathered them that they dismiss them as losers and have little contact with them. But fathers are human. Anyone who sets out to find out more about his absentee father's life, as we did, will probably uncover startling similarities. It can be a difficult but healthy exercise. Knowing this missing information can give you hope and maybe even allow you to forgive.

THE TIMING OF THIS project turned out to be crucial. I never dreamed that each of our fathers would develop serious illnesses during the time it took to bring this book to publication. Doctors diagnosed George's father with prostate cancer in the summer of 2006. He is undergoing treatment and his prognosis is good. However, Sampson's father's health declined irreversibly, and sadly, in May of 2007, he passed away. And my own father, to my surprise, suffered a tremendous setback just when it seemed he had conquered all his demons. It started in the spring of 2006, when Dad's kidneys failed. He was hospitalized for several weeks and had to go on dialysis, which really depressed him. Dad struggled to do his work for his master's degree from his hospital bed. "I've got to get my reports in," he told me.

Complications followed swiftly. Early one morning, Dad went into cardiac arrest and his heart stopped. He was essentially dead for ten minutes, until the doctors resuscitated him. The episode left him with brain damage, and he lay in a coma for several weeks. My relatives and I began considering our alternatives. It was a painful discussion for all of us. We went home that night and prayed.

The next morning, he opened his eyes.

But those ten minutes he spent without oxygen have had a heartbreaking effect. Dad doesn't speak much now, and he can't walk. He'll probably never recover completely. His speedy progress toward his master's degree, his dreams of constructing a retirement home in the South, have all been derailed, probably permanently.

The changes in his life have been difficult to witness.

Over the past ten years, I've grown so used to seeing my father boldly set his goals and meet them. I had visions of him going on tour with us to promote this book. I couldn't wait to show him off and give him a taste of how fame feels. He's earned it.

I've been resilient through so many hardships in my life, but I've come up against the one thing that could blow me backward and knock me off my feet. I used to juggle a thousand things and prided myself on being able to handle everything gracefully. Not anymore. I used to think that anything I set my mind to, I could do. All my life, I've believed that my determination has defined my destiny. It helped propel me to college, medical school, and beyond. But Dad's health problems have shaken me. I didn't foresee them. It seems so unfair, when he so deserves a reward, to deprive him of it. It's been hard for me to accept.

I've learned so much from my father in the decade since he got clean. Probably the biggest lesson he's taught me is that it's a man's job to take care of his family. I always respected family, but watching him in action brought that point home for me.

During that time, Dad made it a priority to take care of his kids and his mother. He considered it his job to go to his mom's house to fix something that was broken. He'd trudge over there in all weather to fix the lights or repair this or that. When I finally bought myself a place to live, I didn't even have to ask Dad for help. After he helped me move my stuff in, he started making plans to help me paint it: "I'll block my schedule out for a couple of days. It won't take long for you and me to get this place together," he told me.

He never came out and said it, but I saw just from watching him that these are the kinds of things that a real man does to support his family. It gave him joy to slip into the role of protector. He sent me the unspoken message that, as a man, people need to be able to count on you.

Kids like me grow up self-sufficient, picking up cues on how to behave from our environment. Our fathers so often aren't there. Eventually their absence begins to define our personalities, making us distrustful and defensive. But when Dad reappeared in my life for good, he showed me how great it feels to be able to turn to someone for unconditional support.

Yes, I was born into a large loving family, the Hunts, but my dad taught me a lesson that my maternal side didn't. Perhaps they couldn't. Maybe this was something I just needed to learn from a man. Watching him showed me that the true measure of manhood can be found in just being a person your family can rely on, no matter what.

Of course, the maternal side of my family always showed me love, and Ma believed in personal responsibility. But I never put it all together and saw the sheer joy that could come from being a man who fulfills his responsibilities to his family until I saw my father doing it.

That changed me. I used to be so caught up in my own life, in becoming a success, that I wouldn't really put myself out for anybody.

Throughout my life, I've always felt blessed whenever I basked in my father's love. He never withheld it, even when he struggled against drugs. He made it clear that he genuinely cared for his children. Because of that, I readily forgave Dad every time he relapsed. I just followed his fatherly advice: I took his negative experiences and tried to pull something positive out of them.

He didn't lose his capacity to love, despite the absence of loving men in his own life. He didn't fall victim to the emotionless style that defines so many men we grew up knowing. For men who are conditioned to be providers but end up living paycheck to paycheck, it's easy to start hating the very idea of feelings and emotions. They're only associated with dreams that didn't come true, with things you never accomplished. Eventually we let society strip us of the vital emotions that cause us to hug a child, to wipe the tears, to offer unconditional support.

Realizing how strong is the impulse for men to pull away from emotions and abandon children, I'm only now grasping how extraordinary my father truly is. He isn't just a good man, I've come to understand. He's a great man.

He absolutely refused to bow down to the trend of fatherlessness that swept through his own life.

Countless men who let society strip them of their fatherly instincts realize the damage that's been done only when it's too late.

It's so common for fathers to finally voice their regrets to their children after the kids are grown. Many men feel as if they blew it. They missed their chance to be a father, so why try to reconcile once their children are grown? Saddest of all are the men who aren't proud of their lives and feel a need, as their health wanes, to apologize.

Why would you want to wait until you're dying to say you're sorry? My dad showed me that the most meaningful way to apologize is through action. Waiting until you're on your deathbed is too late for anyone to get anything out of the relationship.

Yes, my father missed part of my journey; he wasn't there to tuck us in when we were kids. But fatherhood is a lifelong experience. I recognize now in retrospect that that's what those late-night phone calls really were all about. Decades later, he had figured out a way to tuck us in.

And it wasn't too late. I had waited a long time to know the feeling of well-being that comes from having a daddy check on you before bedtime. My dad's life and my life are richer now that he has asserted his rightful place in my life.

So many men are conditioned to believe that a father's main job is to provide for his children. I think one reason fatherlessness is so rampant in poor communities is because low-income men feel that they can't be the provider. And if that's all that a father is supposed to do, well then, he can't perform that task.

Luckily, my father didn't view himself as merely a source of money, because that would have made him feel like a complete failure. We would have been cheated of any connection, because Dad had no stability, no steady job, no reliable income to share with me.

But a father is so much more than a provider. Researchers recently have begun studying something called "father closeness" and realizing its importance in a child's healthy development. One study found that the closer a child's bond is with a father, the more likely the child will be to avoid cigarettes, alcohol, and hard drugs. Another study showed that girls whose fathers give them positive reinforcement tend to display less antisocial behavior.

I wish every child could know the joy of being loved by a father, the way I have known it.

Not long ago, a radio talk show host asked if the three of us had good relationships with our fathers. George and Sam answered no. But I firmly answered yes.

You must admit, that's an ironic response considering that I'm the only one of us whose parents never married. Sam bears his father's last name. So does George. Of the three of us, I'm the only one who grew up without his father's stamp on him. Yet I'm the only one who has a loving bond with his father.

My father has given me something my friends envy, something permanent that didn't cost anything. He delivered it despite a drug addiction. Without ever giving my mother a wedding ring. Without any of the outward trappings of a traditional relationship.

Circumstances prevented me from knowing the most basic facts about my father. I didn't even realize Dad's name was the same as his father's and grandfather's until we researched this book. Yet in the end, none of that mattered.

What mattered most were the nightly phone calls. The solemn "Don't do what I did" discussions after my arrest. The joyful rituals we carved out late in life. The simple assurance that if I needed his attention and his love, all I had to do was call.

Those were all I needed to feel like I belonged to him.

Chapter 4

RAMECK

Forgiveness

For far too many kids who grow up without a father, that void is filled with insecurity and hostility. These feelings are a dangerous combination that eats away at their souls and makes them vulnerable to destructive forces around them. As they grow to adulthood, feelings of rejection and anger simmer and boil over into their relationships at home and at work. As we have shown, fatherlessness is an unhealthy but sadly all-too-common cycle. Fathers who abandon their children often were abandoned themselves.

One powerful step toward ending this cycle is through forgiveness. Forgiving the father who abandoned you, the wrongs done to you, may seem like the last thing you would ever want to do, but take it from a doctor, it can be a powerful medicine for healing. You will never forget how your father's absence hurt you, but you can begin to heal those old wounds. In this chapter, we introduce you to a friend who chose to forgive her father, despite the legacy of pain he left behind. As you will see, forgiving is not about excusing their actions. Forgiveness is about empowering you to grow beyond the pain and loss.

MONICA

Earlier, we told you about Monica, the mother of Kenny, the stand-out kid we've all but adopted. Monica thanks us for every interaction, e-mail, and invitation that we extend to her son, who is now a teenager. As a single parent, Monica says she needs all the backup she can get.

Her manageable life as a suburban wife and mother vanished on the day in 1998 she delivered her baby daughter, Kenny's little sister, Kennedy.

"What's the matter?" Monica asked anxiously during her C-section, when the birthing room fell strangely silent. Since her face was hidden behind a surgical drape, Monica couldn't see the baby. But she could tell something was wrong from the way her husband dropped his head. "It's going to be okay," he assured her, although he didn't make eye contact.

When she caught her first glimpse of the baby, she could see Kennedy had obvious medical problems. Huge moles masked her pretty face. Doctors were slow to diagnose Kennedy with a rare disease called epidermal nevus syndrome, nevus being a medical term for mole. Kennedy, now eight, has the worst form of the disease and will never walk or talk.

When Monica's marriage broke up not long after Kennedy's birth, Monica discovered her inner strength. It was a first for her. She had never felt particularly powerful before, during all the twists and turns her life had taken since childhood.

Monica grew up in Virginia, and when she started school, she noticed that the mothers of her classmates looked much younger than her own mom, a sweet-faced but stern disciplinarian. Monica's world changed instantly when, at age seven, Monica asked her mother an innocent question: "Ma, why're you so old?"

"Because I'm not your mother. I'm your grandmother," came her quiet and unflinching answer. She seemed as if she knew the question would come someday.

Her grandmother showed her a picture that Monica had long seen in her grandmother's bedroom. "This is my daughter. Your mother is my little girl," her grandmother said, as gently as she could. Monica was shocked—she had always thought that *she* was the little girl holding a candy apple in the framed picture. It looked just like her.

That day, Monica learned that after her actual mother had given birth to her in high school, her grandparents stepped in to raise her. And that wasn't all the news: Her parents had gone on to get married and have three more daughters. The rest of Monica's nuclear family was intact and living in New York City. She had never met them.

Monica's grandmother picked up the phone and dialed her daughter, while Monica leaned on her grandmother's knee. It seemed unreal when her grandmother passed her the phone, and Monica heard the voice of her real mother saying, "How are you doing?" That summer, she went to meet her parents and sisters, and everyone agreed that Monica should stay in New York. Like the dutiful person she was raised to be, Monica made the whirlwind mental adjustment to her new family. That fall, she started a new school. It felt as if her identity suddenly had been switched.

But the reunion had its challenges. Her father had an angry side, and she witnessed him beating her mother many times. His temper scared Monica, whose grandparents never raised their voices.

She didn't know what to do about the violence that often jolted her household. At first, she had worshipped her dad. She used to sit on the edge of the bathtub when he shaved, marveling over what a good-looking man he was. But it tied her emotions in knots to see him abuse her mother.

Monica didn't know that her mother was quietly piecing together a plan to get herself and her children to a safer, healthier place.

One day, when Monica was thirteen, her mother put that plan into action. As soon as her father left for work, her mom stripped off her robe. To Monica's surprise, her mother was fully dressed underneath. Beckoning to the hall closet, where the family's suitcases were stacked and fully packed, Monica's mother told them to grab their belongings and leave quickly. They caught a cab to the Port Authority Bus Terminal in New York City, and took a Greyhound bus to Virginia. Monica ended up where she had begun, in her grandmother's house, but this time she had her mother and three sisters, too.

During the next years, Monica had little contact with her father. In fact, she had little contact with any men. As Monica matured, her grandmother and mother wanted to protect her, so they didn't allow her to date anyone except under the strictest of rules.

As a result, Monica said, she married the first guy who expressed an interest in her once she got to college. But after Kennedy came along, the rocky marriage came completely undone. Monica had just started steeling herself to survive as a single mom when, out of nowhere, a shoulder appeared for her to lean on. Her father arrived for a holiday visit, having heard the news about his granddaughter.

He wanted to offer Monica his support. He wanted to meet his grandchildren. Still, he never imagined how profoundly disabled little Kennedy would turn out to be. Monica took him to the hospital on Thanksgiving Day to meet her. After he saw Kennedy's disfigured face, her dad quietly fled to the cafeteria to cry.

On the drive home, he turned to her with something serious in his heart. "I don't want you to feel bad, or to ever think it was something you did that made your daughter turn out like that," he said. "I could not have wished for a better daughter than you. You always listened to us, you did everything we asked. Sometimes things happen and you don't understand it," he added. "Maybe it's because of something I did, and now you have to pay for it," he said soberly.

That day changed everything for both of them. Monica saw a compassionate side of her father, and needing support desperately, she opened up and welcomed it. From then on, they talked frequently. She refused to excuse the battering episodes, but she could forgive. She recognized the stresses he had faced, as a young uneducated man who fathered six children by age twenty-seven, and she understood that he knew no better than to take them out on his wife.

Monica's father's arrival on the scene meant that Kenny now had an attentive grandfather who fixed him lavish breakfasts and horsed around with him. Monica's father also gave her advice on how to raise Kenny to be independent. "Don't baby him. He's got to grow up and be a man," he told her. "He's got to have some responsibility and be able to think on his own."

But their reunion lasted only a few years. In the summer of 1999, doctors diagnosed Monica's dad with stomach cancer. As Monica joined her sister Paulette in caring for their father, she helped him get his affairs in order and came to know intimate details of his life. Her father, she realized, didn't have a relationship with his own father. That fact helped explain many of his parenting failures.

Shortly before he passed away in 2002, he thanked Monica for her love. "I didn't think you would be here for me like this," he said. "Of course I would," she replied.

Then he asked her to forgive him. She didn't hesitate. "If you need me to forgive you so you can go in peace, then I do," she told him. "But you're my dad and I love you."

In fact, Monica realized, if she hadn't let him back into her life after Kennedy was born, she would have missed out on one of the closest friends and supporters she ever had.

On the last day that she saw her father, she remembers, he asked her to bathe him because he did not want the nurses to do it. Performing that final act of kindness toward her dad showed just how far they had come. Her father passed away a day later.

Not a trace of bitterness taints Monica's reflections about her father. Believe it or not, she even gives thanks to God for her topsy-turvy childhood.

Spending her childhood being bounced between two sets of parents ended up turning her into a fierce advocate for her daughter. "A lot of the strength I have to deal with Kennedy is because of the adversity I grew up with," she explained. "I know what it feels like to be abandoned by your parents."

It hurt her, she admitted, when she stood at her father's coffin during the funeral and heard someone say, "Who is she?" Only a few of the people there recognized her.

Yet that moment shaped her. "I never want my child to feel unloved," Monica has vowed to herself.

Monica is a tremendous caregiver, who always finds the right words to say. "I don't believe God allows things to happen in your life to make you bitter. It's only to make you better.

"You look at the mistakes your parents have made, and you can always learn from them," she said. If you don't learn anything else from your father except how not to treat a child, that's still an important lesson, she believes.

Chapter 5

RAMECK

What I Know Best

Somehow I never hated my dad, although I hated the drugs that consumed his life. And as I grew up, I found myself wondering about him constantly, seeking to learn as much as I could about this man who contributed half of my identity. Now that I've got my answers, I know how important it is to examine your father's life and the circumstances that turned him into the man he became. And don't be surprised if you dig up some facts that explain your father's actions, and make him less of a villain in your eyes.

The main thing the three of us recognized while researching this book is that fathers who are emotionally or physically absent tend to have something in common: they lacked role models themselves.

It can be painful beyond belief to swallow your pride and reach out to a father who abandoned you physically or emotionally. In some extreme cases, the hurt may just be too deep for you to forgive. But there are many fathers and children whose relationships are worth salvaging. The hard truth is that you may have to make the first move.

My story is proof that sometimes a son has to take it upon himself to bridge the gap when a father can't. In many failed father-son relationships, the father is so ashamed of how he has messed up that he doesn't have the confidence to reach out to his son. Think about the way men typically act in relationships. Men tend to apologize by showing they care, rather than saying "I'm sorry" outright. Many grown children find their fathers are remorseful later in life but have no idea how to begin to express their sorrow.

Reconciling may not be right for every father-child pair. If you really need your father to apologize for hurting you, and he isn't able to, then your bond may be irreparable. But many people, like me, know that healing takes place when a father feels his son has forgiven his flaws. That's why I kept encouraging my father and why I forgave him even when he didn't forgive himself.

When I finally developed a close relationship with my father, it was too late for him to teach me to drive a car or dribble a basketball. Our relationship couldn't be what I had long hoped for and envisioned. Still, I wanted him in my life, late or not. I really believe in the Serenity Prayer, which says we need to change what we can and accept the things we cannot change.

How to initiate the relationship? If you're uneasy, you probably ought to start with the straightforward approach, and tell him you want to know more about what shaped him as a dad. If you're uncomfortable with that, there are activities that many grown sons can initiate without feeling foolish. It's too late for him to come to your high school basketball game, but it's not too late to watch the NBA finals together.

Even at this late date, there's something you can learn from your dad. He certainly holds the key to half of your ancestry, so asking about his family history is one way to open the door to a useful conversation. Or you can ask your father how he manages his money, fixes a leaky faucet, or prepares a food you remember from childhood.

In *The Pact,* we named three keys to success, "the three D's": Determination, Dedication, and Discipline.

Sampson, who forged a better understanding of his father through the course of writing this book, has come up with three unforgettable F's to help build the bonds between fathers and sons: Forgive, Forge an appropriate relationship, and move Forward.

He began by deciding that it was time to forgive, that it didn't make sense to hang on to the resentment any longer. Why did his father leave? Why didn't he open up more? Why didn't they play sports together? These questions used to tear Sampson up inside, but finally he realized the ill feelings prevented him from growing, from allowing himself to feel emotions, and from communicating with his father. Forgiving his father, he found, allowed healing. It didn't make Sam weak or vulnerable; it enabled him to be strengthened.

The second F is to forge an appropriate relationship. Understand that it won't be perfect. In fact, it can feel downright awkward at first. If you need an idea for an activity, why not invite your father fishing? I know it sounds silly, but I learned while researching this book how I'm not the only man to reach adulthood wishing his father had taught him to fish. I learned from psychologist Mark Kiselica, a fatherlessness expert, that it's common to hear men who grew up without fathers say wistfully that they never had a chance to go fishing with their dads. For some reason, it's a universal yearning. Being in a boat together, dad and son sharing a quiet moment, seems to be the quintessential quality-time activity in most sons' eyes. Your fishing trip might end up being a comedy of errors, if neither of you knows how to do it. But at least you will have reversed a harmful cycle.

During that glorious weekend visit at his father's house, Sampson decided it was time to grow, which brings me to the third F, move forward. You can't change the past, nor can you predict the future, but you can save today by moving forward, making the most of the moments you have left with your father. As the present becomes the past, you'll find that you created some new memories to replace the old ones. And then you will have something to hold on to.

Postscript

So what is the mission that's staring at us, waiting to be undertaken? It's the huge task of halting the rise of uninvolved fatherhood. We desperately need more men willing to stop the cycle, more men willing to break the harmful fathering patterns that existed in their past, more men who will adopt the attitude "Be better, not bitter" and serve as role models to others.

We must do this quickly, because society is rapidly adjusting to the trend of absentee fathers. For the first time in American history, more women are living without husbands than with them. The *New York Times* reported that, in 2005, fifty-one percent of all American women were living without a husband, up from thirty-five percent in 1950, according to the newspaper's analysis of U.S. Census data.

It's time to remind today's fathers of how critical their presence is in their children's lives. How is it possible that people are still having unprotected sex? As Rameck says, "Why aren't fathers sitting their sons down and telling them, 'Never bring a baby into the world that you aren't prepared to love and guide'?" It's also a father's job to tell his daughter, bluntly, "Never let a man disrespect you."

Although we've focused on fathers and sons in this book, we don't want to overlook the critical fact that a father serves as a girl's first role model on how a man should treat a woman. We know one young woman who said she felt so ignored by her father that it led her to her first sexual encounter at age thirteen. As her name made its way around the locker room, athletes and other people guys sought her out, which gave her a rush. "I wanted the love," she said. But although she had a lot of sex partners, she never found one meaningful relationship. "While I was doing it, it really tore my self-esteem down," she said.

Research suggests that if fathers took the time to focus on their daughters, more young women would avoid teen pregnancy and other problems that limit their futures. Having Dad as your cheerleader can help a girl jump over some serious hurdles.

This is a lesson we've learned from Camille, our friend from medical school. Camille's father made her feel that she could accomplish anything. He helped her with her homework. He admired her poetry and kept copies of it in his desk. And he never missed any of her athletic events. At one high school track meet, she ran in a 400-meter race and got so tired halfway through that she contemplated giving up. Suddenly, she heard a familiar voice shouting, "Go, Camille! Go, Camille!" She looked up and couldn't help but smile. There her father stood, with a bag of orange slices, urging her to keep going. The oranges gave her energy, and so did his words. She made it to the finish line.

What propelled Camille to become a successful doctor? She's convinced that it's the support of her father that gave her the courage to stay focused. "Most of my friends who have done very well had a strong father presence," she told us.

Every son and every daughter deserves this kind of dad. Yet so many fathers make excuses—and nothing will change until we make this pattern of behavior inexcusable and obsolete.

We've written this book to give voice to America's fatherless kids. We're saying what they don't have the insight or the courage to say: We need you in our lives, Fathers. We need you to tell us about our shared heritage, to give us your attention, to be proud of us. We don't want to be an afterthought—we want to be part of your identity.

It's so important that talking about fatherhood start to trump men's daily discussions of mindless stuff. Many young people have told us that they followed the advice in *The Pact* and joined with their friends to achieve their goals. We believe that we can channel that same energy, that same positive peer pressure, to change the very way that fathering is viewed. Want to transform our world? We can do it by realizing out collective power to uplift and challenge our friends who are ignoring their responsibilities as fathers. We need to extend an invitation to these men, but it needs to be a warm and welcoming one. We've got to each the men who say, "How can I take care of somebody else when I can't even take care of myself?" We need to let them know that it doesn't cost anything to let a child bask in your attention.

Using Sabu's experiences as a blueprint and working with the National Fatherhood Initiative, we've put together a format that you can use to wake up and energize the fathers in your life and community. To take part, all you have to do is host a roundtable discussion in your community and get men talking about the importance of fatherhood. Join our movement, and start an "Each one teach one" ripple effect in your own city. To learn more, go to www.threedoctors.com.

Remember, we're all in this together.

Acknowledgments

WE WOULD LIKE to start off by collectively thanking our publisher, Riverhead. When we first thought about writing *The Bond,* there were many unforeseen obstacles in the way. But our publisher stood by us, never giving up. To Susan Petersen Kennedy, thank you for believing in us and for seeing the potential in this book. Marilyn Ducksworth is the best director of publicity we have ever met—thanks for being so supportive. To Geoff Kloske, our publisher, thank you for believing in us and keeping the ball rolling. And to our editor, Jake Morrissey, thank you for letting us do what we do. We had an awesome time writing this book with your guidance. And finally to the staff at Riverhead and Penguin for working so hard on this book.

Next, we would like to thank our fathers for participating in this project. We know that it wasn't easy letting the world in on the personal experiences and choices that shaped your lives and our relationships over the years. This process has not only helped our relationships and brought us closer together, but it also has the potential to bring countless families closer together.

We want to thank all the people who helped contribute to this book:

Monica, Najee, Quameen, Will, Reggie, Sabu, Serron, Maurice, Al-Tereek, Darrell, and Shahid. We know that you didn't have to share your intimate and personal stories with us and the world, but we appreciate it from the bottom of our hearts.

We also want to thank Margaret Bernstein, who collaborated with us on this book. Margaret, you brilliantly captured our thoughts and personalities on these pages. And we're grateful to your family for allowing you to devote yourself to the project.

To all our supporters, we love you. There is so much we want to do. We want to be role models for those with dreams. We want to put a human face to education and health that people everywhere can look to for inspiration and motivation.

To Windy Smith, director of the the Three Doctors Foundation, thank you for all that you have done throughout the years. To our volunteers— Lloyd, Sherifa, Yolanda, Gail, Janell, Baron, Michelle, Tanisha, and Maurice—thank you for your commitment and unselfish dedication.

And we want to thank you, the reader, for supporting us over the years. The only reason we have been able to do this at all is because of you. We truly hope you enjoy this book and all the projects that we do.

SAMPSON DAVIS

All praises and glory to God, who has brought me through so many challenges. His miracle lives in me. My purpose in life is to follow the paths He leads me upon.

To Mom, thank you for being you. Your love for life is embodied in everything you do. You are and will always be my hero, To my brothers and sisters—Kenny, Andre, Carlton, and Roselene—I love you all. To my sister Fellease, I miss you so much. I wish you were here.

To Melissa, I love you. You make the difference in my life.

To my circle of friends, thank you for all that you do. Your constant insight, candid honesty, and genuine care keep me going. My work is an extension of each and every one of you.

To my ER family at Raritan Bay, St. Mike's, and Beth Israel hospitals, thanks for the good times. Where else can one say they save lives for a living? Cheers to the *real* ER!

To my brothers, Rameck and George, our bond is a testament of God's reach. Our efforts to give back keep my passion for life alive. Our movement is priceless and ageless. To save one individual makes it all worth it. Reaching thousands has put us in another realm.

In closing, I leave you with this: My phone rang on a Wednesday morning in May 2007, not long after we completed the final draft of this book. It was around six-thirty A.M. My heart raced as I reached for the phone. I knew what it was: My father had passed away.

A few days later, I spoke at to my father's funeral, where a tear trickled from my eye as I said a few words in his honor. I was more grateful than ever that I had used our final months together to make our relationship gel.

While I was there, a cousin handed me one of my old resumes from more than ten years ago. "How did you get this?" I asked. Unbeknownst to me, Pop had made copies of it and had sent them out to all his relatives in South Carolina.

"He was so proud of you," my cousin said, hugging me.

I knew then how important it is to feel a father's love.

I feel my father's presence in everything I do. Pop, I will continue to make you proud, and I hope this book will help to build bridges and close gaps between fathers and their children.

GEORGE JENKINS

I would like to thank all of the men who had on impact on me as I was try-ing my best along my journey into manhood. George Jenkins, Sr., Hey-wood Mack, Robert Williams, Eddie Williams, Joseph Williams, Ronald Williams, Luther Williams, James Graves, Bernard Williams, Sr., Shahid Jackson, Sr., Albert Brown, Jean Charles, Dr. Kenneth Chance, Dr. George Mcgloughlin, Dr. Robert Johnson, Mr. Lonnie Wright, Dr. Cosmo Desteno, Dr. Robert Saporito, Dr. Dennis Mitchell, Dr. Allan Formicloa, and Dr. Ira Lamster. The time I spent with each of these gentlemen was invaluable. I have taken something from each of them that has helped shape me into the person I am today, and I want to say thank you.

I also want to thank Sam and Rameck, as we raised each other into men, and taught each other countless lessons on manhood through our friendship.

RAMECK HUNT

I would first like to start by thanking God. Without His guidance and wisdom, I wouldn't have even been able to come up with the idea for this book.

I also would like to thank my family, especially my father. I love you, Dad. Observing you reaffirmed my belief that we can achieve anything we want to achieve in this world and still be a good person while doing it.

I want to thank my brothers from other mothers, Sampson and George. Thanks for being there for me when I needed you throughout my life, as I will always be there for you. I love you guys.

And I would be remiss if I didn't acknowledge those great fathers and men who contributed to this book (and you, too, Monica). Not only those who contributed to this book, but the many fathers out there who are great dads. You are terrific examples for all of us.

Now I want to do something unconventional.

Although we wrote this book from a male's perspective, I have long realized how important fathers are to daughters. So I want to acknowledge the different women I've met who've inspired me to write this book. Even if you weren't fortunate enough to have your dad play an important role in your life, know this: You are God's gift to this earth. You are a blessing. A father's love is so important for a woman's self-esteem and self-worth.

About the Authors

Sampson Davis, George Jenkins, and Rameck Hunt are practicing physicians and authors of the *New York Times*–bestselling *The Pact* and *We Beat the Street*. They are the founders of the Three Doctors Foundation, which seeks to inspire and create opportunities for inner-city communities through education, mentoring, and health awareness. The Three Doctors, all still friends, live in New Jersey.